Spiritual Education

Spiritual Education

Literary, Empirical and Pedagogical Approaches

Edited by
Cathy Ota and Clive Erricker

sussex
ACADEMIC
PRESS

BRIGHTON • *PORTLAND*

Editorial introductions and organization of this volume
© Cathy Ota and Clive Erricker, 2005. All other chapters
© Sussex Academic Press, 2005.

The right of Cathy Ota and Clive Erricker to be identified as Editors of this
work has been asserted in accordance with the Copyright, Designs and
Patents Act 1988.

2 4 6 8 10 9 7 5 3 1

First published in 2005 in Great Britain by
SUSSEX ACADEMIC PRESS
P.O. Box 2950
Brighton BN2 5SP

and in the United States of America by
SUSSEX ACADEMIC PRESS
920 NE 58th Ave.   Suite 300
Portland, Oregon 97213-3786

British Library Cataloguing in Publication Data
A CIP catalogue record for this book is available from the British Library.

Library of Congress Cataloging-in-Publication Data
Spiritual education : literary, empirical, and pedagogical
approaches / edited by Cathy Ota and Clive Erricker.
p. cm. — (Spirituality in education ; v. 3)
Includes bibliographical references and index.
ISBN 1-84519-017-3 (alk. paper) — ISBN 1-84519-018-1
(alk. paper)
1. Religious education—Study and teaching. 2. Religious
education—Teaching methods. 3. Children—Religious life.
4. Spiritual life. I. Ota, Cathy. II. Erricker, Clive. III. Series.
BL42.S695 2004
207'.5—dc22
                                        2004000771
                                        CIP

Typeset and designed by G&G Editorial, Brighton
Printed by MPG Books Ltd, Bodmin, Cornwall
This book is printed on acid-free paper.

Contents

Spiritual Education

Literary, Empirical and Pedagogical Approaches

Introduction

CATHY OTA AND CLIVE ERRICKER

T his is the third volume in the series on Spirituality in Education published by Sussex Academic Press. It is based upon selected papers from the third conference on Children's and Young People's Spirituality that took place in Winchester, UK, in July 2002. It represents a further development in the significant interest in spirituality in education being explored internationally since its emergence as an academic field of enquiry within the International Journal of Children's Spirituality in 1994 and the series of conferences that have ensued since 2000 in Chichester, UK, from which the first volume in this series emerged, *Spiritual Education: Cultural, Religious and Social Differences, New Perspectives for the 21st Century* (2001). A follow-on conference took place in Haifa, Israel in 2001, from which the second volume was published, *Spirituality and Ethics in Education: Philosophical, Theological and Radical Perspectives* (2004), edited by Professor Hanan Alexander. Conferences then took place at the University of Victoria, Vancouver Island, Canada in 2003; and at Bishop Grosseteste College, Lincoln, UK in 2004. The present volume continues the series and promotes the continuing development of the emerging academic field of Spiritual Education, which is designed to impact across national and disciplinary boundaries in educational development.

Who is this book for?

The purpose of this book, and the series as a whole, is to disseminate research and debate on spirituality within education and the humanities. Spirituality is understood in a broad sense and through the perspectives of different disciplines, but with a clear focus on its importance for democratic societies. In particular, this debate is concerned with the spiritual growth of children and young people, and ways in which that can be addressed in the institutions that seek to educate them, whether these be secular or religious. The intended readership for this book is lecturers, teachers and students in teacher education and schools, theological and religious education, youth work and social and health care, as well as those more broadly concerned with values in contemporary society. There is an increasing tendency for education to become more technicist and bureaucratic in design, focusing on skills outcomes that are seen as specific to particular disciplines, of economic benefit, and having social utility. The idea of the spiritual suffers as a result because it is not measurable in terms of the data and tests used to determine progress and development within our educational institutions and by government agencies. Despite this, politicians continue to use language, increasingly so, that is closely associated with qualities that are reminders of the importance of what we might call 'spirituality'. Terms such as freedom, choice, conviction, will, trust, betrayal, spirit, faith, truth, rights, responsibilities and care are frequently deployed in the social pedagogy of our time, but they are not investigated, discussed and interpreted by young people as an important and central aspect of their education.

These terms are powerful and influential; they can also be dangerous, deceptive, persuasive and coercive. They are at the heart of what we might call a discourse of spiritual values. The power of this discourse can be evidenced by its ubiquity in public life, especially politically and commercially, but also when we witness the attention given to it in relation to the public discussion of family values. Education into this discourse is vital for democratic life, especially as it becomes increasingly more complex through the influence of globalization and plurality. Before we can effectively address what such an education should look like, we need to engage with important socio-cultural and pedagogical issues. This is the rationale that informs this book, the series and conferences on which it has been based, and the *International Journal of Children's Spirituality*.

The Structure of this Book

The division of the book into three parts reflects three different sources drawn upon within the debate over and research into spiritual education. *Part I*, **Empirical Approaches**, provides us with the qualitative and quantitative research data and findings that enable us to map the plurality of issues identified in different research locations. The contributions identify the problematics of representation in religious and cultural education with regard to Native Americans, factors in the effectiveness of spiritual development in different religious education programmes, complexity in the construction of identity for 'Asian' girls in Britain, and issues arising from children's interpretations of narrative texts with moral messages. They reveal three key areas to be investigated which are at the centre of spiritual education: representation, identity construction and nurture/enculturation. *Part I* also identifies a fourth important issue: the agency of children and young people and how that is addressed in education programmes.

Part II, **Literary Approaches**, draws on a range of types of writing and literature across differing genre and disciplines. Here we encounter the importance of research and debate in spiritual education informing itself as an inter-disciplinary field of investigation. A connecting theme is forms and contexts of communication. These range from fictional stories through to theological and psychological literature. We are asked to reconsider the importance of key concepts and faculties often marginalized in education: grace, play, metaphor, irony, imagination and *qi* ('vital force'), that point to ways in which the spiritual is not to be reduced to, or translated into, a purely rationalist vocabulary. At the same time, we are alerted to the dangers in constructing a specialist spiritual vocabulary that separates spirituality off from 'normal' human experience or from enquiries in differing disciplinary contexts. We need to see things differently rather than see different things.

Part III, **Pedagogical Approaches**, draws on themes in the first two sections but in these writings the emphasis is on relating pedagogical processes and the influences upon them-both enabling and disabling. This section identifies significant tensions in contemporary education systems and in wider society. These are of different kinds but the concerns expressed centre on ways in which institutionalized education and religion has lost sight of the spiritual. Key tensions emerge concerning the interface between modernity and postmodernity, tradition and individualised notions of subjectivity, authority and empowerment. Whilst these chapters speak to the complexity of addressing spiritual education in differing ways, whether it be with regard to the aesthetics of reading a biblical text or the rupture between institutionalized religion and contemporary society, they all point to a similar problem being identified. The processes of change toward a more pluralized, postmodern contemporary consciousness within young people and a more secularized society have invited, within both education and religion, institutionalized responses of a reactionary kind that result in alienation and loss of a sense of the spiritual within institutionalized life. These chapters consider different ways of, and draw on different experiences in seeking to address this spiritually vacuous pedagogical condition.

Key Issues

Overall, there are key issues that can be identified, both in the writings in this volume and earlier volumes in this series, which have started to inform the impetus and direction of spiritual education, in the context of the conferences on children's spirituality held so far. The first is that of the agency of children and young people and the need to take their agency with utmost seriousness. This is not just about 'child-centred learning' as a way of pointing out that children are the subjects of education rather than passive recipients of it. We need to continually remind ourselves that we should not construct and then deliver a programme of education, in whatever context or subject, as though children are participants but it is we who really know what they should learn. We should not presume that education does not occur elsewhere in non-institutionalized and more random ways. We should be prepared to reconsider how we do what we do by being sensitively attuned to the responses of children and young people; we are not repositories of truth or knowledge, or even a process of education devised by us, that simply requires handing-on. All this is easy to say, but we seldom get it right and, if we are not careful, we delude ourselves into thinking we have got it right because we haven't given children the opportunity to tell us we got it wrong.

The second key issue follows on from the above. How healthy are the values of contemporary democratic societies? There is a corpus of writing that contests these values are insufficient and that addressing spiritual education is an area in which a significant critique can be developed. Here, the notion of the spiritual has a political force that challenges the tendency toward bureaucratic, materialist and economic interests in contemporary democratic, capitalist societies.

A third key issue is related to both the above. When we speak of spiritual education we are not speaking of a separate subject or discipline but something that infuses education generally and changes both its priorities and character. Key themes here are processes of enquiry, the relational character of such processes recognizing the integrity and depth of inter-action required, and the inter-subjectivity involved.

We hope that this publication will help to further enquiry into and interest in spiritual education, and young people's spirituality, as a priority in education. Most importantly, we hope it will influence those who are the next generation of professional educators to envisage wider horizons and greater possibilities.

Empirical Approaches

Part I presents four diverse studies, in terms of cultural location (and dislocation) and pedagogical implications. They all consider, in different ways, how "western" cultures cope with "difference". I shall refer to these with reference to the broader issues raised in contributions to this volume.

Marian De Souza's chapter on "Spirituality and Religiosity in Catholic and Coptic Orthodox Schools: Implications for Religious Communities" is a quantitative study conducted in Australia, with the responses of the students themselves providing the data on which she bases her findings. The most significant observations De Souza offers refer to the striking differences between Catholic and Coptic students in relation to the influence of religious professionals (Priests and Confession Fathers, respectively) on their spirituality, which was more positive in the Coptic response, and the influence of their school community, which was more positive in the Catholic response. These may be evidence of the newer arrival of the Coptic community and the relative strengths that exist in each community to accommodating the spiritual and relational needs of its youth. However, De Souza alerts us to the pace of change in the Australian environment and adaptations this will require, particularly in relation to how both educators and students continue in their "spiritual journeys" by finding new and creative means of spiritual exploration and belonging. This need has some significance in relation to her observations that Catholic students felt a heavy accent was placed on cognitive rather than affective learning in the final year of school and the newer Coptic community's reliance on a "marginalized ethnic subculture" rather than being integrated into an increasingly pluralist mainstream culture. These two observations cross reference to issues raised in Jane Erricker's chapter below and the chapters in **Part III** by David Tacey and Clive Erricker.

Ann M. Trousdale's chapter, "'And What Do the Children Say?' Children's Responses to Books About Spiritual Matters" is a qualitative study into the effect of narrative in stories for children with moral messages and religious themes. Early in her chapter Trousdale makes an important reference to Bakhtin on the question of authoritative discourse that "seeks to tell us how to think", and she discriminates between this narrative, which does not. Thus, response to narrative allows the reader to communicate what of value they have found within it without the sense of authoritative interior persuasiveness that authoritative discourse resorts to. This distinction is of significant interest in a number of these studies but in differing ways, for example, in Tacey's and Pike's in **Part III**, and Pridmore's in **Part II**, and beyond those in an implicit sense. Trousdale's methodology seeks to be open to the children's responses but it is interesting to note the tension she encounters between apparently significant messages in the texts and children's contrary readings of them. For example, she notes that the questions these young children asked and the conclusions they arrived at were not necessarily consistent with those she expected the texts to convey. In addition she also notes the persuasiveness of pictorial illustration compared to the influence of written narrative.

Christina Welch's quantatively and qualitatively based research into the representation of Native American culture: "North American Indian Spirituality in the World of Western Children: (Neo-) Colonialism in a Post-Colonial Society" reveals some significant problems in terms of representation within Hampshire schools in the UK. Most importantly she observes that even despite some schools attempts to present pupils with different representations of the condition of Native American culture in contemporary society, a normative romanticised representation persists which is then developed into a romantic substratum of idealised and escapist fantasy within western society. In effect, the utility of the normative representation of Native Americans acts as a simulacrum for spiritual identity within urbanised western society: an unrealisable panacea for social ills and individual freedom unconsciously exploited in the classroom and, we might infer, consciously exploited by corporations such as Disney with the making of Pocohontas, to which Welch refers. Pocohontas, as she came to be known, actually died in Kent, England, of influenza at a young age, having married an Englishman (Welch does not refer to that but it is additional evidence to the critical comments she makes about Disney representation). Welch's references to the influence of visual representation echo and extend Trousdale's. She also makes clear the overall influence that host cultures have over the images created of other cultural groups who cease to have influence in contemporary society, local or global. This study alerts us to ways in which spirituality can be idealised and ephemerised for pragmatic commercial purposes that institutionalised education has little power to resist and may well collude in, by default.

Jane Erricker's "Issues of Identity for 'Asian' Girls in Britain" is a qualitative study considering how identity construction of mainly Muslim, but some Sikh and Hindu girls, is influenced by growing up within a "mainly white" host culture in the south of England. One of the key issues that she focuses on is agency and the extent to which the girls willingly adopt hijab as an expression of Muslim identity. She also investigates relationships they establish with "non-Asian" friends within their peer group and how they negotiate issues of authority with parents in their community. Again Bakhtin is relevant here with the concept of authoritative interior persuasiveness. To what extent are the girls adopting authoritative discourse as their own views? Is there a sense in which they *choose* to do this, and, if so, how does that affect the ways in which we understand the complexities of identity construction, authority and agency? In particular, this chapter complements the research in de Souza's contribution and raises issues that are also evident in Trousdale's research and the contributions of Clive Erricker and David Tacey in **Part III**.

The studies in this section have raised questions about the role of religion and culture in young people's lives and how they influence relationships and identities. The next section deals with more philosophical and linguistic issues central to spiritual education.

Chapter 1

Spirituality and Religiosity in Catholic and Coptic Orthodox Schools: Implications for Religious School Communities

MARIAN DE SOUZA

THIS CHAPTER PRESENTS RESEARCH FINDINGS that indicate similarities and differences in the perceptions of students from Catholic and from Coptic schools in Melbourne, Australia regarding the influences of and their connectedness to their families, friends and their religious tradition. There were two projects which investigated primary and middle secondary students' perceptions and experiences of both their spirituality in terms of their sense of connectedness to the human and non-human world, and their religiosity. Additionally, some findings from a study of senior secondary students in Catholic schools that are pertinent to this discussion are also presented.

A questionnaire was used as the research instrument for both the main projects. However, some modifications to the terminology related to specific religious practice and culture were made each time so that the questionnaire was appropriate for each project. There were two sections to the questionnaire: In Section A the questions related specifically to the students' cultural and religious backgrounds while in Section B, students were asked for responses to a series of items that focused on the relational aspect of their lives:

- their inner lives – their sense of self and well-being;
- the world and others – their relationships, the people they considered important, the influences that determined their values, attitudes and actions;
- the mystery of the existence of God or a Supreme Being – their sense

of a Divine Presence or Greater Power working in their lives or in the world;

- and the influences of their religious tradition/community on their spirituality.

Context

Over the past decade, there has been a growing concern about the spiritual and emotional well-being of many young people in Australia. The rising number of fractured and dysfunctional families, the explicit and implicit pressures and demands of a materialistic society, the rapid pace of change, and the diminishing role of mainstream religious institutions have all contributed to the situation many young people find themselves in. Some have experienced a sense of frustration and, indeed, alienation through their experiences of conventional educational frameworks where, for the most part, the focus has largely been on the achievement of goals which will equip young people for the workplace within a society dominated by globalization, economic rationalization, environmental devastation, and a powerful, sometimes destructive, force that combines media and telecommunication influences. Others strive gallantly to cope with exhausting schedules which require endless decisions about choices related to lifestyle and career; for instance, which television programmes, sporting and recreational activities, music groups and fashions they should support, and, most importantly, which subjects they should take which will lead them to fruitful (that is, high income-generating) career paths. In such a scenario, it is not surprising that the spiritual needs of many young people are not being met. There is also a growing recognition, particularly amongst youth and adolescent health workers (O'Connell Consultancy 2000) that this has serious implications for their mental, physical, social and emotional well-being. Solutions to address the problems that have emerged during middle and senior secondary years of schooling sometimes take the form of alternative programmes that focus on the development of life-skills, resilience, and the promotion of a sense of connectedness amongst young people at risk. However, little appears to have been done in the exploration of intervention strategies that are designed to promote spiritual well-being which could be introduced during the earlier years of schooling at state level.

Within this largely secular context, the aim of Catholic and Coptic schools to nurture and develop a community in faith has the potential to promote in their students a deep sense of connectedness to "The Other" in community, Creation, the Cosmos and a transcendent Other, and to authenticate their own sense of self. Harris (1998) discusses the spirituality of young people as a connectedness which has a relational and communal character. This aspect leads young people to a raised consciousness about social justice and community (Eckersley 1997; Harris 1998; MacKay 2000, 2001). The alienation so many young people may feel in relation to the mainstream Christian Churches (in terms of hierarchical structures and local parish levels) has not diminished the deep sense of connectedness that binds them to "the Other". Sometimes this is demonstrated in a passionate response to action for the marginalized in their communities and, indeed, an expression of their spirituality may be seen in a growing awareness of their responsibilities as stewards of the earth and all of creation. This was evident to Flynn & Mok (1999) who recently conducted a study involving 8,310 Year 12 students in seventy Catholic schools in New South Wales, Australia. Describing their visits to the schools as a "privileged and graced experience", they said:

> We were regularly confronted by tangible expressions of *the presence of the Holy Spirit in the lives of youth* today. We sensed their genuine goodness, honesty and integrity. We felt the depths of their searching regarding life and God as they reflected on their experience of Catholic schools and the place of God in their lives. (Flynn & Mok 1999: 1)

It is more than probable that many teachers in Catholic and Coptic schools will empathize with Flynn and Mok's experience, and recognize this deeply spiritual dimension in the lives of the students with whom they interact on a daily basis.

Research

In order to introduce appropriate intervention programmes for primary and secondary students, an ongoing investigation of the influences and expressions of the spiritual lives of young people in Australia is needed as this will have the potential to inform the development of such programmes. For the most part, such studies need to be situated in schools where spirituality is integral to their foundational base. Certainly, religious schools can be recognized as such. The two main research projects presented here investigated Grade 5 and Year 9 students' perceptions and expressions of their spirituality and religiosity. Two distinct religious groups of students were included in the projects, one group attended Catholic schools (Engebretson, de Souza & Salpietro 2001) and the other group attended Coptic Orthodox schools (de Souza & Rymarz 2002). In addition, some references will be made to relevant findings from a third research study that investigated Year 12 students perceptions of RE in Catholic schools (de Souza 1999).

Research project 1 – The perceptions of middle school students in Catholic schools (Engebretson, de Souza & Salpietro 2001)

Forty schools initially agreed to take part in this project and the aim was to involve 1,200 students. However, due to time constraints some schools withdrew at the actual time of the survey. Further, in many cases, parental consent forms were not returned so that at the final count there were 578 students (240 primary and 338 secondary) who participated in the study. It is possible that the returned consent forms came from parents who were more involved in their faith traditions through the schools, parishes or religious communities. Alternatively, some parents may not have responded because of language difficulties. These were some of the factors that were considered in the final interpretation of the findings.

Research Project 2 – Coptic Orthodox middle school students' perceptions (de Souza & Rymarz 2002)

There has been an increasing number of Copts who have settled in Melbourne since the 1970s and, as the community grew and developed, they saw the need to establish Coptic Orthodox schools as an important step in maintaining the special and unique identity of their community. By 1991, the first Coptic school opened in Melbourne and it currently has an enrolment of approximately 700 students from Prep to Year 12. The founding of this school was a significant achievement for the Copts in Australia as it was the first Coptic school to be established outside of Egypt. A second school was opened in 1995 and it currently has an enrolment of approximately 300 students from Prep to Year 11.

Given the fact that both the Coptic schools were quite new at the time of this project, with one only being a few years old, there was, comparatively, a small number of students who responded to the questionnaires, and they were evenly balanced with respect to gender (fifty males and fifty-nine females). However, the numbers declined from younger to older students.

Research Project 3 – Year 12 students' and teachers' perceptions of their religious education programmes in Catholic schools (de Souza 1999)

Where relevant, some reference will be made to findings from this earlier study which involved 227 students from eleven Catholic secondary schools in Victoria, Australia. These included metropolitan and regional, single sex and coeducational schools, and schools with religious or lay principals.

The Findings

A discussion of the overall findings of these projects are beyond the scope of this chapter. The focus, instead, will be on the relevant aspects of the religious and cultural backgrounds of the students from Section A of the questionnaire and on some items from Section B of the questionnaire which relate to students' perceptions of different influences on their spirituality in terms of the people in their lives, their religious traditions and their schools.

From Section A of the questionnaire a summary of the responses from students in Catholic schools (Project 1), indicating the religious and cultural backgrounds were as follows:

- 578 students in total, of which 240 were primary and 338 were secondary, and 280 were females and 294 males.
- 472 were Catholic (80 percent), fifty-two were of other Christian traditions, seventeen were of non-Christian traditions and thirty-five stated they had no religion.
- 508 students were Australian born, thirty-five were Asian born, eleven were born in a European country, six were born in another English-speaking country, five were born in a Middle Eastern country and twelve were born elsewhere.

Four students did not respond to the gender variable and two students did not indicate their religious affiliation.

A summary of the responses from Coptic students (Project 2) for the items relating to their background showed that:

- Forty-eight students were in the 11–13 age group, thirty-two students were between 15 and 16 years, and twenty-three students were between 16 and 17 years. Six students did not give their age.
- Nearly two thirds of the students were born in Australia (sixty-two) and approximately one third were born in Egypt (thirty-nine). Six were born elsewhere and two did not indicate their country of birth.
- The mothers of ninety students and the fathers of ninety-eight students were born in Egypt. This factor appeared to have had implications for the students' responses regarding their cultural and ethnic identity.

The Importance of Religion

The next item from Section A that is relevant to this discussion is the importance of religion. A large majority of students from Catholic schools, 82 percent, were positive about the importance of religion in their lives. These ranged from "very important", "fairly important" to "of some importance". Seventeen percent returned negative responses and 1 per cent did not respond to this item. While there was little difference between the positive responses from male and female students at the primary level, at the secondary level female students did respond more positively than males (thirty-nine female to thirty-one male responses for *very important*; fifty female to thirty-four male responses for *fairly important*; thirty-eight male to twenty-eight female responses for *not very important*, and sixteen male to five female responses for *of no importance at all*). It is possible that the positive nature of these findings for the Grade Six students was linked to the fact that it was a year during which most would have been prepared for and received the Sacrament of Confirmation. These experiences may have heightened the importance of religion and the religious community in their lives. Another influential factor could be related to the family background in that the parents who did consent to their children participating in the study may have been involved at a familial level in their religious communities.

The responses to the corresponding item from Coptic students were also very positive. Overall, of the 109 students 104 indicated that religion was very important while the other five indicated that religion was of some importance. Age and gender did not appear to have much effect on the distribution of responses. These findings suggested that the aim of the Coptic community to hand on their religious heritage to their younger members appeared to be successful. One factor that may have contributed to closeness and the influence of the elders within this community could be that a very large majority of the students had both parents born in Egypt. Thus, their parents' identity was possibly strongly linked to the cultural and religious identity of their homeland, a place where many of their people have suffered/are suffering from persecution for their religious beliefs. This situation may, indeed, have acted as a spur to strengthen their resolve to maintain their particular religious heritage in the secular, pluralistic society within which they now lived since the strengthening of communal bonds in the face of adversity, through shared beliefs and practices, is not an unusual outcome.

At this point it is interesting to note responses from the earlier research study that investigated the perceptions of Year 12 students in Catholic schools on their religious education programmes (Project 3). These indicated that 52 percent of 227 students (17–18 year olds) agreed that religion was important in their lives, 22 percent were undecided and 26 percent disagreed. Thus, a decline in the importance of religion for these students as they progressed into senior secondary school was indicated. The positive responses from senior Coptic students was a distinct contrast to these findings.

Influences on Students' Spirituality

From Section B of the questionnaire students' perceptions of different influences on their spirituality is focused on for this chapter.

The first item presented here is about the students' relationships with others. Responses from students in Catholic schools to two variables – *family influence* and *friends' influence* – are presented in table 1.1.

Table 1.1   Responses from students in Catholic schools indicating influence of family and friends (in percentages)

	Family		Friends	
	Y	N	Y	N
Primary	98	2	100	—
Secondary	94	6	98	2

Over 80% of all students responded positively about the influence of the media.

Total no. of responses: 568. Six students did not respond.

On the whole, this was a positive response and there was little difference between primary and secondary students in Catholic schools in relation to the importance and influence of their family and friends. Also, there was a significant majority (over 80 percent) who indicated that they were influenced by the media.

Table 1.2   Influences on Coptic students' understanding of right and wrong

Influences	Yes	%	no	%
Family	104	95	5	5
Priest	88	81	21	19
Peers	85	78	24	22
Religious teachings	84	77	25	23
Teacher	83	76	26	24
TV/Media	79	72.5	30	27.5

Table 1.2 shows the different influences on the Coptic students' understanding of right or wrong. From this it can be seen that 95 percent of students indicated the family, 81 percent indicated their priest, 78 percent indicated their peers, 77 percent indicated their religious teach-

ings, 76 percent indicated their teacher and 72 percent indicated television/media.

These figures, once again, indicate that families and religious communities play a very important role in the lives of these students. This conclusion is further supported by the results presented in table 1.3.

Table 1.3   Influences on the thoughts and actions of Coptic students

	Parents		Confession Father		Bishop		Friends		M e d i a	
		(%)		(%)		(%)		(%)		(%)
Agreed	96	88	90	82	72	67	72	67	59	54
Undecided	10	9	12	11	21	19	23	21	24	22
Disagreed	3	3	6	6	15	13	13	12	26	24

Total: 109 students

In general, ninety-six of 109 students were positive about the influence their parents had on their thoughts and actions, ninety students responded that their Confession Father influenced their thoughts and actions, seventy-two students agreed that their friends were influential and so was their Bishop. Fifty-nine students mentioned that they were influenced by TV/media. There were some students whose perceptions of the influences of TV/media (22%), friends (21%) and the Bishop (19%) showed some indecision, but only twelve (11%) and ten (9%) showed some indecision about whether they perceived their Confession Father or their family, respectively, as influential in shaping their thoughts and actions. A small minority disagreed that their parents (3%t) or their Confession Father (6%) had been influential while 13 students (12%) and 15 students (13%) respectively did not agree that their friends or their Bishop had influenced their thoughts and actions.

The largest negative response (24%) from Coptic students related to the influence of the TV/media which was quite different to the responses of students from Catholic schools where a significant majority perceived the media as an influential agent. This result also indicates that Coptic students differ from their peers in mainstream culture for whom TV/media plays an important and significant role.

The responses from tables 1.1, 1.2 and 1.3 are a clear indication that, in students' perceptions, their families were strong influences in their thoughts and actions and friends were clearly seen as more influential for students in Catholic schools than for Coptic students. However, for this latter group, their religious links were strong factors in influencing their thoughts and actions as evidenced by the responses relating to their Confession Father and their Bishop. Such links were not mentioned by students in Catholic schools and would certainly be a distinguishing feature amongst Coptic students. Table 1.4 shows the responses from students in Catholic schools about sharing thoughts with an adult/s or with their friend/s.

Table 1.4   Students from Catholic schools –Sharing thoughts

	With adults		With friends	
	Y (%)	N (%)	Y (%)	N (%)
Primary	92	8	94	6
Secondary	78	22	91	9

Total no. of responses: 568. Six students did not respond.

In general, a larger majority of primary students (92 and 94 percent respectively) indicated they shared their thoughts with adults or friends often or sometimes. Seventy-eight percent of secondary students were less positive about sharing their thoughts with adults but 91 percent indicated they often or sometimes shared their thoughts with their friends. In general, there was a greater number of male students who responded negatively to these two variables than female students, and it is possible that there were some students who responded negatively to both these two variables, perhaps indicating some degree of marginalization and alienation amongst them.

Table 1.5   Coptic students – Able to share thoughts and problems with . . .

	Confession Father		Friends		Parents		Older relatives		Bishop	
		(%)		(%)		(%)		(%)		(%)
Agreed	82	76	81	74	75	69	61	56	51	47
Undecided	14	13	18	17	14	13	21	19	33	30
Disagreed	12	11	10	9	20	18	27	25	25	23

Table 1.5 shows the corresponding responses from Coptic students – sharing their thoughts and problems.

Given the earlier indication that the Coptic students had a positive relationship with their Confession Father, it is not surprising that eight-two of the 109 students indicated their Confession Father as the person with whom they were able to share thoughts and problems. However, while fewer students had been positive about the influence of their peers on their thoughts and actions, eighty-one indicated that their friends as people with whom they were able to share their thoughts and problems. Other responses indicated parents (seventy-five students), older relatives (sixty-one students), and the Bishop (fifty-one students). There were some students who were undecided about the people with whom they would share their thoughts and actions, and then there were those who provided negative responses. In descending order these were twenty-seven in relation to older relatives, twenty-five to the Bishop, twenty to parents, twelve to their Confession Father, and ten to their friends.

Again, there are clear difference between these responses from Coptic students and the corresponding ones from students in Catholic schools. The former highlights the strong links to and influences of the religious tradition for Coptic students, particularly with their Confession Father and their bishop, whereas any perceived links to parish or priest were not evident amongst students in Catholic schools.

The final subsection of Section B of the questionnaire explored students' perceptions of the influence of the religious tradition on their spirituality. This was included at the end of the questionnaire so that students had time, through the act of responding to previous questions, to reflect on their spirituality as it had been defined for this project. Table 1.6 presents the findings from Catholic schools about whether their religious traditions helped them in their questions about the meaning of life. These are presented according to the religious traditions with which the student identified.

Table 1.6 Positive responses from students in Catholic schools about their religious tradition helping to answer questions about the meaning of life (in percentages)

	Catholic (no. = 204)	Orthodox (no. = 11)	Other Christian (no. = 5)	Non-Christian (no. = 9)
Primary	79	90	80	67
	Catholic (no. = 268)	Orthodox (no. = 11)	Other Christian (no. = 25)	Non-Christian (no. = 8)
Secondary	59	63	44	38

The results here show that 79 percent of positive responses were from Catholic primary students as compared with 59 percent from secondary students; 90 percent were from Orthodox primary as compared with 63 percent from Orthodox secondary students; 80 percent were from other Christian primary compared with 44 percent from secondary students and finally, 67 percent were from non-Christian primary compared with 38 percent from secondary students.

Table 1.7 supports the earlier findings from Coptic students that indicated there were strong ties and influences between the students and their religious tradition. Accordingly, the results were overwhelmingly positive with ninety-nine of the 109 students agreeing or strongly agreeing that their religious tradition helped them to find answers to questions about the meaning of life. Seven students were not sure and two students provided negative responses. The age of the students did not appear to affect these responses.

Table 1.7   Responses from Coptic students about religion helping to answer questions about the meaning of life

Agreed	99	91%
Undecided	7	6%
Disagreed	2	2%

Total: 109 responses

In general, the responses to the above items followed the previous trend where secondary students from Catholic schools were less positive than primary students but there was little difference in the responses from secondary and primary students in Coptic schools.

The final item to be discussed here relates to the influence of the school on spirituality. Table 1.8 shows that 87 percent of Catholic primary students compared to 52 percent of the secondary students were positive about their religious tradition giving their lives some meaning. Other responses indicated that 90 percent Orthodox primary compared to 64 percent secondary, 80 percent other Christian primary compared to 52 percent secondary and 78 percent non-Christian primary compared to 62 percent secondary were positive. Further, the eleven primary students who professed to have no religion also responded positively to this statement and 21 percent of the twenty-four secondary students were positive. This latter finding may have implied that these students were actually responding to their experiences of the broad religious education programme in Catholic schools.

Table 1.8   Responses from students in Catholic schools about their school community nurturing their spirituality

	Catholic	Orthodox	Other Christian	Non-Christian	No religion
	(no. = 204)	(no. = 11)	(no. = 5)	(no. = 9)	(no. = 11)
Primary	87	90	80	78	100
	Catholic	Orthodox	Other Christian	Non-Christian	No religion
	(no. = 268)	(no. = 11)	(no. = 25)	(no. = 8)	(no. = 24)
Secondary	52	64	52	62	21

These results suggest that Catholic schools, particularly at the primary level, do appear to be providing spiritually nurturing environments for their students. However, in the case of the Coptic students, while their responses were quite positive, they did not indicate the same positive levels as those relating to the family and the religious tradition. Table 1.9 presents these findings.

Table 1.9 Responses from Coptic students about their school community nurturing their spirituality

Agreed	79	72%
Undecided	15	14%
Disagreed	12	11%

Total: 109 responses

It can be seen that seventy-nine students had positive perceptions about their spirituality being helped by their school community, fifteen students remained undecided and twelve students responded negatively while three did not respond. In general, there was little difference between the primary and secondary students. Therefore, for at least a quarter of these students, the school was not perceived to be a spiritually nurturing environment.

Finally, a relevant finding from the earlier study of Year 12 students (de Souza 1999) showed that 49 percent of 227 students agreed that their religious education experiences at school had promoted their spiritual development. However, 34 percent were undecided and 17 percent did not agree. One of the factors that led to these responses was the strong focus on cognitive learning in the final year of school with little attention being given to affective learning. Thus, just over 50 percent of the students perceived this as an area that needed to be addressed. However, de Souza (1999) also found that senior students' overall experiences of Catholic schools were very positive. It was a place where many experienced:

- learning about their faith tradition and the sharing of faith nurturing experiences;
- praying together and talking about God;
- becoming involved in social justice programmes;
- voicing their questions, doubts and opinions in an atmosphere of relative freedom;
- being listened to and their voices being heard;
- a sense of belonging and being valued as individuals; and most importantly,
- freedom to continue their own faith and spiritual journeys.

Indeed, drawing on these experiences, it was clear that these students' experiences of Catholic schools was of a community in faith, and for many, these perceptions encouraged them to consider the school community, rather than their parish community, as their "church". This finding has significant implications for future Catholic communities.

Concluding Analysis and Implications

In an overview of all the research projects discussed here, there was a distinct decline in students' perceptions of the nurturing environment of the Catholic school as they moved into their senior years. This is not surprising given their stage of development where they display characteristics of the "Identity versus Role Confusion" (Erikson 1968) stage. However, despite this decline, about half of the Year 12 students still indicated that they had spiritually nurturing experiences in their schools. On the other hand, age did not appear to affect the responses of Coptic students.

Another factor that came to light was that while most students in Catholic schools felt they could talk to their families or friends, there were some students who appeared to have few people, either amongst adults or peers in their immediate circle, whom they felt they could turn to in times of problems or distress. Generally, Coptic students appeared to be more positive as they were inclined to turn to their Confession Father, friends, and then to their parents. The close relationship to their Confession Father was quite a distinctive trait for these students since few students in Catholic schools nominated their Parish priest as somebody they could turn to. It would seem, therefore, that learning and teaching strategies should be further developed, particularly in Catholic secondary schools and in local parishes, to address this need; for instance, by creating active mentoring and peer support networks. Further, the difference in the positive responses from Catholic school primary students compared to those from secondary students about the influence of their school on their spirituality is a factor that could be investigated to highlight those elements that may have contributed to this favourable response. It is possible that secondary schools could draw on the work done in primary schools to create pastoral and nurturing environments to optimize opportunities for students to feel valued and accepted. Such action may prevent the incidence of "at risk" and marginalized students at middle to senior secondary levels.

The less positive findings from Coptic students regarding their schools as spiritually nurturing influences could be due to the fact that both schools were new institutions and were still attempting to develop their particular ethos and identities. Also, perhaps the strong influences of the family and religious community were more significant for these students at this time. Indeed, the strong cultural and religious ties that were expressed by these students and some of the differences that were indicated between them and their peers from the wider society may have certain implications for the Coptic community. Australian society, at the beginning of the twenty-first century, is essentially a multi-cultural society. This has contributed to an emerging shift in the national face and identity of Australians from an Anglo-Saxon/Celtic dominance to a distinctly multicultural one. Thus, one of the challenges facing the Coptic community is the question of how the religious and cultural heritage of the Copts can be preserved and handed on in a pluralist society while at the same time integrating their community into mainstream culture, rather than remaining a marginalized ethnic sub-culture.

Overall, the findings of the research studies indicated that while educators in Catholic and Coptic schools can affirm themselves in their work, and in the vision and connectedness they offer many young people, they must remain ever vigilant so that they are constantly attuned to the nuances and dynamics of their classrooms as the needs of individual students change, always recognizing that they live with a pace of change that requires response.

At the broader societal and educational level, educators in Catholic and Coptic schools are in a valuable position to inform the ongoing discussion on the spiritual and emotional well-being of young people. In general, educators need to:

- work in partnership with parents, governing bodies and the community to promote the spiritual and emotional well-being of young people;
- recognize that the relational aspect of students' lives is a vital ingredient in their spiritual, emotional and, therefore, their intellectual well-being;
- develop inclusive communities that are open to dialogue and that welcome and celebrate diversity in a real and meaningful way thereby promoting opportunities for students to discover "the other" within their classrooms and communities;
- include time and space in the curriculum for silence, solitude and contemplation;
- create sacred spaces in the school which are aesthetic and accessible to all, and which encourage opportunities for inner reflection;
- offer opportunities for students to develop their creative imagination and to experience joy, awe and wonder;
- explore alternative ways to promote knowledge by recognizing the role of the emotions in the learning process;

- appreciate the role of the arts in the enhancement and expression of spirituality;
- encourage students to accept responsibility and commit to action for the common good;
- provide learning environments that develop empathy, compassion and listening skills.

Ultimately, educators need to recognize the importance and value of nurturing themselves in their own spiritual journeys so that they are better able to enrich and inspire their students as they travel along their own individual paths. Perhaps all educators should ask themselves: How can we, in partnership with our students, explore new, creative and meaningful ways to develop our inner lives and connect with "The Other" in community, in Creation, in the Cosmos and beyond?

References

de Souza, M. 1999: *Students' and Teachers' Perceptions of Year 12 Religious Education Programs in Catholic Schools in Victoria.* Unpublished thesis. Melbourne: Australian Catholic University.

de Souza, M. and Rymarz, R. 2002: *An Investigation into the Perceptions of Coptic Orthodox Students of the Influences on their Religious and Spiritual Development.* Unpublished Research Report. Melbourne: Australian Catholic University.

Eckersley, R. 1997: Portraits of Youth: Understanding Young People's Relationship with the Future. *Futures* 29 (3): 243–49.

Engebretson, K., de Souza, M. and Salpietro, L. 2001: *Expressions of Religiosity and Spirituality Among Middle School Students in Victoria's Catholic Schools: A Research Project Conducted by the School of Religious Education: Victoria.* Melbourne: Australian Catholic University.

Erikson, E. 1968: *Identity: Youth and Crisis.* New York: Norton.

Flynn, M. and Mok, M. 1999: *Catholic Schools 2000 Research.* Unpublished report presented to a meeting of the School of Religious Education. Sydney: Australian Catholic University, December 1999.

Harris, M. and Moran, G. 1998: *Reshaping Religious Education.* Louiseville, Kentucky: Westminster, John Knox Press.

Hay, D. with Nye, R. 1998: *The Spirit of the Child.* London: Fount Paperbacks.

Mackay, H. 2000: *Australia at a Turning Point.* Aquinas Lecture, Ballarat: Australian Catholic University, 27 October 2000.

Mackay, H, 2001: Why our young pine for life in the tribe? In *The Age*, 10 March: 7.

O'Connell Consultancy 2000: *Evaluation of the Community Response to Six Incidents of Youth Suicide in Hume Region, June – September 1999.* Community Document for Department of Human Services. Victoria: O'Connell Consultancy.

Chapter 2

"And What Do the Children Say?" Children's Responses to Books About Spiritual Matters

ANN M. TROUSDALE

Story as Spiritual Exploration

THE POWER OF STORY: it is something great spiritual teachers have understood from time immemorial. In the earliest days, of course, stories were told orally; today we more often rely on the medium of print. And yet, while the medium of print does not carry with it the intimacy of the oral storytelling event, the power of story is in no way diminished.

Various theorists have attempted to explain the "psychology" of story – narrative's particular effects upon the human psyche. According to Jerome Bruner, there are two primary modes of human thought, two "distinctive ways of ordering experience, of constructing reality" (Bruner 1986: 11). One is the paradigmatic mode, which describes and explains phenomena according to categories which are related to one another to form a system. This mode of thought, which Bruner also calls the logico-scientific mode, deals in general causes and is concerned with verifiable empirical truth. The second mode of thought is narrative – a mode of thought which seeks not to establish formal and empirical truth, but verisimilitude, life-likeness. Bruner comments upon the "heartlessness" of logical thought, whereas, he says, "narrative is built upon concern for the human condition" (1986: 14). Narrative does not seek to prove a proposition through an array of data or scientific facts; its power is an interior persuasiveness, to use Bakhtin's term (cited in Rosen 1986); it works in us on a level that authoritative discourse, discourse that seeks to tell us what or how to think, does not.

In the late twentieth century, literary theorists began to bring forth various explanations for what happens when readers engage with literary texts. These theorists take us beyond the view that the meaning of a literary work resides on the printed page; according to Louise Rosenblatt (1978) the meaning of a literary work comes into being in the transaction that occurs between the reader and the text. What the reader brings to the event – one's life experiences, one's present preoccupations, one's inner unconscious needs, one's purposes for reading – all influence the meaning the reader will "evoke" in the transaction with the text.

Wolfgang Iser (1978) has pointed out that a writer of fiction leaves gaps, or blanks, in a text, when information is not made explicit, when connections are left to the reader to make. The reader is drawn into the text by filling in those gaps, by supplying what is meant by what is not said. The text continues to guide, to confirm, or correct the reader's inferences, as the reader continually casts forward toward a future horizon of possibilities, while retaining "the past horizon that is already filled" (1978: 111). Thus the reader "composes" the story in his or her own mind; the story is in effect being *rewritten* by the reader, rewritten so as to allow play for the reader's imagination (cited in Bruner 1986: 35).

Among the implications of such theory is the realization that different readers will have different encounters with the same literary work; interpretations will vary according to what the reader brings to the event. This is particularly true as it relates to adults' and children's responses to a story. Adults, in choosing books for children, often assume that children will "read" the same story the adult did, that a story will have the same meaning for the child as for the adult. But this is not the case; children's responses are affected not only by their different positions in life, their often more limited life experiences, but by their developmental levels as well (Trousdale 1987, 1989). So while one might assume that stories can play a powerful role in children's spiritual development, one needs to exercise caution in assuming just what particular stories will mean to particular children.

My interest in the potential which children's books offer in children's spiritual development lies not in those books that are overtly didactic in nature, using narrative as only thinly disguised "authoritative discourse," with an agenda of indoctrinating children or teaching them to believe or think in certain ways, but rather in books that raise important questions for children to consider, perhaps expand their thinking, to lead forth from them insights or questions that are ready to be articulated and explored. In this approach I find myself resonating with such children's authors as Katherine Paterson, whose books treat children's spiritual concerns with respect, taking children's spiritual quests seriously and recognizing that they often involve struggle and questioning.

This essay presents a study of young children's responses to two picture books, *Old Turtle* by Douglas Wood (1992) and *You are Special* by Max Lucado (1997). The books are consonant with both Jewish and Christian belief systems, and I was interested in how children from both traditions would respond to them. I interviewed children from Roman Catholic, mainline Protestant, and reformed Jewish traditions.

Procedures

I used qualitative research methodologies to design the study because I was interested in exploring the children's responses in an open-ended way rather than attempting to prove or disprove a particular hypothesis. Further, qualitative methodologies are an appropriate starting point when one is researching little-known phenomena; it properly precedes statistical sampling (Goetz & Lecompte 1984). I used a multiple case study design to allow for intensive analysis of data. Participants were chosen by criterion-based selection.

I selected children who had received religious education in their various traditions. I wanted to use both boys and girls, not to examine gender differences but in order to hear both boys' and girls' voices. Research in response to literature has shown that children younger than seven, who are still in the preoperational stage of development, tend not to be able to express their response to narrative beyond such comments as "I liked it," or a simple retelling of the story. As they move into concrete operations they begin to be able to organize and synthesize their response (Applebee 1978). At this stage children are moving beyond egocentrism; while their thinking is still linked to concrete experience, it is no longer totally bound by perception. They are becoming able to reason things out (Fisher & Terry 1982: 24–5). The texts I was interested in examining children's responses to are picture books aimed at an audience of young children. Accordingly I chose seven- and eight-year-old children, two boys and two girls from each tradition. I located them through personal and professional reference.

I interviewed the children individually in two separate sessions, five of them in their homes and one at a nearby public library. At each session I read one book to them, stopping at intervals to ask questions about their ongoing response. At the end of the story I asked summative questions and asked them to retell the story to me; I have found in my own research that the retelling of a story often provides insights about children's interpretations of stories that interview questions do not discover.

The interview questions were open-ended. I stressed that there were no right or wrong answers to the questions I would be asking; I simply wanted to know what they thought. I tape recorded the interviews for later transcription and took field notes. I also interviewed their parents about the children's background, interests, and religious education. I analyzed the data using grounded theory methodologies (Glaser & Strauss 1967).

Such qualitative methodologies, with limited sampling, seek not to provide generalizable results. Rather than attempting to provide definitive answers to previously raised questions, these methodologies tend to gain insights and raise questions which lead to further research.

The Texts

Old Turtle (Wood 1992) begins in the days when all beings could talk and understand one another. They begin to express their views about God, quietly at first, each seeing God in its own image: the star sees God as a twinkling far, far away; the antelope sees God as a runner, swift and free; the stone sees God as a great rock that never moves. They begin to argue, and the argument grows louder and louder until finally Old Turtle stops the argument, going on to incorporate all the beings' ideas of God – God is both "swift and free . . . and still and solid as a great rock"; God is both "close by, yet beyond the farthest twinkling light." The animals grow quiet. Then Old Turtle announces that a new kind of being will soon appear. These new beings are intended to be reminders of all that God is, "a message of love from God to the earth and a prayer from the earth back to God". But the humans forget who they were created to be and begin to argue about God, about who knows God and who does not, about where God is and is not, about whether God is and is not. They began to hurt one another and to harm the earth and other creatures. Now the other beings speak to the people, incorporating their new understandings of the universality of God, and the people listen and begin "to see God in one another and in all the beauty of the Earth." Old Turtle smiles; and God smiles.

You Are Special (Lucado 1997), a toy fantasy, tells the story of Punchinello, a Wemmick who is clumsy and inept. The other Wemmicks give each other stars or dots; stars for being talented or beautiful, and gray dots for being scared or lacking in ability. All the other Wemmicks give Punchinello gray dots and his self-esteem suffers, until he meets Lucia, a Wemmick who has no dots or stars. She explains that the dots and stars do not stick to her because she goes every day to the workshop of Eli, the woodcarver, who lives on the hill overlooking the village. She suggests that Punchinello visit Eli too. He does and Eli tells Punchinello that it doesn't matter what the other Wemmicks think; what matters is what he, their maker, thinks, and he thinks Punchinello is "pretty special." He explains to Punchinello that "the stickers only stick only if they matter to you. The more you trust my love, the less you care about their stickers" he says (1997: 27). He invites Punchinello to come visit him every day, and, as Punchinello leaves, he realizes Eli means it, and a dot falls off.

The Participants

Catherine and Patrick: A Roman Catholic Background

Catherine and Patrick are from the Roman Catholic tradition. Catherine was seven years, seven months old at the time of the study. An African-American child, she has a bright, open face and a ready smile, which reveals the fact that she has lost several baby teeth. Catherine has a 17-year-old sister who, her mother told me, is "very spiritual and that rubs off on Catherine." Catherine enjoys dance, art, and reading; she proudly told me that she reads at a sixth-grade level. Her father is project manager with one of the local gaming industries and her mother is a physical trainer.

Catherine attends a Catholic parochial school and catechism classes at church. Her mother says that she is raising her children Catholic because she was raised Catholic, but that she herself does not claim "a particular religion." She presently attends a large, non-denominational charismatic church and takes Catherine to programmes there. It is important to Catherine's mother that the girls hear different views, and makes her own views clear when they conflict with Roman Catholic teachings. Religious observances at home include grace before meals and prayers in the morning.

Patrick, who is of Caucasian descent, was seven years and ten months old when I interviewed him. Patrick is a burly child, described by his father as very active and "loud," even "pushy" – especially in contrast to his nine-year-old brother who is "small, soft-spoken and more timid." Patrick has already surpassed his older brother in size. Patrick's parents are both engineers at local chemical plants.

Patrick also goes to a Catholic parochial school, which he told me, he does not like. When I asked him if he had religious education at school, he replied, "That's mostly the main thing. Take out your religion book, take out your religion book, take out your religion book, take out your religion book." Patrick's religious curriculum is particularly focused this year in that he is learning portions of the *Catechism* in preparation for his first communion in the spring.

He has also been exposed to Protestant traditions. Before he began attending Catholic school he went to a Mother's Day Out at a Baptist church, and during the past few summers has attended a Methodist day camp. In terms of religious practices at home, his father told me that "we do a pretty good job of going to church every week, say grace, that's about it." According to his father, Patrick does not talk much about religious beliefs or ask questions, but occasionally he "talks about saying a prayer for somebody"; just recently he had said a prayer and lit a candle for an aunt who was having trouble conceiving a child. A week later she announced she was having twins. "He's talked about that," his father said.

Despite his very active nature, he does have "a tender side," his father said. He "still likes to snuggle with his mother," and while he does not particularly enjoy reading alone, he does enjoy sitting and reading with her.

SUSIE AND KEVIN: A MAINLINE PROTESTANT BACKGROUND

Susie and Kevin are from the mainline Protestant tradition. Susie, blonde and blue-eyed, was seven years, six months old at the time of our interviews. She has a younger brother, who was three years old. Susie is an avid reader. She told me that reading is her favorite subject at school, and at home she likes to read and play with her little brother. Her father is an opthamologist and her mother a full-time homemaker.

Susie "learns about God" at the private Episcopal school she attends and at Sunday school in a United Methodist church. Her father is Roman Catholic, and she occasionally attends church with him. The family's religious observances at home include grace before meals, prayers at bedtime, and observance of Christian holidays.

Kevin, at eight years and five months of age, was the oldest child in the study. He is also the eldest of three children in his family; he has a brother who was four and a sister of two. His mother teaches maths at a public high school; his father, employed at local chemical plant, has recently heard a call to ordained ministry.

Kevin is an athletic child, "a real good little soccer player," his mother says, and is a member of the school basketball team. He has attended public school for the past two years; prior to that he attended an Episcopal day school where he went to chapel every day. Now his formal religious education takes place at "a really cool" Sunday school class at a large urban mainline Protestant Church. His mother emphasized, however, that she hoped that Kevin's religious education occurs "every day, from the examples his parents are setting for him."

Kevin apparently spends some thought on religious matters, though his questions tend to be "pretty concrete," his mother said; question such as "Where *is* Bethlehem?" However, he recently asked them, "Who made God?" "We had to say that's an unanswerable question," his mother said. "Nobody made God; God was. And he's willing to accept that."

His mother describes him as both sensitive and a "boy-boy. He likes all the rough-and-tumble, but you can hurt his feelings. He's a sweet kid." Like Patrick, he is the "polar opposite" of his brother, who is a very active and aggressive child and who, his mother said, does not seem to have Kevin's sensitivity.

HANNAH AND DAVID: A REFORMED JEWISH BACKGROUND

Both Hannah and David attend religious school at a reformed Jewish synagogue. Hannah, the youngest child in the study, turned seven as the study began. She likes to read, particularly books about cats and other animals; her mother told me that she wants to be a veterinarian when she grows up. Hannah told me that she enjoys playing soccer and, after school, "hanging out with her friends." Her mother described Hannah as very competitive and a "moody" child who likes things to go her own way, getting upset when they do not. She attends public school, where her mother told me she is an excellent student, striving to be first in all her subjects. She has an older brother, eleven.

Hannah told me that she "learns about God" at the synagogue's religious school. Her family is not particularly observant. Her mother is not Jewish; she was born a Catholic but began attending the Unitarian church after her parents' divorce. She married a Jewish man whose family was "kind of loose on the religion too," though when the first child was born he felt a "family pull" to go back to synagogue and have his children attend the religious school. They do not observe Jewish traditions in the home but celebrate the "big holidays" with Jewish friends. Her mother said that Hannah does not ask many questions about religion per se, though she does talk about such matters as dressing up as Esther to celebrate Purim.

Hannah's parents are musicians, both playing in the city's symphony orchestra. They both also have what they describe as "day jobs." Her father is an editor and producer at a classical recording company, and her mother teaches violin at a nearby university and in the local schools.

David was eight years, four months old when the study began. He had two younger sisters, five and two years of age. David told me that he enjoys electronics, "like computer games, Nintendo, stuff like that." His mother said that she would describe him as "silly, extremely silly," but also "emotionally sensitive," caring about other people's feelings. He is also "very bright," his mother said; "smarter than I was at his age." She said that he enjoys all the subjects at the local university's laboratory school which he attends. David told me that he "learns about God" at "my Jewish Sunday school and synagogue."

David's parents are scientists, his father a physics professor at the local university and his mother a molecular biologist at a biomedical research center. When David was born she stopped working full-time and works now only on the week-ends, when her husband is at home with the children. David's mother is Jewish and his father is Catholic. She told me that she is "a little more culturally Jewish than religiously," though the family does say hamtozee, the prayer before meals, and observe Sabbath with challahs and juice for the children. They also have a Seder meal at home for Passover. The family "occasionally" attend services at the Catholic church if her husband initiates it.

They do not discuss religious matters much at home; if David asks questions she tries to answer them, and he "seems to be satisfied" with what she tells him. She was very clear, however, that she feels it important for her children to have a Jewish identity; "I do mention that he's very lucky that he's a part of a small group and instill that feeling of how special it is to be Jewish."

Discussion of Findings

What can a study of this sort reveal about children's spiritual insights, their perceptions of God or of an ethical life? What do their responses reveal about the extent to which these perceptions are shaped by their particular religious traditions? How might these perceptions be colored by their own individual ideas and their home lives? And, finally, what impression upon such perceptions might books like *Old Turtle* and *You Are Special* make upon them? These questions certainly lie at the heart of this study and the children's responses do begin to shed light on such questions, but their basic, literal responses to the books in question also raise interesting issues.

Old Turtle

THE CONFLICT

I stopped reading the story mid-point in the beings' argument to ask the children what the beings were arguing about. The fact that they are creating God in their own images is not made explicit through any author intrusion; it is a gap left in the text for the reader to fill in. Most of the children readily filled in that gap. They are arguing "about God," as David said, "and they're saying [God is] just like them." As Catherine explained, the star would think God was a twinkling far, far away "because stars do that." Only Susie did not make the connection at this point, but four brief paragraphs later she did: "They think that what they are is what God is," she realized.

The argument intensifies when the beings' descriptions of God contradict one another. They insist on their own perceptions, thereby limiting God to projections of themselves and implicitly denying others' perceptions. This was a fine point which Kevin picked up on, pointing out that their description of God is "something that would be like them and not be like the other animals and things."

When Old Turtle stops the argument, going on to affirm the beings in their perceptions of God while taking them beyond those limited perceptions, she takes them beyond dichotomies and extends their understanding of God into the realm of mystery: "God IS." The children's responses to the question, "What is Old Turtle doing?" ranged from the literal to the theological. As Patrick said, "He's telling them what God is and stopping the fight." Susie, Catherine, and Kevin pointed out the inclusivity in Old Turtle's point; as Susie and Catherine said, Old Turtle was telling the beings that "God is everything." Kevin took it a step further, pointing out that "he's saying that all of the animals are right, except they need to be put together ... if you put them together that's what God is. And they shouldn't argue because they're all right." David and Hannah, the Jewish children, said that Old Turtle was "telling them what God is." When I asked them what they thought at this point, they expressed agreement with Old Turtle. Hannah commented, simply, "I think it's right"; as David put it, what Old Turtle said was "pretty much true."

When I asked the children about the humans' arguments about God, it was clear that the accompanying illustration affected – and in some cases overpowered – their response to the written text. On these pages, the written text forms a narrow column accompanied by a three-quarter page spread, a haunting depiction of a devastated landscape in the foreground of which lie dead animals and a human skeleton. The children clearly found this illustration a powerful one. The text tells that the people forgot that they were a message of love and began to argue about God, "about who knew God and who did not; and where God was and was not; and whether God was and was not". A brief description of their destructive actions toward one another, the earth, and the animals follows; this is what the illustration depicts.

Catherine, engrossed in the illustration, stopped my reading of the story to puzzle out what the text and illustration meant. "How'd the forest begin to die?" she asked. We discussed pollution and how the forest seems to have been burned. Then, looking at the human skeleton lying near the muzzle of a not-quite-so-decomposed antelope, she asked, "The antelope ate the people?" I said that they're both lying there dead, so it looks like they hurt one another and hurt the animals. She still considered the picture. "And so what did the people do, do you think?" I asked. "Killed the earth," she replied.

Three of the other children had a similar interpretation; they "killed the animals and everything," said Hannah; they "ruined the earth," said Kevin; they "hurt the earth, just kind of destroyed it right now," said

David. Patrick focused on the humans' conflicts with one another: "The people fought, they hurt each other's feelings and hurt them in a lot of different ways," he said. Only Susie seemed to focus chiefly on the written text, incorporating the content of the argument into its consequences: "They were so angry that other people didn't believe what they thought that they killed people," she said.

Finding a Lesson in the Story

I did not consider either book to be preachy or overly didactic, but I have found that asking young children if they find a lesson in a story can reveal what they consider its central issues. Not all of the children found a lesson in *Old Turtle*; Kevin and David said they did not. David explained that the story "tells you something. You just learn about something in the story," specifically, "what God is." Susie, Catherine, Hannah, and Patrick found lessons, which had to do with fighting or arguing. For Susie it was simply "don't fight"; for Hannah it was specifically "don't fight about God," and for Catherine it was "don't start an argument about God." Patrick seemed to combine both senses of teaching and a lesson, a teaching about God and an injunction – one in which God is not specifically mentioned. The lesson for Patrick was "God is everywhere and you shouldn't hurt people just to hurt them."

Both the beings of the earth and the humans learned this lesson, but the explanations the children gave about why the beings and the people changed revealed variations in interpretation, two more spiritually-oriented than the others. For Kevin, Susie, David, and Hannah the beings changed because of what Old Turtle said, and the humans changed because of what the beings said. This was a point not explicitly made by the author; it was a gap that was filled in by the children, who apparently accorded sufficient authority to Old Turtle and, later, to the beings of the earth, to be able to change other people's minds.

The other two children, Catherine and Patrick, both from a Roman Catholic background, saw a different causality at work, one of a more spiritual nature. For Patrick, the star came to see that God was near because, as Patrick explained, God "is close to the people and in their hearts" – apparently imputing to the star an epiphany of some sort. Catherine had no response to the question about why the beings changed, but she did to the question why the people changed. Her reason and Patrick's reason were the same; they changed because "they saw God in one another," a statement of a spiritual revelation that is explicit in the text but which was, apparently, more salient to them than to the other four children.

You Are Special

A LITERAL INTERPRETATION

As with *Old Turtle*, the children's responses indicated that they understood the story on a literal level, but their interpretation of the story did not go beyond the literal, concrete level. Max Lucado is a well-known Christian writer, and while he does not make an explicit spiritual connection in this story, he clearly intends the story to have a spiritual dimension (in fact, some adults whom I've talked to find the story overly didactic and obvious). Eli, the Wemmicks' maker, knows and cares for each one and encourages Punchinello to spend time with him daily to put such concerns as other people's opinions of him into perspective. The connection between Eli and God was not readily apparent to the children in this study. When I asked them if Eli reminded them of anyone, not one of the children said he reminded them of God. In fact, Kevin, David, and Hannah said he didn't remind them of anyone they knew. Patrick, Susie, and Catherine said that he did, each mentioning members of their own families. Eli reminded Patrick of his "mom," Catherine of "my mom and my Granny," and Catherine of her 17-year-old sister – for a very specific reason. As a relative newcomer to town and one of the few African-American children in her school, Catherine had also suffered rejection at the hands of her peers. She told me that she had been teased by some of the children, who also played pranks on her, such as giving her candy that "didn't taste good." She told me that her sister, who picked her up from school every day, told her not to worry about what the other kids thought. And so, she said, Eli is "kind of like my sister."

It was only when I explicitly asked them if Eli reminded them of God that the children said yes – "now that you *mention* it," as David said. I shall discuss the children's responses to this question in a later section.

Finding a Lesson in the Story

After my question about whether Eli reminded them of God, and they all made the connection, I asked them if they thought there was a lesson in the story. All of the children did, but for five of the six it had nothing to do with God, or the benefits of visiting Eli in his workshop every day, or resting secure in the knowledge of Eli's – or God's – love. For four of them the lesson had to do with self-esteem or autonomy. For Patrick and Kevin the lesson had to do with maintaining one's self-esteem despite others' opinions. As Patrick put it, "It doesn't matter what anybody else thinks. It matters what you think." The lesson for Kevin was similar: "Don't mind what people say; just remember you're special in your own way."

The lesson for David and Hannah had less to do with other people's opinions and more to do with one's own opinions of oneself. For David the lesson was, "Well, it doesn't really count if you're bad or not. It just depends who you are and you're all special in your own way." David had used the adjective "bad" previously, not in an ethical sense but in a performance sense; Punchinello was "bad" at doing what the other Wemmicks did. I believe that was his meaning here. For Hannah the lesson was, "You should think for yourself."

For Catherine the story had raised memories of being the object of teasing, so for Catherine the lesson did not have to do with self-esteem or any sense of autonomy but with compassion: it was "not to tease anybody because it's mean and hurts other people's feelings."

Only Susie's lesson revealed a link between dealing with peer relationships and God: "If someone's treating you bad, just don't believe and believe in God."

Perceptions of God

At the end of reading both books I asked the children questions that were designed to elicit their perceptions of God. What influence upon their responses did the literary texts, their religious training, and their own individual experiences and insights have? Here I found a rich interplay; in some cases the children seemed to be influenced by both text and tradition; in some cases their responses seemed more predominantly influenced by the text; in one child tradition seemed to play the predominant role with one story and her own intuitive ideas with the other. In only one child, Patrick, was there a consistent pattern with both books.

After reading *Old Turtle*, I said, "All of the beings seemed to have their ideas about what God is like. Do you have any ideas about what God is like?" Only Patrick, from a Roman Catholic tradition, included both what the text suggested and teachings from his religious tradition in his answer. Patrick said, "God's like everything. And God's like a person but he is invisible and all around." Susie, a Protestant, had a similar response, though she seemed to draw more heavily from her tradition than explicitly from the text. Susie said, "I think that [God] is everywhere and he's a person."

Catherine, from the Roman Catholic tradition, and David, from the Jewish tradition, seemed to derive their ideas directly from the text, and both of them collapsed dichotomies in their answer, in accordance with Old Turtle's view. As Catherine said, "I think he's powerful and in other ways gentle." David's response revealed careful processing of the text. During the reading of the story he had remarked to me that he found Old Turtle's inclusive description of God "really interesting." At the end of the story, when I asked him if he had any ideas about what God was like, he looked around at the open expanse about us (we were sitting on his patio) and said, "Well, he's very big." Then, the wheels obviously turning in his head, he added, "Well, he could be small." His response indicated that he had understood the limitations in a unitary, polarized perception of God, and accordingly expanded this first observation to include its opposite as well.

When I asked Hannah, also from the Jewish tradition, if she had any ideas about what God is like, she replied "Not really." A moment earlier Hannah had told me that she thought what Old Turtle said about God was "right." Although she had intuitive understandings of God, apparently she did not reserve for herself the authority to describe God outright.

As I have mentioned, in *You Are Special*, the children did not, of themselves, make the connection between Eli, the woodcarver, and God. But when I asked them specifically whether Eli reminded them of God in any way, they all said yes – "now that you *mention* it," as David said.

In this case, perhaps because of the way the question was phrased, five of the children's responses revealed a connection between the story and the influence their religious education, four explicitly using both text and tradition in their answers. With the sixth child, Hannah, the role of her religious education was uncertain.

Of the four whose answers explicitly incorporated both text and religious education, one was from the Catholic tradition, two from the Protestant, and one from the Jewish tradition. Patrick's response was articulated in terms of relationship: "if you trust God's love it doesn't matter what people think. Because God loves you no matter what." Kevin said that Eli reminded him of God in that he was "a person who just cares and doesn't mind about anything else." Catherine had a similar view: "Because he doesn't care what anybody else thinks, and he's nice, and he cares for those Wemmicks." David's response was similar, if a bit more tentative: Eli reminded him of God because "he told him that he was special in his own way and that's what they say God does." While apparently relying on what he had been taught, here again, the Jewish child seemed reluctant to define God for himself.

Susie's response did not explicitly use teachings from her Protestant tradition but it seemed that what the book said to her was consonant with it. Susie was the one child who had connected Eli to God in the "lesson" she found in the story. When I asked her if Eli reminded her of God, she nodded then said simply, "'Cause it doesn't matter what other people think."

Hannah, who had said in response to *Old Turtle* that she didn't have any idea about what God was like, now offered an opinion. She said Eli reminded her of God "a little bit. Because God would try to tell him what

Eli said–to not think what other people said." It was uncertain whether this view derived from religious teaching or from her own intuitive understanding of what God would do.

Conclusions and Implications

The study does suggest that such books as *Old Turtle* and *You Are Special* may have an influence on children's spiritual development. The fact that all of the children understood the limitations in a single, polarized, exclusionary view of God in *Old Turtle* suggests that the book does offer the possibility of expanding children's thinking, particularly as revealed in David's initial description of God as "very big," then his amending that description to include "very big's" polar opposite. And the fact that four of the children found the "lesson" in *Old Turtle* to be an injunction against "fighting" or arguing about God and David's seeing the book as teaching one "what God is like" – a view he said he agreed with – testify to the inner persuasiveness of the narrative.

Yet there was sufficient diversity in the children's responses to caution us against assuming that all children will make the same meanings of the same literary text. The reasons which the children gave for the beings' and humans' "changing" in the story, implicitly learning the lesson, varied considerably. For two of them, it apparently derived from the authority they themselves ascribed to Old Turtle and later to the beings, a causality they inferred. For two of them, the reason was more theological in nature, and reflected the words of the text itself.

There was no consistent pattern in how the children used the interplay of text, tradition, and their own perceptions to respond to the stories, with one exception. The exception was Patrick, who incorporated both text and tradition in his responses. It was also Patrick who spoke most consistently of trusting in a personal relationship with God. Patrick, it may be remembered, was the child described by his father as "active, loud, and pushy," who complained to me about the emphasis on religious education at his parochial school ("Take out your religion book, take out your religion book, take out your religion book, take out your religion book"). Despite his negative reactions to the religious education in his school, Patrick seems to have a strong sense of a relationship with a loving God.

The most significant finding from *You Are Special* was that the children did not of themselves understand the allegorical nature of the story. They interpreted it on a literal, concrete level, in terms of issues in their own lives, variously issues of self-esteem, peer relationships, and dealing with other people's criticism. Catherine explicitly related the story to her own experience of being mistreated by her peers. It might seem that she of all the children would have found the lesson in the story to have to do with maintaining one's self-esteem under such circumstances, which was what her older sister had helped her to do. But the lesson for Catherine had to do with compassion toward others.

When I asked the children whether they saw any similarity between Eli and God, they seemed easily to be able to incorporate Eli's character into what their traditions had taught them about God or, in Hannah's case, her own instinctive understanding of what God would do under similar circumstances. Still, when I went on to ask them if there was a lesson in the story, seeking to discover what they saw as the central issue or theme, five of the six held to their perception of the story as one that had to do with self-esteem, peer relationships, or dealing with others' opinions of oneself. Only Sarah incorporated God into what she saw the lesson of the story to be. On the whole, the children's understanding of the story in terms of their own concrete experiences seemed rather firmly entrenched.

The children from Christian traditions tended to be more definite in expressing their ideas about what God is like, to speak of a personal relationship with God, and, in two instances to describe God as a person, reflecting their traditions' teaching. David and Hannah, from a reformed Jewish tradition, tended to be a bit more tentative in describing God (and once, in Hannah's case, reluctant to do so), but their responses revealed a perception of God's goodness and an instinctive understanding of God, or of what God would do under certain circumstances. The exception to this tentativeness was David's telling me that God was "very big," then amending that description to include its opposite as well. His response here was not tentative, but amended to be inclusive. I did not find distinct patterns of difference between the Roman Catholic and Protestant children.

What are the implications of the study for us? They are several. First, the fact that the children did not "read" *You Are Special* on the allegorical level that might be obvious to adults should serve as a cautionary word to us in assuming that children will interpret stories on the same level that we do, and, specifically, to take into account children's developmental levels in choosing books for them. They fact that they were able to see a connection between Eli and God when I explicitly asked them about it suggests that their next reading of the story might resonate on deeper levels of spiritual insight. Or perhaps children at their developmental level are simply not ready to make this connection, and to force the issue with them would be unwise. Stories are more powerful for children when they themselves fill in the "gaps," and arrive at their own connections and realizations. They have a sense then of "owning" the story.

Nevertheless, both books also offer the opportunity for rich discussion with children about spiritual issues which they are ready to perceive, such as how we relate to one another and to the earth and its creatures. When adults take the role of encouraging open-ended discussion, rather than seeking to impose their own ideas of what stories mean, we give children the opportunity to deepen their breadth and level of understanding as they are ready to. At the same time we give ourselves the opportunity to learn something from and about the children.

This study of course is limited in scope in terms of its participants, texts, and setting. A study across ages would give insights into what aspects of faith children are ready to incorporate into their understanding at what ages and would perhaps shed light on their processes in doing so. Greater insights could be gained in working with children from a wider range of religious traditions; particularly, it would be interesting to study the responses of orthodox Jewish children, whose tradition focuses more on relationship with God than does the reformed tradition. And of course, it would be instructive to study the responses of children from the third religion that springs from the Abrahamic base, Muslim children.

There are, of course, many other books that deal with spiritual issues than these two, books that offer further discussion about the nature of God and of how we are to relate to the earth and its creatures.

The study is also limited in that I worked with children on an individual basis. It would be instructive to discover how children's perceptions and understandings might be expanded and influenced by hearing their peers' views in opportunities for group discussions.

Narrative is just one way to encourage children's spiritual development. There is also a place for direct teaching about one's faith tradition, for worship, for encountering God in the beauty of God's creation. Narrative is only one way, but it is a potentially powerful way. And while there is no panacea for the ills that beset our world today, it seems that, if Catholic, Protestant, Jewish, and Muslim children were to internalize the central themes of books like *Old Turtle* and *You Are Special*, there might perhaps be greater hope for understanding and acceptance and for some progress toward peace in the world.

References

Applebee, A. N. 1978: *A Child's Concept of Story: Ages Two to Seventeen.* Chicago: University of Chicago Press.

Bruner, J. 1986: *Actual Minds, Possible Worlds.* Cambridge, MA: Harvard University Press.

Fisher, C. J. and Terry, A.1982: *Children's Language and the Language Arts*, 2nd Edition. New York: McGraw Hill.

Glaser, B. F. and Strauss, A. L. 1967: *The Discovery of Grounded Theory: Strategies for Qualitative Research*. New York: Aldine.

Goetz, J. P. and Lecompte, M. D. 1984: *Ethnography and Qualitative Design in Education Research*. New York: Academic Press.

Iser, W. 1978: *The Act of Reading: A Theory of Aesthetic Response*. Baltimore, MD: The Johns Hopkins Press.

Lucado, M. 1997: *You Are Special*. Sergio Martinez, Illus. Wheaton, IL: Crossway Books.

Rosen, H. 1986: The Importance of Story. In *Language Arts* 63 (3): 226–37.

Rosenblatt, L. 1978: *The Reader, the Text, the Poem*. Carbondale, IL: Southern Illinois University Press.

Trousdale, A. M. 1987: *The Telling of the Tale: Children's Responses to Fairy Tales Presented Orally and Through the Medium of Film*. Doctoral dissertation, The University of Georgia.

Trousdale, A. M. 1989: Let the Children Tell Us: The Meanings of Fairy Tales for Children. *The New Advocate* (Winter), 24–36.

Wood, D. 1992: *Old Turtle*. Cheng-Khee Chee, Illus. Duluth, MN: Pfeifer-Hamilton Publishers.

Chapter 3

North American Indian Spirituality in the World of Western Children: (Neo-) Colonialism in a Post-Colonial Society

CHRISTINA WELCH

THIS CHAPTER DEALS WITH the popular visual representation of North American Indians in the UK today and draws attention to the effects that these representations have had on some ninety Hampshire school children and their perceptions of North American Indians. With an emphasis on post-colonial methodologies that emphasize the benefits and/or detriments to North American Indians of representations, it examines in brief some of the historic visual representations of North American Indians available in the UK, explores the role of the UK hobbyist movement in the contemporary representation of Indian-ness to the UK public, and scrutinizes the teaching of North American Indian spirituality within the education system. Arguing that representations can have a strong educative element, and that popular visual representations are especially influential in forming perceptions of the world, this chapter concludes that contemporary popular representations of North American Indians in the UK tend toward (neo-)colonialist.

In regard to the terminology used within this chapter North American Indian/s refers to North American Indians, whereas Indian refers to Western representations of these peoples. Post-colonialism as a methodology refers to the analytical reflection on, and challenge to, the dominating and subordinating cultural practices of Western colonialism (Moore-Gilbert 1997: 12) with the West being a politically, culturally and economically based hegemonic project (Hesse 2002: 161). Post-colonial in regard to time refers to the UK today when colonial domination is alleged to have ended (Goldberg & Quayson 2002; Hardt & Negri 2000; McClintock 1993). I recognize that these terms are inherently problematic.

Psychology of Representation

Today we in the UK live in a culture saturated by visual representation. Images are everywhere and are used to entertain, to educate and to inform. Scholars from a wide variety of academic fields have written extensively on the effects of visual representation upon our perceptions of other peoples and their lifeways, and especially upon how these representations form, and influence established, stereotypes of these peoples (Bell 1992; Bloom 1999; Churchill 1998; Deloria, P. 1998; Deloria, V. 1988; Ellingson 2001; Francis 1992; Gidley 1994; Jahoda 1999; Kashima 2000; Kilpatrick 1999; Krech 1999; Kuper 1988; Kushner 1999; Maxwell 1999; Mihesuah 1996; Pickering 2001; Root 1998; Schmidt 2000–1a&b; Schneider 2003; Stedman 1982). Whilst one may speculate as to whether one image alone is sufficient to create a stereotype, it would not be uncontroversial to say that the cumulative effect of a particular type of representation is likely to lead to an assimilation of that type of image by those to whom it is presented. This is particularly an issue in regard to children.

Many academics have specifically highlighted the effects that visual representation has upon our children (Hirschfelder, Molin, & Wakin 1999; Huhndorf 2001; Reese undated; Rossiter 1997; Saplin & Searle 1992), influencing perhaps permanently their ways of perceiving the world. Representation is power, a power well able to construct and manipulate perceptions of reality (Foucault 1977; Hall 1997). Yet representations of North American Indians have rarely come from these peoples themselves. Presented, represented and re-presented for centuries by an endless series of Westerners, North American Indians have only recently gained access to the mass mediums that allow them to present themselves to themselves and to others. Yet due to the globalism that restricts the output of products to major corporations (Williams Undated) and the commercialism that restricts the stock of High Street stores to only the most profitable items (Hawthorne 1989: 261) even this is somewhat limited.

With the way that different peoples and their worldviews and spiritualities are represented to our children having long lasting effects upon the ways that our children perceive these other peoples, it would seem reasonable to assert that inaccurate representations should be avoided, especially in education. Certainly this has been the case in regard to representations of Jewish and coloured peoples. Gone from school text books, and on the whole from popular culture (Kushner 1999) due to their unacceptability let alone inaccuracy, are representations that depict people of colour as frizzy-haired minstrels and Jewish people as having large noses and big wallets. Yet this has not been the case with some other peoples, especially North American Indians (Anon Undated) whose histories and spiritualities are available as subjects within the English education system at secondary level; in particular, the American West 1840–1895 in History (which I will not be discussing here), and in Religious Education (RE).

However, it is not just through formal education that children learn about other cultures, indeed much of their knowledge comes from wider popular culture (Hirschfelder 1999: 139–40; Bird 1996: 1–12; Berkhofer 1978: 71–111), such as TV and other visual media. And it is predominantly from popular culture that children in the UK today are learning about North American Indians, their history and their spirituality. I use the singular specifically, as generally these diverse and dynamic groups of peoples are represented in a homogeneous and static manner with a propensity towards turn-of-the-twentieth century Plains culture.

Contemporary and Historic Popular Representation

Popular visual representations of North American Indians are commonplace in the UK today. Postcards, calendars and greetings cards regularly depict Indians (notably Heron Cards, Pomegranate and Taschen, Taschen 1997 a&b), while their lifeways and spiritualities inform a plethora of New Age environmental-icon style books (Ash 2001?; Bierhorst 1994; McGaa 1990; McLuhan 1971; Meadows 1996; Versluis 1993; Wa-Na-Nee-Che & Freke 1996). Indians frequently appear on TV in Hollywood Westerns and serials such as *Dr Quinn: Medicine Woman*, while a variety of films are easily available in High Street shops, including the recently re-released blockbusters *Dances with Wolves* (Orion 1990, 1998) and *Last of the Mohicans* (Morgan Creek 1992, 1998). Further, TV advertisements have recently featured North American Indian themes (painted faces, feather-bonnets, tipis and bows and arrows being the common signifiers) and interior designers have also got in on the act. The BBC *Good Homes* magazine (April 2001) and its day-time DIY TV show *Housecall* (*Cherokee Chic*, 25 April 2001) both featured North American Indian style rooms. Indian-ness is a concept well known to the UK public.

Images aimed specifically at children are also prolific; from films such as Walt Disney's *Pocahontas* (1995) and Dreamworks's *Spirit: Stallion of the Cimarron* (2002), visual representations of North American Indians abound. Toy manufacturers Lego Duplo and Playmobil both produce Indian playsets for young children, Winnie the Pooh and friends appear in Indian dress[1] (feathers in hair and buckskin clothing), plastic bow and arrow sets are easily obtained for pocket-money prices, and Dream Catchers are commonplace. Further, the children's comic *The Dandy*[2] now finds Desperate Dan with a young female Indian sidekick named Little Bear. Clad in a very short buckskin dress with a feather in her hair, Little Bear and the other residents of her tipi village function as foils to Desperate Dan's antics. In an effort towards toward political correctness Little Bear is studying to be a medical doctor, however her Western looks and outfits (reminiscent of Disney's *Pocahontas*), and the inclusion of totem poles in a Plains setting imply superficiality. It would seem that UK adults and children alike are subject to a multitude of representations, predominantly visual, of Indians. However, the majority of these popular images are relatively stereotypical and tend to perpetrate a Western myth of North American Indian lifeways. Further, many of the images tend to homogenize North American Indian peoples into a single group, often represented as distant in time and combining imagery from areas such as the North-West with those of the Plains.

The Contemporary Legacy of Historic Representation: De Bry, Catlin and Curtis

Western stereotyped visual representation of North American Indians is by no means a recent phenomenon, indeed its history can be traced back to at least the fifteenth century. One notable example of such imagery can be found in the much re-printed publication of *America* by Theodore De Bry. Reprinted fifty times in four languages between its initial publication in 1590 and its final reprint in 1655, this work Europeanized many of the original illustrations of artists such as John White;[3] the English watercolour painter who accompanied Sir Walter Raleigh into Virginia in 1585 (Kupperman 2000: 42–5). De Bry, in providing a frame of reference for his classical Western audience, gave White's naturalistic depictions of the Pomeoc people the Greco-Roman look that was common to artwork of the time. However, the mistranslations of such images were then carried forward into later representations of North American Indian peoples, becoming normative in the process; for example, illustrations directly lifted from De Bry can be found in several later works dating to well into the nineteenth century, including a publication from the French Geographical Society in 1835 which stands as clear testimony to the perceived authenticity of these reprints (Pratt 1989).

Along with the misrepresentations of White's images, De Bry included the illustrations of the Huguenot artist, Jacques Le Moyne de Morgues who accompanied the French into Florida in 1564. However, Le Moyne represented his subjects as directly opposed to Christian civilization, engaged in savage rituals such as cannibalism, child-sacrifice and idolatry[4] (Ellingson 2001: 11, 45, 103). With North American Indians then portrayed as normative in looks, but abnormal in nature such representations played into and perpetrated the image that these New World peoples were Other to the Christian West; visual imagery indisputably showed that North American Indians were the barbaric savages of earlier traveller tales.

But what has this antiquated tome to do with contemporary understandings of North American Indians? Simply that De Bry's illustrations can still be found informing people about prior contact North American Indians without reference to the issues surrounding their representational origins.

Stephanie Moser (1998) has highlighted the crucial role that visual representation has played, and continues to play, in influencing popular and scientific understandings of pre-history by arguing that recreations of ancient life have typically represented theories current when the recreations were produced. Understandings of De Bry echo this, arguably saying more about the West than the peoples they purport to represent. Yet, in 2002 The America Museum in Bath ran an exhibition of De Bry prints (*Strangers in the Land: First Encounters between Europeans and American Indians)* stating that the prints were examples of "the earliest and most authentic depictions of American Indians" (The American Museum leaflet 2002). Certainly the exhibition provided the visitor with examples of early depictions of North American Indians, however their representational authenticity is not without question. Yet no mention is made by the museum of the potential problems with the De Bry images.

In the adjoining room however, a further exhibition (*The North American Indian – as varied as the land*) informs the visitor of the great effects that "confused . . . image(s) of the American Indian" have had on "the minds of . . . generations of children" (The American Museum 2002) – representing De Bry as authentic hardly sits well with this sentiment. But whilst De Bry's often savage images of North American Indians and their religious practices may have faded somewhat, the plethora of Plains imagery with its feather-bonnets and horse-backed warriors has taken its place in the minds of our children; many a child continues to dress in feathers, war whoop and shoot the cowboy kid next-door!

This Plains image can be seen to have firm roots, although not its seed, in the paintings of the mid-nineteenth century artists such as George Catlin (1796–1872). Catlin, an American watercolour painter, travelled more widely and portrayed more scenes of North America and its indigenous inhabitants than any other artist until the advent of photography. While much has been written upon Catlin and his works, it is sufficient here to note that he had a Romantic love of the peoples he likened to Ancient Greeks and Romans (Jacobs 1995: 117, 121; Moore 1997: 142, 161). His paintings typically featured horse-backed warriors, exotic-looking chiefs, scenes of buffalo hunting and of savage rituals;[5] all of which he supplemented with tales of Indian daring, courage, strength and agility. His paintings and written works had, and still have, great public appeal. Not only did Catlin tour his works and collection of North American Indian artefacts to great acclaim around American and European cities, but a children's book *The North American Indian* by Old Humphreys was based upon his written and artist works.

Humphrey's *The North American Indian* was published by the London Religious Tract Society in 1855, and featured tales told by a trapper to three young boys aged between six and twelve years of age. As they listen to the old man's recollections of rituals such as the Mandan Medicine-Lodge ceremony,[6] they compare the warriors exploits and brave-ness to their own playtime adventures and accidents (Humphreys 1855: 188–9). This comparative attitude toward North American Indian life was mirrored in contemporary newspaper reports of Catlin's 1848 touring exhibition. *The London Times* for example noted that fox-hunting seemed "a puny pastime" when compared to the "grappling of a bear or the butting of a bison" (Catlin 1848: 209). Both adult's and children's representations of Indians in the Victorian-era tended to emphasize the *Boys Own* aspect of North American Indian lifeways. However, their spirituality was another matter and nothing short of conversion to Christianity was deemed acceptable, as the reservation schools proved testimony to (Barker 1997; Enochs 1997). But that aside, noble savage heroism ensured that the brave warrior-like image of the North American Indian was the popular one.

Like the representations in De Bry, some of the images that Catlin made were lifted for use in later publications and often mistranslated in the process. However, not all of Catlin's images, it should be noted, were entirely accurate, several works were done in Paris based purely on recollections and tales-told round the evening camp-fire.[7] However, so popular was the be-feathered image of the Plains Indian, that Catlin's 1832 portrait of the Mandan second chief *Mah-To-Toh-Pa* (Four Bears)[8] was used several times to represent Indians of different times and different locations. With his floor-length feather-bonnet and fringed painted buckskin outfit Four Bears became the eighteenth-century Ottawa leader *Pontiac* in a popular nineteenth century publication about the North American Indian wars, and the mythical Iroquois trickster *Pawpukkeewis* in the illustrations of Henry Longfellow's epic poem

Hiawatha (1855) (Ewers 1999: 16–17). The mid-nineteenth century it seemed could not get enough of eagle feathers. With the plethora of *Boys Own* representations, whether accurate originals or inaccurate copies, popular visual representations concentrated on the Plains image as normative for the Indian in general.

However, perhaps doing more than anyone else to ensure that the enduring image of the North American Indian remained a feather-bonneted one, regardless of the reality of this image, was Buffalo Bill Cody and his Wild West Show. First seen in Britain in May of 1887, Buffalo Bill toured the UK for several years with his cast of almost one-hundred North American Indian men, women and children. With huge publicity and extravagant sets, which included the original Deadwood stagecoach that the Indians attacked twice daily along with a settler cabin and its pioneering inhabitants, Cody ensured massive audiences wherever he went (Gallop 2001). Advertised as reality, this elaborate tale-told-as-fact show portrayed Indians as Romantic savages; blood-thirsty but heroic, a worthy enemy for the US cavalry-men. And it is this image of the Indian that continued into the Hollywood Westerns where John Wayne, virtually single-handedly, ensured the safety of honest Christian frontier-folk from those wild and savage be-feathered "injuns" in films such as Stagecoach (United Artists 1939) and The Searchers (Warner Brothers 1956) (Kilpatrick 1999; Stedman 1982).

Since the 1970s though it is more likely to be the Indian depicted as trying to save the frontier from the barbarism of civilization than vice versa, as more recent films have taken a politically-correct stance on the representations of the North American Indian. In *Dances with Wolves* we are presented with the kindly Sioux who welcome the White hero into their midst, allowing him to save them from the barbarity of the US Cavalry, and in the *Spirit*, the Lakota are firmly set as the good guys of the American West. From the too-bad-to-be-true North American Indians of by-gone years we now have too-good-to-be-true images, with reality residing somewhere in the middle; lost amongst the representations that continue to say more about Western representers than about North American Indians.

Possibly the most prolific of such representers is the photographer Edward Sheriff Curtis (1868–1952). Although his late nineteenth and early-twentieth century black and white images remained virtually unknown to the public until the mid-twentieth century, today his Romantic historic photographs can be found gracing numerous publications, as well as appearing on postcards, greetings cards, posters and calendars. His work fits the contemporary too-good-to-be-true portrayal of the Indian; at home in nature, spiritual and proud. While Curtis took an enormous range of images and detailed much of the varied tribal lifeways of the time, although not altogether accurately for he travelled with wigs and costumes to ensure he got his authentic Indian look, it is typically a Plains style feather-bonneted warrior or a distant tipi that exemplifies his work.[9] These images showed the North American Indian that Curtis wanted to exist, and continue to represent the type of Indian that is often imagined today.

As demonstrated in the above examples, visual representations, albeit often biased and stereotypical representations, of Indians have not been uncommon in the UK since the 1600s and they remain as popular as ever. Whilst the touring shows of Buffalo Bill may have gone, public displays of Indian-ness remain in the form of media presentations (as already discussed) and in UK Powwows, gatherings of UK individuals who display aspects of Indian costume, dance and spirituality to the fee-paying public.

Powwows in the UK

Recently I have been engaged in field research with the UK Powwow movement. This loosely organized community of individuals dress, dance and sing as North American Indians, typically in contemporary regalia, although some choose a more historic mode of dress. These performances provide an opportunity for like-minded people to get together in little publicized events, but a few times a year Powwows go public. The year 2002 saw the thirty-sixth annual Powwow at The American Museum in Claverton, Bath (a museum of predominantly pre-twentieth century North American arts and crafts), and the first Powwow at the English Heritage site of Battle Abbey in Hastings, West Sussex. These events serve as both entertaining and educational, displaying to the public the elaborate costumes of the dancers as well as the variety of dances and songs that North American Indians perform during their own contemporary Powwows. However, they also inform the audience about aspects of North American Indian spirituality. At Bath, The Master of Ceremony explained the sacrality of the circle in which the dancers performed, and the reasons for invocations to the Great Mystery. At Hastings the show ground was also ritually smudged and the audience requested to treat the area as they would a church; with great respect. Further, the audience was asked to walk around the outside of the area from East to West to honour the directions as the Indians do. The inherent sacredness of the dance area and the event, was clearly emphasized to the fee-paying public.

But why should this have any relevance to children and their under-standings of North American Indians and North American Indian spirituality? Apart from the effects that these displays have on percep-tions of Indian-ness to children in the audience, one reason is because the majority of UK Powwow dancers became interested in North American Indians as children watching Hollywood Westerns. But these adults have gone on not only to continue playing at being an Indian; to dress and dance as one, but also to take on aspects of North American Indian spirituality.

Of the UK Powwow dancers that explicitly practice aspects of North American Indian spirituality, the majority do so in a Lakota Plains style, smudging, sweat-lodging and praying to Wakan Tanka. It would seem that these adults are able to live out their childhood fantasies of feather-bonnets and fringed buckskin, while expressing a form of spirituality that many North American Indians and academics (Western and Native) find unacceptable in non-Natives (Aldred 2000; Churchill 1998; P. Deloria 1998; V. Deloria 1988; Mesteth, Standing Elk & Swift Hawk 1993; Miskimmin 1996). The issues surrounding such appropriation I will not be going into here, but my point is that it is Plains lifeway that is generally, though not solely, represented as *the* normative lifeway and spirituality for *the* North American Indian.

Perceptions of North American Indians by Hampshire, UK School Children

To assess the influence of representations of North American Indians within popular culture and in education upon UK children, and to test the dominance of Plains imagery, I have been engaged in empirical research with approximately ninety Hampshire County school children aged from seven to twelve years of age. As far as I have established no junior schools in Hampshire cover this topic and only a few include North American Indians in their RE curriculum at secondary school. Resources for the subject vary from home-produced handouts to books and materials provided by the Hampshire Teaching Resource Centre.

Methodology

Having located a pre-secondary school sympathetic to my research aims, I was able to question their junior children (aged seven to eleven years) in two group settings (seven to nine years of age, and ages nine to eleven). The teaching staff ensured that the language used in my questions was age appropriate, and the answers were given to me orally. The children were asked a range of questions to ascertain their perceptions of North American Indian peoples[10] and where they had seen these representations.[11] The children were also asked to identify an object; a Dream Catcher, and tell me if they knew of a Guiding song *We*

Are The Red Men. Their parents were also asked to complete a questionnaire detailing films, videos and books that the children would have been exposed to, and whether the children had been to any Disney theme park (alongside the Buffalo Bill Wild West Show, toys in Indian-style dress and other Indian merchandise such as jewellery, posters and collectable figurines are widely available at the Disney parks). The parental questionnaire was used to supply more detailed information concerning sources of representation.

As regards the secondary school, I questioned a class of Year 7 pupils (aged eleven to twelve years) from one of the institutions that used an officially produced text book as a teaching aid, to elicit perceptions of North American Indian peoples based on the premise that the class had recently spent a term (approximately twelve one-hour lessons) learning about these peoples.[12] The teacher approved the questions as suitable for the children. The students were also shown a series of images to look at in terms of their accuracy; catalogue pictures of children's playsets which combine tipis with totem poles and display Indians alongside cowboy playsets (Lego Duplo & Playmobil), and three black-and-white photographs; an anonymous 1930s postcard of an English lady standing in a suburban garden wearing a knee-length fringed buckskin dress with Western shoes who was sporting a feather in her hair and holding a tomahawk, plus two recent photographs of a First Nation Canadian youth wearing modern Western dress in urban locations (Thomas 1997, 1994). They were also asked to identify a Dream Catcher, and if they knew the Guiding song. Further, the class was shown two short clips from the Hollywood films *Maverick* (Warner Bros. 1998) and *ThunderHeart* (Columbia Tristar 1992) to comment on in relation to their perceptions of North American Indians. The *Maverick* clip showed an Indian chief expressing exasperation at the normative Western stereotype of the be-feathered tipi dwelling Indian, while the *Thunderheart* excerpt showed aspects of reservation life; abandoned rusting cars, dilapidated shacks, jeans-clad children playing in rubbish-littered dirt streets. The children worked in groups of no more than three students and wrote their answers on sheets of paper that re-stated the questions.

I based the majority of my questions upon a North American study conducted in 1974 by the League of Women Voters, the findings of which appear in *American Indian Stereotypes in the World of Children* (League of Women Voters 1999: 3–8). While North America has very different issues in connection with the stereotyping of North American Indians, such as the controversial use of Indian mascots by sports teams and the celebration of Thanksgiving Day (Frazier 1997; Stedman 1982), I was interested to discover the perceptions of UK youngsters who typically have little or no direct access to North American Indians outside the confines of the mass media with its strong Plains bias – although doubtless this is the case in most of North America also.

Findings

Although by no means an exhaustive study, my research indicated that the junior children had a not inconsiderable (although not necessarily accurate) understanding of North American Indians. Indeed, the children's knowledge and interest in North American Indians was immense, not a single child was unable to express something about North American Indians. However, the children's perceptions were typically based on Plains culture with feathers and tipis featuring high on their list of descriptions (although huts in the forest was a well-known alternative dwelling place despite little thought having been given to the differing geography of such accommodation). Indians were described as people with painted faces, feathers in their hair and buffalo-skin clothing who kill their food with bows and arrows, who use totem-poles to tie up captives while tomahawking them to death, who dance around fires war-whooping and who communicate with smoke signals and drums; understandings that were typical of the Victorian era when the colonialist displays that were The World's Fairs and Wild West shows confirmed to the general public the reality of the Indian savage (Altick 1978; Maxwell 1999).

From the parental questionnaires and responses from the children it was clear that they had taken their perceptions of North American Indians from representations available in wider society, from the occasional Hollywood Western (Warner Brothers' *Calamity Jane* (1953) was mentioned by an eight year old), through children's favourites such as Dreamwork's *An American Tail: Fievel Goes West* (1991) and Walt Disney's *Peter Pan* (1953) and *Pocahontas* (1995). As there can be little doubt that popular representations greatly influence the understandings of our young children, it may be interesting to see if Dreamwork's overtly pro-North American Indian animated film *Spirit: Stallion of the Cimarron* makes any difference to children's perceptions of Indians the future.

The power of popular representation was perhaps expressed most strongly in that very few of the children questioned did not recognize the Dream Catcher that I had asked them to identify. Although this surprised the class teachers, these items are often found in High Street stores as well as being a regular feature in various fundraising catalogues used by schools and children's activity clubs.[13] In the contemporary West, Dream Catchers appear to signify Indian-ness as much as feathers, tipis and totem-poles, although understandings of this object appear to be as partial as perceptions of these other Indian signifiers.[14]

At the secondary school the overall perception of North American Indians was little different. Despite twelve weeks learning about a variety of North American Indian peoples, their histories, spiritualities and contemporary lifeways, from several divergent locations (geographic and temporal), when asked similar questions to those put to the junior children the secondary pupils tended to recall only Plains-style clothing and housing, with buffalo-hunting being a typical occupation. It would seem that the representations that typify popular culture were not replaced by those taught in this secondary school module. Despite teaching that resulted in examination results well above the UK national average[15] it would appear that the pervasiveness of stereotypical popular representation has led to the students failing to properly internalize the recently taught non-stereotypical understandings.

When questioned about the playsets, the Year 7s felt that they accurately represented North American Indians, and would be appropriate for young children to learn about Indian peoples. They expressed surprised when the totem-pole/tipi anomaly was pointed out. In regard to the photographs, most of the class thought that the postcard lady was the most authentic Indian due to her outfit which acted as a potent signifier. Again surprise was expressed that the young man in the photograph was Native. Thus, despite these children being taught about differing Nations and about modern North American Indian lifeways, homogeneity and statis ruled the day with signifiers of Indian-ness not being undifferentiated and the concept of contemporary Native peoples rejected in the face of historic stereotypes.

In regard to the film clips several children expressed surprise that North American Indians spoke English, and that they wore modern Western clothing. Once more the concept of modernity and Indian-ness was lost on the majority of the class despite their previous tuition on the subject. Yet when shown and asked to identify a Dream Catcher this item was almost universally recognized. While the secondary teacher expressed surprise at the dominance of popular knowledge over and above the recent formally taught material, such questioning reinforced the findings from the junior children that representations, especially popular visual representations, of North American Indians are hugely influential. The secondary school teacher is incorporating some of the research materials in his future lessons to ensure that his students confront their stereotypes of North American Indians and thus learn more effectively (Walker 2002).[16]

Although I was unable to question students at the other secondary school, the teacher provided me with the worksheets used by the class. Here there was a very strong emphasis upon Lakota Plains culture as *the* normative spirituality for North American Indians *per se*. Indeed, the course suggested that Vision Quests, Sweat-lodges and Sun-Dances summed up the entirety of North American Indian spirituality. Whilst the work sheets written by the previous teacher were reasonably knowledgeable about Lakota culture, the emphasis on the word "the" homogenized the wide diversity of North American Indian cultures and beliefs into a single entity, and totally ignored the possibility that North American Indians could hold alternative spiritual beliefs, such as Christianity (Weaver 1998; Kidwell, Noley & Tinker 2002). Further, the course had a focus upon the historic with the regular use of past tenses to describe all activities. Here the children were encouraged not only to believe that Lakota lifeways typified North American Indian-ness, but that Indians were distant in time.

The Otherness of North American Indians was perhaps most strongly demonstrated in the popularity of a Guiding song *We are the Red Men* that all the children were asked to elaborate on. *Red Men* is mostly sung by Brownies, Guides and Scouts at campfire sing-songs, but is not unknown as an action song in infant and pre-schools. The UK Guiding Organisation in one of their songbooks suggest that the words "maybe . . . a parody of a genuine song" (1976: 12) and add that the performance should be done with "solemn dignity." But as the accompanying actions are frankly pantomime-ish (1976: 13) and with words that include "long-nosed squaws", perhaps the British Guiding movement should re-think its policy regarding this song.[17] In North America, the Scout and Guide movement removed *Red Men* from its publications in 1994 for reasons of racism, and they informed me that the song has not been sung since the 1960s due to its unacceptability (Susan 2002; Austin 2002).

Conclusion

From the sixteenth century onwards then popular visual representations have tended to reflect contemporary Western attitudes of the representer, rather than depicting the reality of the subject/s. The historic images I have very briefly, and with great generality, run through have assisted in shaping contemporary representations of North American Indians. Obviously manufacturers of goods today will only make products that are going to sell, and the time-tried and/or stereotypical image of the Indian continues to sell well. Even publications available for the enthusiast tend toward the Romantic and unless someone takes the trouble to research about the representations that are available to them, few will question the accuracy of the representations in *Haiwatha*, or the authenticity of a Curtis poster. The continuous exposure to the Plains image of the North American Indian, regardless of its origin, has had a lasting effect.

Children are growing up in the UK with representations of North American Indians that would not be sanctioned of many other peoples or religions; their understandings of these peoples is at best partial and stereotypical, and at worst inaccurate and derogatory. Yet even with formal education, ingrained images of the Indian as depicted in wider culture remain almost impervious to less misrepresentational teachings. In North America moves have been made to rectify stereotypical and derogatory imagery of North American Indians, but as yet little has been done in the UK. Indians as predominantly portrayed, and perceived, as historic tipi-dwelling be-feathered savages (and makers of Dream Catchers!); (neo-) colonialist in the extreme. The idea that North American Indians might live modern lives is almost unthinkable, as is the conception that they may not hold traditional beliefs.

Granted there are few North American Indians living in the UK and as such there is little pressure to change misrepresentations, nevertheless, rectifying inaccuracies should not purely be a result of insider complaint. We are allegedly living in a post-colonial society where respect for other peoples is paramount. Yet, the visual representations of North American Indians in UK popular culture speak more of colonialism with its continuing re-presentation of the same old Indian-ness. In continuing to allow popular culture to virtually be the sole informant of a people's identity, not only do North American Indians remain dialectically opposed to Western norms, but they continue to be defined as an homogeneous and historic peoples, and how post-colonialist is that?

Notes

1   Produced by Disney July 2001. See <www.prdailynews.co.uk /archiveukeuro_july.htm> for images.
2   *The Dandy* is produced by D.C. Thomson & Co. Ltd.
3   "Chiefe Herowans wife of Pomeoc and her daughter of the age of eight or do years" by White c1558 was subtly altered in De Bry's "Pomeoc mother and daughter" c1590. See Kupperman 2000: 44–5 for these images.
4   For Le Moyne's "Tupinamba Cannibal Feast" (De Bry c. 1590) see Jahoda 1999: 103. Both "Savage Cruelty" (child sacrifice) and "Savage Religion" (idolatry) were reprinted in Picart's *The Ceremonies & Religious Customs of the various Nations of the Known World* (1733–39) and can be found in Ellingson 2001: 11, 45.
5   See Moore 1997 for many examples of Catlin's work.
6   The 1970 film *A Man Called Horse* (20th Century Fox, director E. Silverstein) portrays Catlin's Mandan Medicine-Lodge ceremony.

7   "Mandan Scalping an Enemy, 1835–7" (Moore 1997: 187) is an excellent
    example of painting done by Catlin purely based on recollections.
8   See Moore 1997: 142 for Catlin's portrait of *Mah-Ta-Toh-Pa*.
9   See Davis (1985) and Pritzker (1993) for examples of Curtis' work.
10 Can anyone tell me anything they know about the people that we call
    Indians? Where might they live? What might they wear? What jobs might
    they do?
11 Can you tell me where you have learnt about the Indians you have talked
    about?
12 Having been taught most recently about the Sioux Indians, do you think
    there are any other Indian peoples? Can you tell me where Indians live?
    What jobs they do? What they wear? Can you name a famous Indian and
    what they were/are famous for? Did all Indians go on a vision Quest? Can
    Indians be Christian?
13 Fund Raising Direct, Preston: Webb Ivory: Burton on Trent.
14 Tipis are rarely understood as being the property of woman, and both
    totem-poles and Dream Catchers are typically removed from their mythic
    bases.
15 Seventy-one percent of students gaining grades A–C in final RE exams for
    the year 2001.
16 The teacher has requested that he not remain anonymous.
17 The UK Guiding body have no record of this song in current publications,
    but it is very well known in Hampshire and continues to be part of their
    repertoire.

References

Aldred, L. 2000: Plastic Shamans and Astroturf Sun Dances: New Age
    Commercialization of Native American Spirituality. In *American Indian
    Quarterly*, 24 (3): 329–352.
Altick, R. D. 1978: *The Shows of London*. Cambridge, MA: Belknap Press of
    Harvard.
Anon. Undated: *Fact or Fiction? Do you have the right to any faith you want?* Online:
    <http://users.pandora.be/gohiyuhi/art00001.html>.
Ash, S. 2001: *Sacred Drumming* (foreword by W. Black Elk). Old Alresford:
    Godsfield Book.
Austin, L. (Records Administrator and Archivist, Girl Guides of Canada) 2002:
    Personal Correspondence. 12 February.
Barker, D. K. S. 1997: Kill the Indian, Save the Child: Cultural Genocide and the
    Boarding School. In D. Morrison (ed.), *American Indian Studies: An
    Interdisciplinary Approach to Contemporary Issues*. New York: Peter Lang, 47–68.
British Broadcasting Corporation (BBC). 2001: *Housecall*. BBC1. 25 April.
Bell, L. 1992: *Colonial Constructs: European Images of Maori, 1840–1914*. Auckland:
    Auckland University Press.
Berkhofer, R. F. Jr. 1978: *The White Man's Indian: Images of the American Indian
    from Columbus to the Present Day*. New York: Vintage Books.
Bierhorst, J. 1994: *The Way of the Earth: Native America and the Environment*. New
    York: William Morrow and Co.

Bird, S. E. (ed.) 1996: *Dressing in Feathers: The Construction of the Indian in American Popular Culture*. Oxford: Westview Press.

Bloom, L. (ed.) 1999: *With Other Eyes: Looking at Race and Gender in Visual Culture*. London: University of Minnesota Press.

Catlin, G. 1848: *Catlin's Notes of Eight Years' Travel and Residence in Europe, with His Native American Indian Collection*. Vol. II. London: G. Catlin.

Churchill, W. 1998: *Fantasies of the Master Race: Literature, Cinema and the Colonisation of American Indians*. San Francisco: City Lights Books.

Columbia Tristar. 1992: *Thunderheart*. Directed/produced by M. Apted.

Davis, B. A. 1985: *Edward S. Curtis: The Life and Times of a Shadow Catcher*. San Francisco: Chronicle Books.

Deloria, P. J. 1998: *Playing Indian*. London: Yale University Press.

Deloria, V. Jr. 1988: *Custer Died for Your Sins: An Indian Manifesto*. London: University of Oklahoma Press.

Dreamworks. 2002: *Spirit: Stallion of the Cimarron*. Directed/produced by K. Asbury and L. Cook.

Dreamworks. 1991: *An American Tail: Fieval Goes West*. Directed/produced by P. Nibbelink and S. Wells.

Ellingson, T. 2001: *The Myth of the Noble Savage*. London: University of California Press.

Enochs, R. 1997: The Catholic Missions to the Native Americans. In Morrison, D. (ed.), *American Indian Studies: An Interdisciplinary Approach to Contemporary Issues*. New York: Peter Lang: 195–216.

Ewers, J. C. 1999: The Emergence of the Plains Indian as the Symbol of the North American Indian. In A. Hirschfelder, P. F. Molin, and Y Wakin (eds), *American Indian Stereotypes in the World of Children: A Reader and Bibliography*. Maryland: Scarecrow Press Inc, 11–20.

Foucault, M. 1977: *Discipline and Punish: The Birth of the Prison* (translated by A. Sheridan). London: Allen Hall.

Francis, D. 1992: *The Imaginary Indian: The Image of the Indian in Canadian Culture*. Vancouver: Arsenal Pulp Press.

Frazier, J. 1997: Tomahawkin' the Redskins: "Indian" Images in Sports and Commerce. In D. Morrison (ed.), *American Indian Studies: An Interdisciplinary Approach to Contemporary Issues*. New York: Peter Lang, 337–56.

Gallop, A. 2001: *Buffalo Bill's British Wild West*. Stroud: Sutton Publishing.

Gidley, M. (ed.) 1994: *Representing Others: White Views of Indigenous People*. Exeter: University of Exeter Press.

Girl Guide Association 1976: *Musical Fun with the Brownie Pack*. London: Girl Guide Association.

Goldberg, D. T. and Quayson, A. (eds) 2002: *Relocating Postcolonialism*. Oxford: Blackwell.

Hall, S. 1997: *Representation: Cultural Representations and Signifying Practices*. London: Sage Publications.

Hardt, M. and Negri, A. 2000: *Empire*. London: Harvard University Press.

Hawthorne, S. 1989: The Politics of the Exotic: The Paradox of Cultural Voyeurism. In *Meanjin*, 48 (2): 259–68. Heron Cards, Hitchen, Hertfordshire, UK.

Hesse, B. 2002: Forgotten Like a Bad Dream: Atlantic Slavery and the Ethics of

Postcolonial Memory. In D. T. Goldberg and A. Quayson (eds), *Relocating Postcolonialism*. Oxford: Blackwell: 143–73.

Hirschfelder, A. 1999: Toys with Indian Imagery. In A. Hirschfelder, P. F. Molin, and Y. Wakin (eds), *American Indian Stereotypes in the World of Children: A Reader and Bibliography*. Maryland: Scarecrow Press Inc, 139–69.

Hirschfelder, A., Molin, P. F., and Wakin, Y. (eds) 1999: *American Indian Stereotypes in the World of Children: A Reader and Bibliography*. Maryland: Scarecrow Press Inc.

Huhndorf, S. M. 2001: *Going Native: Indians in the American Cultural Imagination*. London: Cornell University Press.

Humphreys, O. 1855: *The North American Indians*. New York: Robert Carter and Brothers.

Jacobs, M. 1995: *The Painted Voyage: Art, Travel and Exploration*. London: British Museum Press.

Jahoda, G. 1999: *Images of Savages: Ancient Roots of Modern Prejudice in Western Culture*. London: Routledge.

Kashima, Y. 2000: Maintaining Cultural Stereotypes in the Serial Reproduction of Narratives. In *Personality and Social Psychology Bulletin*, 26 (5): 594–604.

Kidwell, C. S., Noley, H. and Tinker, G. E. 2002: *A Native American Theology*. New York: Orbis Books.

Kilpatrick, J. 1999: *Celluloid Indian: Native Americans and Film*. London: University of Nebraska Press.

Krech, S. III. 1999: *The Ecological Indian: Myth and History*. London: W.W. Norton and Co.

Kuper, A. 1988: *The Invention of Primitive Society: Transformations of an Illusion*. London: Routledge.

Kupperman, K. O. 2000: *Indians and English: Facing Off in Early America*. London: Cornell University Press.

Kushner, T. 1999: Selling Racism: History, Heritage, Gender and the (Re) production of Prejudice. Online: <http: //www.sagepub.co.uk/journals/ details/ issue/sample/a011065.pdf>.

League of Women Voters. 1999: Children's Impressions of American Indians: A Survey of Surburban Kindergarten and Fifth Grade Children: Conclusions. In A. Hirschfelder, P. F. Molin, and Y. Wakin (eds), *American Indian Stereotypes in the World of Children: A Reader and Bibliography*. Maryland: Scarecrow Press Inc: 3–8.

Lego Duplo. 2001: *Big Chief Brown Bear's Camp* catalogue number 2436.

Maxwell, A. 1999: *Colonial Photography and Exhibitions: Representations of the 'Native' and the Making of European Identities*. London: Leicester University Press.

McClintock, A. 1993: The Angel of Progress: Pitfalls of the Term "PostColonialism". In P. Williams and L. Chrisman, L. (eds), *Colonial Discourse and Post-Colonial Theory: A Reader*. New York: Harvester Wheatsheaf: 291–304.

McGaa, E. (Eagle Man) 1990: *Mother Earth Spirituality: Native American Paths to Healing Ourselves and Our World*. New York: HarperSanFrancisco.

McLuhan, T.C. 1971: *Touch the Earth: A Self-Portrait of Indian Existence*. Oxford: Abacus.

Meadows, K. 1996: *Earth Medicine: Revealing Hidden Teachings of the Native American Medicine Wheel* (revised edition). Shaftesbury: Element.

Mesteth, W. S., Standing Elk, D. and Swift Hawk, D. 1993: *Declaration of War Against Exploiters of Lakota Spirituality.* Online: <www.acis.org/war.html>.

Mihesuah, D. A. 1996: *American Indians: Stereotypes and Realities.* Georgia: Clarity.

Moore, R. J. Jr. 1997: *Native Americans: A Portrait: The Art and Travels of Charles Bird King, George Catlin, and Karl Bodmer.* New York: Stewart, Tabori and Chang.

Miskimmin, S. 1996: The New Age Movement's Appropriation of Native Spirituality: Some Political Implications for the Algonquian Nation. In *The Papers of the Algonquian Conference, 27*: 205–11.

Morgan Creek International. 1992, 1998: *Last of the Mohicans.* Directed/produced by M. Mann and L. Hunt.

Moore-Gilbert, B. 1997: *Postcolonial Theory: Contexts, Practices, Politics.* London: Verso.

Moser, S. 1998: *Ancestral Images: The Iconography of Human Origins.* Stroud: Sutton Publishing Ltd.

Orion. 1990, 1998: *Dances With Wolves.* Directed/produced by K. Costner.

Pickering, M. 2001: *Stereotyping: The Politics of Representation.* Basingstoke: Palgrove.

Playmobil, 2001: *Mounted Warrior* catalogue number 3876, *Wolf Clan Hunters* 2874, *Totempole Warriors* 3873, *Natives' Teepee* 3871, *Camp Thunder* 3870.

Pomegranate. Undated: *Native American Women: Curtis Stationery Set.* Calgary: Pomegranate Communications, Inc.

Pratt, S. 1989: *The European Perception of the Native American, 1750–1850.* Unpublished doctoral dissertation.

Pritzker, B. 1993: *Edwards S. Curtis.* London: Bison Group.

Reese, D. Undated: *Teaching Young Children about Native Americans.* Online: <http://111.ed.gov.databases/ERIC_Digests/ed394744.html>.

Root, D. 1998: *Cannibal Culture: Art, Appropriation and the Commodification of Difference.* Oxford: Westview Press.

Rossiter, G. 1997: The Shaping Influence of Film and Television on Young People's Spirituality: Implications for Moral and Religious Education. Part 2. In *The International Journal of Children's Spirituality*, 1 (2): 21–35.

Saplin, B. and Seale, D. 1992: *Through Indian Eyes: The Native Experience in Books for Children.* Philadelphia: New Society Publishers.

Schmidt, R. 2000–1a: *The Harm of Native Stereotyping: Facts and Evidence.* Online: <http://www.bluecorncomics.com/stharm.htm>.

Schmist, R. 2000–1b: *Quotes on Native Stereotyping.* Online: <http://www.bluecorncomics.com/stquotes.htm>.

Schneider, D. J. 2003: *Stereotypes and Stereotyping.* Online: <http://www.ruf.rice.edu/~sch/Stereotype%20Book%20Chapters.htm>.

Stedman, R.W. 1982: *Shadows of the Indian: Stereotypes in American Culture.* Norman: University of Oklahoma Press.

Susan. 2002 (Sunshine Scouts, Canada): Personal Correspondence. 13 February.

Taschen. Online: <http://www.taschen.com>.

Taschen. 1997(a): *The North American Indian: The Complete Portfolios.* Germany: Taschen.

Taschen. 1997(b): *The North American Indian: Photographs by Edward Sheriff Curtis: 30 Postcards*. Germany: Taschen.

The American Museum. 2002: *The North American Museum: As varied as the land*. Claverton, Bath.

Thomas, J. 1997: *Bear Thomas, Buffalo Harbour, New York, 1997*. Online: <http: //www3.sympatico.ca/onondaga11/attitude.html>.

Thomas, J. 1994: *Bear Thomas – General Store, Toronto, Ontario, 1994*. Online: <http: //www3.sympatico.ca/onondaga11/dreamescape.html>.

United Artists. 1939: *Stagecoach*. Directed by J. Ford.

Versluis, A. 1993: *Way of Native American Traditions*. London: Thorsons.

Wa-Na-Nee-Che (D. Renault) and Freke, T. 1996: *Native American Spirituality*. London: Thorsons.

Walker, M. 2002: Personal Conversation. 20 March.

Walt Disney/Buena Vista. 1995: *Pocahontas*. Directed/produced by E. Goldberg.

Walt Disney/Buena Vista. 1953, 1998: *Peter Pan*. Directed/produced by C. Geronimi and W. Jackson.

Warner Brothers. 1998: *Maverick*. Directed/produced by R. Donner.

Warner Brothers. 1956: *The Searchers*. Directed by J. Ford.

Warner Brothers. 1953: *Calamity Jane*. Directed/produced by D. Butler.

Weaver, J. (ed.) 1998: *Native American Religious Identity: Unforgotten Gods*. New York: Orbis Books.

Williams, G. Undated: "Bestriding the World". Online: <http: //www.mediachannel.org/granville.shtml>.

Chapter 4

Issues of Identity for "Asian" Girls in Britain

JANE ERRICKER

"Hijab is not merely a covering dress but more importantly, it is behaviour, manners, speech and appearance in public. Dress is only one facet of the total being." *Mary C. Ali*

THIS CHAPTER is concerned with the problems that "Asian" children, or young people, have in adapting to life in Britian, either because they have been moved from another country to live in Britain, or because their home and community culture represents a different set of norms and expectations from those they experience in school and in the wider community. It concentrates on girls as the problems often have a gendered aspect.

The reflections I present in this chapter have grown out of a series of experiences that I, and the Children and Worldviews Project team, have had both as researchers and as teachers.

The initial set of experiences was those we, Clive, Cathy and Jane, had interviewing young children in a primary school that was 99 per cent "Asian" (their word) children who were Muslim, Hindu or Sikh. We have written more specifically about those experiences elsewhere (Erricker et al 1997). The second set of experiences were those Clive and I had while teaching Madressa school teachers in a local Muslim community, and conversations with members of the community. These two sets of experiences have led me to consider the lives of young people, particularly girls, who are growing up in social situations that accept them as "same", in the small community, and define them as "other" in the larger, host community. I wanted to determine how these girls construct their identities, given that the relationships which are the raw material for that construction would be reflecting back very different perceptions. In the small community of which these young people are a part (their religious or cultural community) they would be the "same" and approved of, and in the larger community (a British town or city in which they were part of a minority group) they would be seen as "other" and not necessarily understood. Now I realize that this is not an unusual situation for any of us. All of us are parts of different, overlapping communities (Griffiths 1995) that to a greater or lesser degree will accept us, reject us or simply tolerate us. The difference with the communities that I am considering is that the difference and the reaction is greater, and that there is a positive choice by some of the young people to emphasize the difference. What interests me most about the situation of the girls in these communities is the way in which discourses of gender, "race" and power interact and intersect and how these girls claim agency and power as they bridge the two communities they inhabit.

This chapter is the very beginning of my research in this area, taking data from several sources that were not necessarily intended to answer these questions. But it *is* possible to ask these questions of this data, and from the answers to those questions begin to construct what eventually will be a much larger and more focused study. Here I hope to show how identity construction is influenced by the social situation of children and young people, and how the social situation that is used for this construction varies with the age of the child/young person. This will lead me to the importance of a particular community for adolescent girls and to a discussion of the way in which they choose their behaviour, that is, questions of agency and control. In looking at these issues I am trying to avoid judgements based on simple ideas of social justice, gender or "race" and instead am suggesting, like Griffiths (1995), and Kincheloe and Steinberg (1997), that "in the reality of the lived world such categories rarely appear in the 'purity' implied here, as they blend and blur, undermining any effort to impose theoretical order" (p. 3).

Theoretical Framework

I am interested here in the construction of identity by the children we interviewed. Identity construction is complex and is dependent on relationships, as Carol Gilligan (1982) says in her notion of the self that gives us a sense of the process of self construction as ongoing. Her "self" is attached, relational and subjective. She says:

> we know ourselves as separate only insofar as we live in connection with others, and that we experience relationships only insofar as we differentiate other from self. (Gilligan 1982: 63)

The construction takes place in temporal and spatial contexts, as Morwenna Griffiths (1995) explains. In her model the individual creates her own identity but not in isolation from circumstance or context:

> The individual can only exist through the various communities of which she is a member, and, indeed, is continually in the process of construction by those communities. [The web] emphasises that the concept "community" must be understood to include both those it is possible to know personally and also the wider society and its political categories . . . The proposal is that self (the self, the individual) is constrained by overlapping, various communities, each of which is itself changing. Such plurality is the norm, not the exception. (Griffiths 1995: 93)

In order to understand the importance of relationship in the construction of identity by the subjects of my research, in the way that Griffiths suggests above, it is important to appreciate the nature of the communities in which they live. The children in this study are of "non-European" descent, easily identified by particular signifiers as "other" from the social majority (nationwide rather than neighbourhood). In the words of Banks they are members of an ethnic group,

> An ethnic group may be defined as an involuntary collectivity of people with a shared feeling of common identity, a sense of peoplehood, and a shared sense of interdependence of fate. These feelings derive, in part, from a common ancestral origin, a common set of values, and a common set of experiences. (Banks 1981: 41)

This common ancestral origin and common set of experiences means that some are dark skinned, dark enough to be identified as "other", some wear "unusual" clothing as identified by the social majority, e.g. shalwar khameez, hijab, and some have non-Christian religious commitments, made obvious by the specific activities of daily prayer, fasting etc. Their overlapping communities therefore fall easily into two groups, those of "similar" social minority people, and those of "different" social majority people. And they are facing and interacting with at least two different community cultures as defined by Figueroa (1991):

> In broad terms culture refers to characteristic constellations of conceptual constructs, symbolic systems, beliefs, values and behavioural patterns shared by a group or set of groups, differentiating it from other groups or sets of groups, thus defining identity. (Figueroa 28)

It is possible that the communities I am talking about would fall under the category that Weeks has described as follows:

> The strongest sense of community is in fact likely to come from those

groups who find the premises of their collective existence threatened and who construct out of this a community of identity which provides a strong sense of resistance and empowerment. Seeming unable to control the social relations in which they find themselves, people shrink the world to the size of their communities and act politically on that basis. The result, too often, is an obsessive particularism as a way of embracing or coping with contingency. (Weeks in Bauman 2001: 100)

It will be interesting to see if the data suggests this. Bauman explains this possible particularism by suggesting that the choices faced by such communities are stark ones:

> The prospect opened up by the nation building project to ethnic minorities was a stark choice: assimilate or perish. Both alternatives pointed ultimately to the same result. The first meant the annihilation of the difference, the second meant the annihilation of the different, but neither allowed for the possibility of the community's survival. The purpose of the assimilatory pressures was to strip the "others" of their "otherness": to make them indistinguishable from the rest of the nation's body, to digest them completely and dissolve their idiosyncrasy in the uniform compound of national identity. (Bauman 2001: 93)

The communities that these young people belong to have not assimilated. They remain distinct and distinguishable in their dress and behaviour and in that sense may be said to be rowing against the tide, as identified by Bauman. He sees communities in Western culture under threat as they cease to work because, in the West,

> the growth of individual freedom may coincide with the growth of collective impotence in as far as the bridges between private and public life are dismantled or were never built to start with; or, to put it differently, in as far as there is no easy and obvious way to translate private worries into public issues and, conversely, to discern and pinpoint public issues in private troubles. (Bauman 1999: 2)

He goes on to say:

> What . . . can bring us together? Sociality, so to speak, is free floating, seeking in vain solid ground on which to anchor, a visible-to-all target on which to converge, companions with which to close ranks. There is a lot of it around – wandering, blundering, unfocused. Lacking in regular outlets, our sociality tends to be released in spectacular one-off explosions – short-lived, as all explosions are. (Bauman 1999: 3)

This critique of "Western" community life is one that I think we would all understand and recognize. Individual freedom has come with a price – the loss of close, supportive, welcoming and safe communities. Every now and again something happens that makes us feel like a community again, but it is always short-lived. It may be an event in our street, our town or own country: the death of a neighbour, a local celebrity, the Queen Mother, or the World Cup. But as Bauman says, it is just a one-off explosion. But does this apply to these small, ethnically and religiously distinct communities to which these young people belong? In the face of larger community breakdown they seem to be holding on to common beliefs and values, common behaviour and common goals. But the result of this must be a tension that increases with each successive generation, as the influence of the "outside world" becomes harder to resist. It is these influences and these tensions that we are exploring in the identities of the young people we spoke to.

In order to analyse the construction of their identities we need to look at the relationship between their community and their identity. As I said previously, identity is constructed as it is situated in time and space. Griffiths says, "The individual can only exist through the various communities of which she is a member, and, indeed, is continually in the process of construction by those communities". And Benhabib (1992) eloquently asks my research question for me when she says:

> Identity does not refer to my potential for choice alone but to the actuality of my choices, namely to how I, as a finite concrete, embodied individual, shape and fashion the circumstances of my birth and family, linguistic, cultural and gender identity into a coherent narrative that stands as my life story . . . the question becomes: how does this finite, embodied creature constitute into a coherent narrative those episodes of choice and limitation, agency and suffering, initiative and dependence? (Benhabib 1992: 161)

So, "we collectively make ourselves but not in conditions of our own choosing" (Griffiths 1995: 70), and within those conditions we look for autonomy and control in order to make ourselves how we wish to.

Griffiths asks us not to look for one aspect of power as predominant over another or others, but instead asks us to see the influences on identity construction as a web. She has used this feminist framework specifically for analysing women's autobiographies and she argues that women have more complex and conflicting aspects of their lives with which to create a coherent single identity. Although she is concerned particularly with women I suspect the same holds true of anyone and certainly for our young people.

There are two aspects of Griffiths' web integral to its formation and which are relevant to my discussion today. One is an understanding of autonomy and the other is that individuals belong to overlapping communities. Both of these have implications for understanding how our identities form within, or in relation to, structures of power / authority. Notions of gendered autonomy and overlapping communities are part of the strands of the web which may at times be at odds with each other. Griffiths argues that autonomy has been assumed to be a non-gendered concept. Yet in its implications of independence and public action it is also implicitly andro-centric. She says that,

> My dependent close relationships feel as though they increase freedom more than they diminish it. I can live my life more as I would want to when I have dependent close relationships with a range of other people. (Griffiths 1995: 30)

This is an important idea. It resembles Gilligan's notions of identity developed in relationship and highlights the importance of close, nurturing and accepting communities in women's lives. However, Griffiths goes on to say that paradoxically "women continue to want to run their own lives and do so in their own way. In other words, they want autonomy, in the sense that autonomy means deciding for oneself" (Griffiths 1995: 136). So how does a sense of automony reconcile itself with being part of community that is also an organization with, as we have said before, shared behavioural patterns and maybe an "obsessive particularism"? Hopefully our data will start to answer that question, and indicate how we might find out more.

Methodology

This chapter draws on data collected by members of the Children and Worldviews Project research team between 1994 and 2001. The dataset mainly consists of open ended interviews with children between the ages of 7 and 16 in two settings: an inner city primary school and at a faith community.

In both settings the aim of the interviews was to use a qualitative approach that enabled the children to talk about their lives and what was important to them. This approach to research is underpinned by a keen awareness of the impact of power within adult-child relationships. Practically this has meant that over time the project team has developed and refined a style of interviewing along the following principles:

- to ensure that the interviewing environment is as comfortable as possible (physically and relationally);
- to establish good rapport with the children/young people and clearly demonstrate that you are interested in listening to what they have to say;
- to ask open-ended questions which allow children/young people to respond freely and deeply, without feeling there is a right answer;

- to allow the child/young person to talk at length about issues which are important to them;
- to follow the lead of the child/young person and pursue issues that they raise as significant to them.

In acknowledging the complexity of young people's lives, as well as the prerequisites for a process where young people are able to narrate these experiences, the research methodology has centred on young people, "not as actors whose behaviour must be measured, but as documents that reflect the culture of which they are the bearers" (Shimahara 1988: 81).

While doing this work we were and are very aware of the problems of white middle class female (or male) researchers talking to girls (or boys) from different ethnic and of religious backgrounds. Like Haw, we are looking for "how the discourses of gender and 'race' articulate with each other" and we accept too the need for "a methodology which would enable an analysis of the complexity and interrelatedness of these discourses and would be sensitive to the issues of power" (Haw 1998: 3).

Interviews were carried out in a primary school and at the Madressa school, by one or more of the Project team – Clive, Cathy and Jane. Although we are aware of the difference the gender of the researcher could make to this work, the gender of the researcher was not considered as an issue at the time. It was only during analysis of the data and the collection of subsequent data, that this analytical category was used. Interviews with two of the male leaders of the community are also quoted here in order to contextualize the young people's comments.

Results and Analysis

In this results section of this chapter I have divided the data into that obtained from the primary school, and that taken from the community. Conclusions will be drawn from all of the data together.

Conversations from the Primary School

The primary school concerned is in a large city in the south of England. The city has large populations of people who are of Indian descent, or who have recently emigrated from the Indian subcontinent. The group is by no means homogeneous, with many different languages represented – of which Hindi, Gujarati and Punjabi are just three. Some of the group are Hindu and some Sikh and some Muslim. We spoke to children in year 3 and year 5.

Year 3 Conversations

The children in year 3 talked at length about their families. They appeared aware of their families' origins in the Indian subcontinent, but did not mention their religious affiliations. The result of questions about India was more description of family relationships. They talked at length about the houses they lived in and enquiries about differences between Britain and Pakistan mainly brought comparisons of the houses.

When one child, F. said that the family was going back to Pakistan, there was no explicit indication that this might be because of any racism that they had experienced, though the family was concerned about the general crime level in Britain. These children's identities were completely bound up with their families, and external influences were only appreciated in terms of how they would affect the family.

Year 5 Conversations

The first interview that we are concerned with here involved a group of the girls R, Sh and H, and two boys D and S in year 5 (aged about 10 years). When they were asked to introduce themselves four out of five of them identified themselves as belonging to a particular religious group, as one of their first statements.

H: my name is H and I'm a Sikh and I believe in my religion and I have got four brothers and one sister.

Like the younger children, they were eager to talk about their families and asked for details of the interviewers' family lives as well. D talked mainly about his family at the beginning of the interview, but later talked about his Muslim religious beliefs and explained aspects of doctrine to the interviewer. Another child, S, showed a detailed knowledge of ritual. The children were very keen to argue over points of doctrine and ritual, reminding us of a Piagetian intense interest in rules. But there was little sense of disagreement or discomfort with the demands of their faith in terms of belief or behaviour, or obviousness awareness of their difference from the surrounding majority community. Even though they were not all of the same faith, the impression from their conversation was one of affirmation of their cultural similarities and an understanding and acceptance of religious differences. There was also no sense of gender conflicts from this mixed group interview.

However when two of the girls, R and H, were interviewed separately a slightly different picture emerged. They had a grasp of different frameworks of identity and gender role and they knew that there were differences in practice in England and in India. For example, they knew that boys were valued more than girls:

R: you have to cut it cos, cos you know like in India right, in every Indian religion they don't like girls much because they say that when the girls get married they go to a different sort of house and they sort of really like boys to happen instead.

They also knew that their roles would be different from those of their English contemporaries;

H: yes, like do you know when we go and that person is married, they have to go to the boy's house and you know the boy's parents, you have to do some work like for them.

The girls had also suffered racial abuse, and knew that they were identified as different by members of the social majority;

R: people calling other people like, like us, like English people calling us Pakis and that, that should be changed
Q: hmm, do you experience some of that yourself?
R: sorry?
Q: do people do that to you?
R: sometimes, yes
Q: yes?
R: like a gang will go up to people and they say
H: the NFs
Q: the NFs? There's a lot round here is there?
H: yes, they try to get us out of the city, they think this isn't our city, but do you know, India isn't our city either
Q: why do you think they're like that?
R: it's because of our skin
Q: yes?
R: like we're black and all that, dark brown
Q: yes
R: and like you're a bit white and pink, that's why

This extract contains the incredibly poignant view that *"they try to get us out of the city, they think this isn't our city, but do you know, India isn't our city either"* where it is clear that, rather than being allowed to have two "cities" or identities, they aren't allowed to have either.

In summary, the year 3 children gain their sense of identity from the family they belong to. They describe themselves as having these brothers and sisters, aunties and uncles who do this and parents and grandads who say that. Pakistan is a place where the family is going to return or where aunty has come from. They did not mention their religious communities, though of course we cannot infer much from this as they might well do so on another occasion. The data here is inadequate for anything but a very tentative indication.

The year 5 children appear to have a clear view of their membership of a religious community, and what that entails for them in terms of religious duties. The girls know how they, as females, are valued within their community and are aware that it is different in the wider community. They are beginning to have an awareness of gendered identity. They know that they are discriminated against because of their "difference" and have their own ideas about how that can be addressed. Their identities are constructed within their small community, and in opposition to discrimination from outside. They know that they have ambitions that might clash with their parents' expectations but they don't see that as an immediate problem.

Conversations from the Community

In retrospect I realized that the conversations from the primary school brought up similar issues to those raised in conversations with members of the Muslim community that we became involved with. This community is a Muslim community in the South of England. There are other similar communities scattered around Britain and the world and they keep in close communication. The members of this community meet on Fridays for prayer and Saturdays for the young people to learn about their faith in Madressa school. These conversations took place on a Saturday. They are best contextualized by the words of two of the elders of the community, M and J, who explain the difficulties the community has with their young people.

J. If you talk to Mulla, one of the problems is education in the community and youth. If you said to him, "What about youth problems?" He would say, "What problems? We go through that phase, everybody. The youth will come out of this phase intact." So this is our aim and what he is promoting in the community. We take these kids through faith school and do everything but we must expect they are going to rebel, they are going to break away, run away, they are going to do silly things, they are going to go gambling, they might womanise, they might do anything. Whatever they do, don't chastise them, be patient. Try to keep them on harness as much as possible. Just pray that they come out of this phase as soon as possible. That is how we work on it. In the Bangladeshi community they say don't send the kids to university, you will lose them. You've got a business running, they can enter that and they will be fine.

We totally disagree with that. We believe the message of the prophet is absolutely clear, that education is paramount "Go and learn", so we have to learn.

Q. So what difficulties does that present for the younger generation here?

J. After school they go and play with their friends and they offer them something to eat and drink and they have to say no. You see it all presents problems. For me in Zanzibar I used to go to a friends house, he would come to my house. Food was not a problem, girl/boy separation was not a problem. For our children it is something they have to deal with and we try to teach them how to deal with it.

M. There the practices and environment were conducive, here they are not conducive.

The elders of the community are aware of the problems, not so much *for* the young people, but *of* the young people. Their attitude is essentially benign, they value education deeply, and they are aware of the tensions their young people face and they are trying to teach them how to cope.

Inevitably the young people's ideas of the problems they face are different.

M (girl aged 15): You can be treated differently and be left out (with your friends) like when they go to bars and concerts . . . everyone hangs out together and I like being with my friends. But when they hang out they go to bars, clubs and stuff. Firstly, I am not allowed there, secondly, I'd just feel out of place in somewhere like that.

Q. Does that cause any questions for you about what you would like to do and what you can't do?

M: Well, we know why we can't . . . alcohol . . . you can't control yourself. But everyone else is doing it, you think, why can't we do something they can do as well.

T. (girl aged 15): They talk about some party and being ill (through drinking) and you think, that was fun? Everyone has such a horrid time, and get ill, yet they make out it was so good, they tell you about being sick and that and you think, I don't want to do that. But just being with your friends can make you high, happy, whatever.

S. (girl aged 13): In my case I'm still so young. It will get more serious later. People accept you in hijab and they are getting to know me better and so they don't ask as many questions. I find it quite hard to explain to them but they just say why? They don't get it.

A. (boy aged 15): I think it's really different (for boys). I don't mind going to the pub, I hang around with my friends wherever they go, so I participate in what they do. If they get drunk I'll do my own little thing…hang around and talk to people and stuff. I know loads of people from our school that go to pubs and everything and not all of them drink, they just go there to hang out and stuff.

Q: Is there a difference between you going to a pub and not having a drink, say, could you? (to girls)

T. They look at us and they see a different person. They look at guys and they just see guys…Muslims in a pub, you wouldn't know, but with us its obvious because we wear hijab. We're Muslims and they can actually see it so we get noticed….My friend says T. oh come it will really be fun. Wear a scarf, a really cool scarf. And I am thinking, OK, can you just imagine me in that place, with these (other) people wearing hardly anything and me in long skirt, long sleeves, scarf and everything. But my friends are so lovely, they want me to enjoy it and every time they go to the clubs they come back and talk about how much fun they have. And they are like "Oh I wish you were there, wish you were there, you were there in spirit". They want me to enjoy it with them but I can't. They try and get around that problem but they can't.

Q. How is it for boys with friends in school?

H. (boy aged 14): My friends are OK because if I'm there they won't have a drink, they'll just get a coke or something. So, if I'm not drinking they won't drink.

In this part of the conversation we get a sense of the difference for the boys and the girls. All of them have restrictions on their behaviour – they can't drink alcohol – but for the boys it is less of an imposition because they are not so obviously different. They are still just "guys" and in a pub it is not so different just not to be drinking. However for the girls even just being in a pub or club is difficult because the dress restrictions are so obvious.

A. I was going to say, with this parents thing, it is different for boys and girls because with the girls the parents watch out for them because, for obvious reasons…
T. …because we're precious
Q. What do you think the reasons are for being stricter on the girls?
A. It's to do with that whole hijab thing again…
T. … because we're more precious

T. Your parents don't let you go out, like with your schoolfriends because they are a bad example. They go in pubs and stuff. But I am not going to do that but they just don't understand.

M. What the parents need to do is trust us enough to go with them but trust us not to do what we know is wrong for us.

A. I thought you just said that you don't want to go anyway though.

T. My mum hardly ever lets me go out with my school friends actually.

Q. Is it different for boys?

A. Yea, parents like their children to make their own decisions, it's not that they can't trust the girls as much, its that . . . girls are more precious (laughter) and with girls, in the end,…I can't say it…

Q. Do girls have to be protected, is that it?

A. Yea

S. People have heard this lots but I'll say it anyway. It's like, if there is a jewel, a really precious jewel, you'd want to keep it safe and hidden…they are precious jewels, get rejected(?) – should this be 'respected'? – and that's why we have hijab and that way you are safer and you keep your self respect and stuff.

T. or M. And we're respected. When I'm walking down the street and there's some other girl a guy will turn round and look at her and wolf whistle, but he'll have respect for me and they don't treat me like a dog (laughter).

However there is no criticism of the practice. The girls accept wearing hijab as what they must do, they know the issues for their non-Muslim friends and they see it as a positive – *"we are respected".* The main tension comes because the parents find it necessary to stop them going out, rather than trusting them to behave in the correct manner when they are out. The girls enlarged on the issue of respect later.

S. If we were to lose our religion we would lose our moral values, our community, we would lose everything about us and have no identity, which I think, is very important to the person. If we were to lose that we would feel really lost and out of place, not knowing where to go and what to do. We would lose our values, community and respect, all the things a person should have coming with religion and I think that is very, very important.

M. or T. In schools if you have self respect people will respect you as well. If you value yourself other people will value you as well. In my school, with my friends, I am usually the last one to hear the gossip, and when one of them fills me in on what's happening I say why didn't you tell me before. They say well you've got morals and you'd think less of us. And I say, no that's not true. They won't tell me what's happening because they think I'll think what they are doing is wrong. They won't say it because they get embarrassed.

S. They come to me for advice as well because they know that I have got respect for myself. I had a friend being beaten up and she came to me because she knew I could help out. A lot of them are actually interested in Islam. They don't know and they want to find out.

S. is very aware of the importance of her religion in identity construction. At the age of thirteen she knows that the community makes her feel
safe. In the community, obeying the rules that it imposes on her, she
feels valued, "in place" and respected. M. knows the downside of this –
"*the last one to hear the gossip*" but she still feels that those outside her
community as well as inside, respect her for what she is. Even though
her identity is constructed in opposition to them, we do not get a sense
of this as negative, unlike the experience of the younger girls at the
primary school. We do not get a sense of this as gendered, in this part
of the conversation.

Conclusions

I found the results of the analysis of this small amount of data unexpected in some ways. I was looking to see how these young people
constructed their identities. What did they use to tell them who they
were? If somebody asks me who I am the answer that I give depends on
many things. In just giving that answer I am admitting to multiple identities, created, but not in isolation from circumstance or context, but
situated and contingent. I am aware that the context in which these
young people were asked about their identities might well affect their
answers (in a religious context, give a religious answer). However, even
with that proviso, I think I can see some trends in the answers they gave.
Firstly, there appears to be a difference with age. The younger children,
when asked (in a roundabout way) who they are, answer that they are
members of particular families. They give details of their families so we
can understand them, and they want to know about our families. Their
contexts are small and immediate, their identity and their protection
comes from those close family relationships. In other work we have
done we have seen both the value of that closeness in dealing with large
issues such as death, and the results of the lack of that protection
(Erricker et al. 1997). The year 5 children immediately identify themselves as members of a particular religious community. They are
beginning to have a sense of their religious community as an arbiter of
behaviour but see no problems or restrictions in that, though they are
aware that they are discriminated against and judged as "other" in the
wider community. The girls know that they are treated differently
because of their gender but see limited problems, treating the issue as
one simply of yet another religious rule. Their context is wider than that
of the year 3 children, taking in the small community, and just touching
on the wider social context.

The young people are fully aware of the wider social context as they
test their identities against "Western" youth with "Western" values and

behaviour. Their identities, still based within the community, are challenged by their close engagement with a different culture and thus are constructed partly in opposition to difference rather than in recognition of sameness. Morwenna Griffiths sees this process as an autonomy:

> The individual deciding for herself is at the centre of a notion of autonomy applicable to the lives of women. This is a freedom to make yourself in recognition of the way the self is made in communities although it is not determined by them. Thus, there is a need for *space* for the self to be formed both in and against various communities of others and also out of the material conditions in which it finds itself. (Griffiths 1995: 142)

Griffiths sees the process as gendered while we would claim that the boys too need that space. For the girls the difference is more obvious making the "against" more of an issue. But for both the idea of space looks like the trust the young people are asking for. The wearing of hijab does not look like an imposition from this data. The girls claim they have respect when their religious commitment is clear in the way they dress and it would appear that as Bauman (1999) suggests, they do not understand the ability to dress as they like, individually, to be freedom,

> To be an individual does nor necessarily mean to be free. The form of individuality on offer in the late-modern or postmodern society, and indeed most common in this kind of society-*privatised* individuality – means, essentially, *unfreedom*. (Bauman 1999: 63)

This makes wearing hijab an empowering choice in the face of a gendered threat of loss of personal identity in the face of perceived male desires. This choice could also be choosing the security of community life above the illusory "freedom" of a postmodern world. The security of the religious community and the positive choice to visibly identify oneself with that community allows the girls to have agency and control that would be denied them in the "free choice" and "individuality" of a Western, postmodern life where community is disappearing.

References

Bauman, Z. 1999: *In Search of Politics*. Stanford: Stanford University Press.
Bauman, Z. 2001: *Community*. Cambridge: Polity Press.
Benhabib, S. 1992: *Situating the Self*. Cambridge: Polity Press.
Carlo, S. When I Covered My Head, I Opened My Mind. *www. islamzine.com* 24/5/02
Erricker, C. in Erricker, C. and Erricker, J. 2001: *Contemporary Spiritualities*. London: Continuum.
Erricker, C., Erricker, J., Ota, C., Fletcher, M and Sullivan, D. 1997: *The Education of the Whole Child*. London: Cassell.

Gilligan, C. 1982: *In A Different Voice.* Cambridge, MA: Harvard University Press.

Griffiths, M. 1995: *Feminisms and the Self: the web of identity.* London: Routledge.

Haw, K. 1998: *Educating Muslim Girls.* Buckingham: Open University Press.

Kincheloe, J. and Steinberg, S. 1997: *Changing Multiculturalism.* Buckingham: Open University Press.

Lister R. 1997: *Citizenship: Feminist Perspectives.* Basingstoke: Macmillan.

Shimahara, N. 1988: Anthroethnography: A Methodological Consideration. In R. Sherman and R. Webb (eds) *Qualitative Research in Education: Focus and Methods.* London: Falmer Press.

Woodhead, M. 1990: Psychology and the Cultural Construction of Children's Needs. In A. James and A. Prout (eds) *Constructing and Reconstructing Childhood – Contemporary Issues in the Sociological Study of Childhood.* London: The Falmer Press.

Part II

Literary Approaches

P ART II consists of six studies that raise important fundamental
questions about what we mean when we speak of spirituality and
how spiritual development can be discerned and promoted.
Whilst complementing the empirical studies, the methods employed in
this section are primarily philosophical and theological, with attention
being paid to the role of language and conceptuality.

Jerome Berryman's "Play as a Means of Grace in Religious Education"
develops his study included within the first book in this series on the
importance of non-verbal communication to spirituality. Here he
concentrates on how a reconceptualisation of grace and play can help
us to recognize why much religious education is manipulative and ultimately spiritually destructive. However, Berryman's argument extends
beyond religious education to a critique of contemporary society that
has lost the understanding of the importance of play, that has replaced
it with the simulacrum of pseudo play, within which grace is absent.
Thus, our relationships are impaired, they lack grace as a giving quality,
the combination of play and creation. With creativity also absent we are
bereft of meaning. Berryman's contention is that religious education (in
the context of Christian nurture) reflects the impoverished model of
wider society, it has internalised, rather than resisted, this modernist
malaise. For educators outside the Christian tradition the force of
Berryman's argument is still salient since, if Berryman is correct, we
might expect the insidiousness of pseudo play to be present in education generally. In this respect there are important links to be made
between Berryman's contribution and those of Priestly and Chater, in
Part III, who critique education within the state system in the UK.

Daniel Scott's "Spirituality in Young Adolescents: Thinking
Developmentally" focuses on Hay and Nye's influential concept,
within spiritual education and the study of young people's spiritual
development, of relational consciousness. He critically examines both
its value and its assumptions. His concern is that the concept of rela-

tional consciousness valorises the spiritual as a separate domain that cannot be located in the broader research into children's development. Scott examines Hay and Nye's categories that constitute relational consciousness from the viewpoints of existing developmental research in educational psychology and especially in relation to cognitive and moral development. He concludes that the concept of relational consciousness exhibits a tendency to think of spiritual development with a model that is too linear to take account of the unsystematic nature of spiritual experiences. There is a need to recognize that spiritual development may take different forms at different times in stages of children's development and that it has a "dark side" associated with loss and abuse, for example, that can affect relational capacity. Also, the unexpected in human experience can offer a wide range of possibility and difference in relational experience. In problematising the idea of relational consciousness Scott raises an important larger question as to how our social and cultural environment impacts upon our spirituality and how we might address such a question. Chater and Priestley are relevant in this respect when discussing the impact of institutionalised education in Part III. Tacey's study is also relevant in this respect, but with regard to religion. Also, if the spiritual is embedded in relationship, what contribution can theology make to this idea? Berryman and Bellous both signal the relevance of this to theology. Finally, are we to assume that it is possible for spirituality to be a universal concept, that it is to be understood as an essential human quality, or does it have to be understood differently by virtue of its contextualisation in different cultures and with regard to different enculturating influences? Wong Ping Ho's study raises issues in this respect, from a Chinese perspective.

John Pridmore's "The Spiritual and the Fantastical – George MacDonald's 'Wise Woman'" resonates with Scott's warning to be careful about presuming the spiritual to be something we can pin down and study the development of in a systematic fashion. Using MacDonald's stories for children and referencing to the work of Priestley, Pridmore locates spirituality firmly in the vagaries of experience. However, he insists that MacDonald's work is important because of the latter's insistence in his stories that it is a matter of "seeing" or "touching" the world in a certain way, and being touched in turn by its unexpected mystery. This is the teaching of MacDonald's Wise Woman, who appears in his books in many forms, and answers all direct questions with answers that are riddles to ponder. There is something analogous to the Hindu concept of maya in what Pridmore is pointing us toward, and the Zen teaching on non-conceptualization. His critical comments on pedagogical provision in education, its didacticism and "artificial analyses", and his positive appreciation of the teaching based on "awkward questions" of MacDonald's Wise Woman resonate with Berryman's emphasis on the need for play and grace.

Joyce Bellous's "Faith and Social Intimacy: Learning for Life" presents a Christian theologically based approach to spirituality developed from a consideration of the importance of faith as the basis of social intimacy. Faith, for Bellous, is the means to living with uncertainty. From a religious perspective it is "holding sure in God". The two parameters of faith that Bellous offers are connected by the analogy of social intimacy. Just as a mother allows her child to take risks and put herself in a situation of uncertainty, but at the some time empowers her to do so, through communicating with her in a socially intimate way, encouraging her, reassuring her and expressing these in various verbal and non-verbal ways, so it is in terms of the believers relation to God. As a result faith is the story that enables us in life and the means to a reality "beyond mere seeing". In effect, faith fulfils both our individual human potential and our common inter-related potential because we move beyond fear. Epistemologically, faith is not what we know for sure scientifically, but still, in a mythological sense, as a whole system of propositions (following Wittgenstein) it is known for sure. This leads Bellous into a discussion of Jesus' teaching which she identifies as complex irony. Thus, having created a division in epistemological understanding, she proceeds to use that hermeneutically in relation to scripture. The result of this interpretation is not that we know in advance what a text means or what results an action will produce, we do not have certainty in that respect, but we have faith as the sure expectation of a positive outcome whatever that outcome may be. In a sense we might say that the outcome is assured as positive because faith is its motivation. To put it another way, using Bellous' analogy, the relationship between mother and child will be assured in its outcome because of the faith and trust involved in the social intimacy of their relationship even if the outcome in any particular case produces unexpected results. The relationship survives, and is possibly nurtured by, whatever result. This is because intimacy is the indicator of commitment and the basis upon which relationships are positively negotiated. The alternative to this commitment generated by faith Bellous discerns contemporarily in a desire for security and a lack of engagement. Thus, for "children to learn to negotiate their own landscape with wisdom and compassion" and for social intimacy to flourish the development of faith is required. Bellous is rejecting the bases upon which modernist society and its educational agendas operate. She is also suggesting that faith transcends or goes beyond the divisions of religious traditions and also the division between religious and secular. Informed by existentialist approaches, in Kierkegaard and Heidegger, she locates in experience as a process of moving forward in uncertainty rather than prior certainty being the basis of action. This resonates with what has been presented within other studies in this section (Berryman, Halstead and Pridmore in particular) but emphasises the radical epistemological rupture required for such a project to work and hints at the significant pedagogical implications entailed.

Mark Halstead's "How Metaphors Structure Our Spiritual Understanding" draws our attention to language. Spirituality does not have a distinctive vocabulary, he argues, but is distinctive in its reliance on metaphor as the method of conveying meaning and, as a result, not reducible to literal statements. This creates hermeneutical difficulties in that we read metaphors in different ways, one example being sometimes for similarity and sometimes for difference. However, the irreducibility of metaphorical language can be judged as elaborate nonsense or referencing to a meaningful truth about experience. Is there any way to decide? Halstead's conclusion lies in the key to metaphors being an explanation of experience, thus, if we work from attempting to convey our spiritual experience in language we enter the linguistic domain of metaphor. What makes the metaphor meaningful to someone else is if it resonates as a way of expressing their own experience or contrasting with it. In education, therefore, this is what we should seek to enable children to develop the capacity to do, as a result this will help will help them develop spiritually. He cites the work of David Hay and John Hammond in relation to religious experience and experiential methods in religious education as examples of this approach. Halstead has much in common with Bellous in terms of the experientialist approach he draws upon and with Pridmore and Priestley when he speaks of the irreducibility of metaphor in relation to spiritual experience. He also leaves us with a puzzling set of hermeneutical problems which partly reference across to Pike's study in **Part III.** These impinge upon issues of agency, authority, representation, and cultural context. When we read metaphors, or any non-literal text, are there limits to interpretation? Is there ever an authoritative interpretation, such as we find within religious traditions and in the way in which texts are interpreted as being representative of the beliefs of those traditions within religious education in schools in the UK. Since it is culture that makes language meaningful, to what extent can we speak meaningfully of spiritual experience in similar terms across cultures?

Wong Ping Ho's "The Chinese Approach to Learning: The Paradigmatic Case of Chinese Calligraphy" follows on well from the issues Halstead has raised. The conceptualisation of the spiritual dimension of human life Wong Ping Ho etymologically locates in *qi,* as an equivalent of the Greek *pneuma and* Hebrew *ruah* and Sanskrit *prana,* thus we have the metaphor of spirit emerge from similar understandings of breath or air in movement as a vital forces animating humans.

But, he is cautious in relating this understanding to Western philosophical categories which operate on a dualistic principle of matter and
spirit. This leaves us with issues of epistemological incommensurability
existing between modern western models and a Chinese model, in his
context, within which the European Enlightenment made no impact.
Tracing *qi* back to Mencius and then introducing the modern Chinese
concept of *jingshen* as an alternative rendition of spirit as a revitalizing
energy acquired through self-cultivation, he then relates this to calligraphy as a pursuit through which this was realized. In Taoist terms a
discipline for following the Way. The important point that Wong Ping
Ho's study allows to emerge is that just as there is no dualism in the epistemological basis of the idea of spirit in Chinese language and culture
and no accompanying sense of individuality relating to spirit, so there
is no notion in calligraphic instruction related to individual creativity
and expression. Learning to do calligraphy, as an expression of self-
cultivation is imitative of the masters not an expression of individual
style, experience or emotion. He argues that the dedication to imitation
and repetition, understood in this way, becomes a spiritual discipline.
It is also meditative, and through this means of expression the dualistic
nature often associated with the spiritual over against the physical or
material is erased. Furthermore, Wong Ping Ho then makes allusion to
how the "new capitalism" can be understood as a western project that
directly contradicts the virtues and goals imbued in the Chinese pedagogy he has described. His argument invites us to reconsider what
Western (and universalist) assumptions we might be bringing to our
understanding of spiritual education and young people's spiritual
development.

The studies in **Part II** address questions concerned with how we are
to characterise spirituality and its relationship with language, culture
and educational development. There is a strong sense, within these
studies, that the frame of reference required to address spirituality is at
odds with that provided by modern educational thinking and that this
applies within both religious and secular contexts.

Chapter 5

Play as a Means of Grace in Religious Education

JEROME W. BERRYMAN

IN *SPIRITUAL EDUCATION* (Erricker, Ota and Erricker 2001), a previous
book in this series, I contributed a chapter about "The Nonverbal
Nature of Spirituality and Religious Language." There I argued that
spirituality is located in our non-verbal communication system and that
the positive and negative richness of this domain can be coordinated in
a series of six diagrams.

The first three diagrams showed aspects of the spiritual life. First, a
pair of opposing forces, full and empty, was compared with an animate-
inanimate polarity. The second figure showed an axis of *anima* (vitality)
and *animus* (animosity) related to an axis of moving-toward versus
moving-away-from. Thirdly, the axis of consuming (being nourished)
versus being-consumed was compared with the forces of controlling
and letting-go. The overall balance of these forces determines the quality
of the spiritual life.

The sounded and soundless signals we use to communicate spiritual
states were also depicted. We will set them aside for another time and
focus now on the connection between the first three figures with what
will be develop here, a master trait for the healthy spiritual life and the
empirical ground for religious language.

This master trait involves the opposing forces of play and non-play
on one axis and creating versus destroying on the other. The play vector
includes the positive tendencies from the three graphs noted above –
animate, full, *anima*, moving-toward, letting go and consuming (being
nourished). The non-play vector sums up the negative extremes –
empty, inanimate, *animus*, moving-away-from, controlling, and being
consumed.

In this chapter play and non-play will be contrasted. We will then say
how and why the theological term, "grace," is used to name optimum

the tendencies of the spiritual life and the empirical ground for the language of religion. In conclusion the implications of this master trait for religious education will be explored.

Play

"What is shared by mass murders, felony drunk drivers, starving children, head-banging laboratory animals, some anxious students, most upwardly mobile executives and all reptiles?" Stuart L. Brown's answer to his own question is that they do not play.

Brown went on to say about animals in the wild that, "Systematic research indicates that play burns up to 20 percent of the survival energy of the young and the growing" (1995: 9). This is true despite the risk of death and damage to the participants and despite the fact that play does not actually provide the hunting, shelter, safety, or other outcomes necessary for survival.

What is play, then? Brian Sutton-Smith studied play for forty years and summed up this experience in *The Ambiguity of Play* (1997). He wrote there that he had finally "got it right." By this he meant that he was able "to bring some coherence to the ambiguous field of play theory by suggesting that some of the chaos to be found there is due to the lack of clarity about the popular cultural rhetorics that underlie the various play theories and play terms" (1997: 7–8).

Sutton-Smith defined a "rhetoric" as "a persuasive discourse, or an implicit narrative, wittingly or unwittingly adopted by members of a particular affiliation to persuade others of the veracity and worthwhileness of their beliefs" (1997: 8). He divided the seven rhetorics into the ancient community-minded views and modern ones, which arose after about 1800 when play began to be studied in a systematic, scientific way.

The ancient views of play concluded that its action was related to power (status, victory), fate (magic, luck), community identity (festivals, cooperation), or frivolity (nonsense as opposed to work). Modern views see play as involving progress (adaptation, growth), the imaginary (creativity, fantasy), or the self's concerns (peak experiences, leisure). "In general each rhetoric has a historical source, a particular function, a distinctive ludic form, specialized players and advocates, and is the context for particular academic disciplines" (1977: 214).

The ambiguity of play, then, is not the result of its diversity of forms, experiences, the many kinds of players, the variety of play agencies, or the multitude of play scenarios. It is because the study of play has so many different starting points. Ludic practice and value statements, based on the rhetorics, have also become conflated. This is why there is no general theory of play that encompasses children and adults as well as animals and humans.

In addition to Sutton-Smith's rhetorics reason I would like to add a second reason for the difficulty of constructing a general theory of play. If it is true that play is located in our non-verbal communication system, then making the translation from the non-verbal to the verbal is problematic. To elaborate on this idea we must turn to Terrence Deacon's *Symbolic Species: The Co-Evolution of Language and the Brain* (1997). This may also provide a clue for a general theory of play, the development of which we will leave for another time.

Humankind developed symbolic referencing by means of the co-evolution of language and the brain. A second communication system also developed parallel to but independent from language. It is a non-verbal system. It uses different parts of the brain and provides the communication environment, which gives additional and sometimes contradictory meaning to language. This is why someone could wish you "Good morning," in a way that could ruin your day.

There are two nonverbal levels of referencing, according to Deacon. They are "iconic" and "indexical." We share these two kinds of referencing with other species. Iconic referencing is limited to the awareness of what is like and unlike. Indexical referencing links events such as smoke and fire.

The tokens of meaning for symbolic referencing are not connected in any way to what they refer to except by social agreement. How we say things, then, carries at least as much meaning as what we say.

Since play is signaled by our nonverbal communication system – a smile, the cocking of the head, a twinkle in the eye – we can only describe what we do when we play. The description I find most succinct and complete is that of Catherine Garvey in her book *Play* (1977). Play is pleasurable, has no extrinsic goals, is spontaneous and voluntary, involves active engagement, and has systematic relations to what is not play such as creativity, problem solving, language learning, the development of social roles, and a number of other human cognitive and social phenomena (1977: 4–5).

There is nothing we can say or do in a non-playful way that we cannot also say or do in a playful way, depending on our nonverbal communication. There is no way to make a one-to-one translation from playing to symbolic referencing. This would be like trying to make a literal translation of crying or laughing into words. We need to look, then, in the direction of physicality, a kind of showing what play is rather than toward verbal precision.

Some human beings are better at "showing" and being sensitive to nonverbal communication than others are. One such group is adult artists. They retain a special sensitivity to their iconic and indexical referencing, which makes them adept at playing with words, movement, stone, color, sounds, and other media. A second group, which is especially sensitive to iconic and indexical referencing, is children. They have no choice but to be in tune with their nonverbal system of communication, since their symbolic referencing is just developing.

Vestiges of the nonverbal can be found in the verbal by noticing the connotations of our symbolic referencing. We will use the work of Howard Gardner (1994) to develop this idea. The roots of connotation are in the pre-object-formation ways of knowing. The same seven ways in which we create meaning, according to Gardner, involve connotation in different ways. This has been amplified in Gardner's *Creating Minds* (1993). Connotation communicates by what Gardner calls modes and vectors, a kind of deep body knowing. This probably begins in a global way and then develops more specificity in centers of sensitivity such as the mouth. Examples he gives of modes and vectors are moving towards, and away from, wholeness and particularity, being empty or full, and opening and closing. This approach has been used in our depictions of the spiritual life.

Instead of stressing denotative language to fashion our understanding of play and non-play we have employed connotative language. Instead of seeking logical precision we will use the suggestiveness of narrative and connotation.

Non-play

The opposite of play may at first seem to be seriousness. For many people play is considered negative, silly, and a waste of time. This is a classic problem that Huizinga (1955) dismissed in the following way. Seriousness seeks to exclude play while play includes seriousness. This makes play a higher order concept than the play versus seriousness dichotomy suggests.

Another opposite of play commonly suggested is work. The problem with the play versus work dichotomy is that for some people their work is play. Besides, one needs to work at any game to play well. A new, more complex, level of play is achieved by practice that is worked at. This makes work and play the necessary rhythm of life rather than opposing vectors of force.

What I would like to propose for the opposite of play is "emptiness." When we are at play, we are full of life, connected to the game and to the players in the game. Synergy abounds. When we cannot play we are maintaining life at best. For example starving and depressed children do not play, as mentioned above. You can see how emptiness fits into the negative tendency of the play versus non-play opposition. As we have already noted, the negative extreme involves being empty, inanimate, *animus*, moving-away-from, controlling and being-consumed.

Emptiness may be caused by the strong pull of an imperative to feel good without expending energy. This least-effort impulse is ancient. It is probably rooted in the conservation of energy needed to face unexpected dangers. It helps avoid burning out from such unrelenting stress.

This concept of emptiness needs to be distinguished from the classical idea of emptiness used by the mystics. The mystic becomes empty to make room for God. It is one's self-concern that is emptied. The presence of God fills up the "space" left empty, so the mystic does not remain empty. The net result for the mystic is to be filled with energy of the highest kind, the creative energy of the human creature at play with the Creator.

The emptiness of non-play remains empty. The non-player becomes isolated over time from play with the deep self, with others, with nature, and with God. They are haunted by this, sometimes unconsciously, and are compelled to suck the life out of others to appear lively to themselves as well as to others! Such people are parasites and dangerous to any host that sustains them.

People who cannot play do not necessarily present themselves as dull. They often appear sparkling and brilliant, because they must be attractive to draw others to them. If this fails they must achieve positions of power so that others can be compelled to be in their company. Either way, attracting or compelling, their compulsion is to consume the energy of those around them to remain alive.

It is not surprising that energy sponges have been identified as evil and personified as satanic. They are, indeed, the historical enemies of life. In Hebrew and Greek, for example, "Satan" means enemy or adversary.

A classic portrayal of someone who can't play and yet is glittering with intelligence and attractive power is Milton's Satan in *Paradise Lost*. This is an epic of an empty one.

Whether you take a positive or negative view of Milton's Satan you still must consider that he is at times lying, deceiving himself, or mad. This ambivalence gives depth and intrigue to this figure, but more importantly for our purposes, Milton has taken seriously the difficulty of discerning the difference between play and pseudo-play in his monumental character. Jesus' heroic and straightforward goodness is rather boring by comparison.

Another example from literature, more widely read today, is from William Golding's *Lord of the Flies* (1954). The boys, who are stranded on an island, build their first civilization around Ralph and his leadership in meetings called by the conch shell. He was someone who could play with delight, as the first pages of the novel show.

Ralph did a surface dive and swam under water with his eyes open; the sandy edge of the pool loomed up like a hillside. He turned over, holding his nose, and a golden light danced and shattered just over his face. (1954: 12)

Jack was Ralph's opposite. His play was not play for the sake of play. It was to attract people to him. He was empty and based his leadership at first on the power of position. It was "because I'm chapter chorister and head boy. I can sing C sharp" (1954: 21). He also had a knife and when he learned to disguise his face with paint and hunt he opposed Ralph's reasoned and cooperative approach to leadership by control based on violence and deception. He compelled others to follow him and tried to disguise his parasitic leadership as play.

Jack's rise to power can be traced in the novel by the degeneration of laughter among the boys. It signaled play during the leadership of Ralph but it became the sound of derision when voiced by Jack and his followers. Jack's power was used to create fear – fear of him as the leader and a larger fear, the dread of the "the beast," which he kept vividly alive in his followers' imaginations. Fear of the beast reinforced in his followers the need for his power to protect them and insured his control over them. When Jack invited Ralph and his few remaining followers to join his tribe he said, "We hunt and feast and have fun. If you want to join my tribe come and see us. Perhaps I'll let you join. Perhaps not" (1954: 127). His idea of fun had nothing to do with real play, as described by Garvey. It was pseudo-play used as a ploy to keep his power over the others to rob them of their energy and creativity.

A later invitation to pseudo-play was made by Jack, "Who'll join my tribe and have fun?" (1954: 137) This fun involved a frenzied dance of death at night. Simon – who had climbed the mountain alone and faced the beast, which turned out to be a dead pilot still attached to his parachute and shifting about lifelike in the wind – crawled out of the bushes exhausted after his ordeal on the mountaintop.

The other boys were dancing and singing in the dark on the beach. "Kill the beast! Cut his throat! Spill his blood. Do him in" (1954: 139). Simon, perhaps unrecognized, became the victim of their lust and was killed in their frenzy. That was what "fun" and "play" and "laughter" had come to mean under the rule of the empty one.

There are times when people, who would rather play than fight, must fight against such energy-draining forces and the people who embody them. Life must be guarded against those who can only simulate life, because involvement in any game on their terms is destructive and robs others of life.

To help guard against the danger of pseudo-play we need to be more specific about our description. To do this we will use Garvey's description of play to guide our comparison:

Play	**Pseudo-play**
1. Play is pleasurable.	1. Pseudo-play is numbness, a restless but hollow simulation of life.
2. Play has no extrinsic goals.	2. Pseudo-play is parasitic. It destroys the life of the host to maintain its own survival.
3. Play is spontaneous.	3. Pseudo-play is obsessed to attract others to claim their souls, their vitality.
4. Play requires engagement.	4. Pseudo-play is detached, but appears involved. Disguises are assumed to maintain relationships.
5. Play nourishes such activities as creativity, language learning, and learning social roles.	5. Pseudo-play exploits others for their energy to gain a sense of being alive. Pseudo-players cannot create creating in others. They can only rob others of their creativity.

Theologians have tried in various ways to say that evil is emptiness. This has been true from the early church's *privatio boni* to the *das Nichtige* of Karl Barth in the twentieth century.

In theological terms the opposite of evil is not so much logical good but experiential grace. We turn now to a discussion of grace, because that term provides a rich enough concept to identify the master trait of spirituality.

Grace

Grace has been used to refer to the quality of relationships in all four of the cardinal directions we experience relationships: with the deep self, with God, with others, and with nature. The word is used in both religious and secular contexts, which may be one of the reasons why it is still intelligible to people in a post-Christian age. The profound popularity of the song "Amazing Grace" is an example.

Grace has deep Judeo-Christian roots, but it also has roots in Greek mythology. The graces are three sister goddesses who are givers of charm and beauty. Perhaps this etymology is another reason why the word "grace" remains alive and awake while the related Christian terms such as justification, salvation, redemption, and reconciliation, which carry ponderous overtones of a slave economy and the courtroom, seem dead or at least asleep. These venerable terms, at most, plod instead of evoking the pleasurable ease and suppleness of movement that grace does.

The history of theology, worship, and pastoral care could be written as a study of how theologians and communities have conceptualized and lived out the meaning they give to grace. Such a review would take us too far afield for this discussion and it is too filled with passionate modern advocates of ancient controversies. To name positions taken by theologians such as Augustine of Hippo, Thomas Aquinas, Luther, Calvin and others would draw in too many of these controversies and too much feeling for our discussion to keep its focus. The same problem would occur if we were to give examples about how communities, such as Protestant Puritans or Catholic Jansenites, have lived out what they thought about grace. Instead, we shall make our discussion as neutral as possible.

The meaning of grace can be divided into three kinds of usage, following the basic parts of speech. Grace as change is a verb. When grace refers to a person, place, or thing it is a noun. When it is used to qualify verbs or nouns it becomes an adverb or adjective.

First, then, let us examine the verb "to grace". The first thing to note is that grace promotes change in a positive direction. It causes and helps one move in the direction of being full of grace. The second thing to notice is that the experience of this action seems to originate from both outside and inside of a person. Thirdly, it might come as an irresistible cause or as something one needs to cooperate with to effect change. Either way grace is gratuitous. You can't earn it or force it in any way.

The second use for the term grace is not about grace as a means but as an end. The end state of grace is being full of grace, being graceful. It is a person, place, or thing.

An old term of address is "Your Grace." People are named Grace. Grace is the prayer we say at meals. Graceland is a famous home. Grace has also been thought of as a substance, which flows from God especially through the sacraments. The angel said to Mary, "Hail, Mary, full of grace."

Today, however, grace usually refers to a quality of relationships rather than a substance. The power of the substance metaphor, however, remains vivid and potent. This is because one can feel "full of grace", but then it leaks away and we must move on. The word shifts to its verbal usage again.

One might choose to be graceful, even desire to be graceful, and yet not be graceful. There is a gap. Even when once begins to act gracefully, like someone in training, the action can be awkward. Grace as an end-state occurs when it becomes more than a habit. You are graceful without trying. It is no longer a matter of conscious effort. God and such people are those who can grace others by their being.

Thirdly, "grace" is used as a modifier. Action can be graceful. A person, place, or thing can be graceful. A musical note, which embellishes the melody or harmony, is called a grace note. Play can be graceful. When one is learning to play a game the player may be awkward but only when measured by standards above the level one is presently playing. Graceful play is relative to one's experience in the playing of the game.

There is one more point to be made about grace before turning to an example from J. R. R. Tolkien's hobbits. Christians consider God's graceful relationship with humankind as a Trinity. This experience, given theological nuance, brings to the understanding of relationships a three-in-one symbol. The relationship with God is with one who is beyond, the Creator God; it is with the one who walks beside us speaking and in intelligible human form, in Christ; and it is the creative power within, the Holy Spirit. All of this richness remains within a single relationship of gracious, gifted, overflowing energy. The lure of the beyond, the support of a companion to identify with, and the push from within to move toward what is holy are all at work, all of the time, in all of our relationships whether we acknowledge this reality or not.

The offer of this sort of relationship is always there, a gift to be accepted, neglected, or rejected. To reject it resists being part of the gracious movement of life. No matter where one begins – beyond, beside or within – the whole relationship is also at work in the lovely system of the whole cosmos.

Let us now consider an example of grace from J. R. R. Tolkien's *The Lord of the Rings* (1966) to get a feel for what the trinitarian awareness of grace is like. Frodo does not prevail because of intelligence, physical strength or will power. At the Crack of Doom he and Gollum wrestle for the ring, but Frodo has already given in to its power. Gollum overcomes the weakened Frodo and bites off his ring finger. At last Gollum has his Precious (the ring), but he loses his balance and falls into the fiery abyss. The ring was unmade by the intense heat and the quest was over.

The only reason Gollum was present to help unmake the ring was because of actions that seemed foolish at the time. It was Frodo's graceful charity that allowed Gollum to live. Neither he nor Sam trusted Gollum, but despite the danger to Gollum and from Gollum he helped them get where they needed to go and then ultimately accomplished what Frodo no longer could do. Frodo's merciful instinct that spared Gollum was shared with Bilbo Baggins in *The Hobbit* (Tolkien 1966). He too allowed Gollum to live. Two generations of hobbits, being their own graceful selves, contributed to the successful ending of the quest, which could not have been anticipated by simple, linear, billiard ball causation.

When we compare Frodo and Gollum we can also see how the loss of grace can change a person. Gollum, who was also a hobbit, became obsessed by the power of the ring until he became unrecognizable. Frodo's nature also changed because of the ring's power, so that the story could not end with him living happily ever-after.

When one's nature is graceful, like Bilbo Baggins and Frodo, it does not always change those around one. Neither Sarum nor Gollum changed, but when one steps back and takes a larger view it was a kind of cosmic grace that brought a successful end to the quest.

Let us then sum up with a diagram to show the master trait for spiritual health and the teaching of religion:

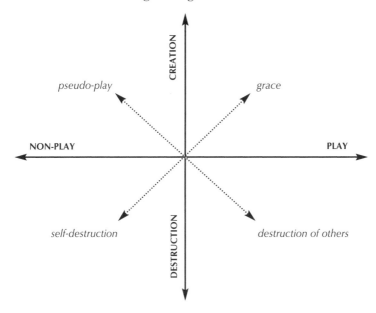

Play is the summary of the animate, full, *anima*, moving-toward, letting-go and consuming for nurture. Non-play is the summary of inanimate, empty, *animus*, moving-away-from, controlling and being-consumed. If we look in the upper right quadrant of the force vectors we see the combination of creation and play. This is what I call grace, because it is a term rich enough to include all that the force vectors in the diagram imply. If you look in the upper left quadrant you will find what we have called pseudo-play like that of Satan or Jack. In the lower right quadrant is the combination of play and the destructive forces that destroy others to save the self at all cost, even if it involves the death of millions and a whole nation, as in the case of Hitler and numerous other such rulers throughout history. In the lower left we find forces that compel self-destruction such as Gollum's.

We turn now to the implications of grace for religious education.

Grace and Religious Education

Religious language, at least in the Christian Tradition, needs to be grounded in the non-verbal experience balance of forces we have termed grace. When it is not so grounded human spirituality is distorted when it is drawn into the language system of religion.

Religious language is a powerful language domain. When it is grounded in the vectors of force to destroy others it becomes extremely dangerous. This produces fanatical and unholy wars as well as a lust for martyrdom. A more subtle danger, however, is pseudo-play, so it will be our focus here.

Four examples will be described to illustrate the danger of pseudo-play. In all four games there is a lack of concordance between verbal and nonverbal communication. The religious words are not grounded in the quality of relationship they claim to identify, name and express or denote. This is especially tragic for children, because when trusted adults talk in this way with children, the children learn such discord *as* religious communication.

This discord – religious language taught with the non-verbal signals of the destruction of others, the destruction of the self, or of pseudo-play – leaves children in a double bind. They are wrong non-verbally if they respond to what is said and they are wrong verbally if they respond to what is shown. The pain of such discord can overwhelm the need for relationship and children may withdraw from using religious language because of this pain. They can even become empty, attempting to live amid broken relationships and the loss of play by becoming parasites themselves.

Such discord is also tragic for adults. As symbolic referencing develops, adults tend to depend more and more on words and overlook their loss of iconic and indexical referencing. The roots of words pull away from their ground in the nonverbal. We cannot live in a world limited to words-about-words without becoming insane as individuals or as cultures. We become trapped in the irony of our language-given freedom from the domination of the physical world.

Pseudo-play uses this irony to disconnect the verbal from the nonverbal and in order to disguise nonverbal emptiness as verbal play. Four educational games with this underlying current of emptiness are: "Compulsion," "Entertainment," "Manipulation," and "Competition." They overlap, since all involve the disguises of pseudo-play.

Compulsion will be discussed first and illustrated by Eric Berne's *Games People Play* (1964). That book touched a responsive chord in the mid-1960s when it was on the best seller list in the United States for two years. The title still has a vocabulary life of its own today. "Games" are spoken of in a cynical way as a result of Berne's contemptuously distrustful view of most people's way of communicating. He wrote:

> Because there is so little opportunity for intimacy in daily life, and because some forms of intimacy (especially if intense) are psychologically impossible for most people, the bulk of the time in serious social life is taken up with playing games. Hence games are both necessary and desirable, and the only problem at issue is whether the games played by an individual offer the best yield for him. (1964: 61)

Berne's "games" are compulsive and unconscious. His "play" is actually pseudo-play, since it is not freely chosen. A person, young or old, playing any one of Berne's thirty-two negative games from his "Thesaurus of Games" is stuck in a behavior that is destructive by its very action, because it keeps one stuck. His Thesaurus described only five constructive games. The only way to get unstuck, Berne counseled, is to become aware of what game you have been trapped into playing. Instead of "playing tapes" unconsciously you can then choose to play or not play once the game is made conscious and named. In practice, however, it takes a good bit more work to change such behavior. The Rumpelstiltskin effect may work well in the fairy tale, but in daily practice it is neither so dramatic nor final.

When one goes "beyond games," Berne wrote, there is a "jerk-free, game-free conversation between two autonomous adults." This kind of relationship, which includes what he called "awareness," "spontaneity," and "intimacy" sounds more like what we mean by play. It is true that we can be trapped in destructive games, but it is also true that we can't be "beyond games," for games structure all of our lives. We need to attend as much, therefore, to how we play our games as to what games we play. Religious education is a game like any other pattern of behavior. It is critical to signal grace as the non-verbal foundation for this communication system as we draw children into its traditions of verbal expression and safeguards from distortion.

A second dangerous game played in the name of religious education is Entertainment. This game, disguised as play, is destructive because of the one-way flow of energy. The entertainer (teacher) creates passive consumers by such activity. No synergy is possible, since this is about control. Such activity begins to empty children of their spirituality at an early age rather than stimulating it by play.

A third dangerous game disguised as religious education is Manipulation. The ultimate pleasure in this game is also for the teacher. The activity's product is to meet the teacher's need to produce a product. A child tempted to join such a game will be play-burned by the deception so that other invitations to enter into play-like activity will be avoided in the future. Play's links to creativity, language learning, the learning of social roles and problem solving are severed by such action so that the child's spiritual development is arrested by being manipulated into being other-directed.

The fourth dangerous game is Competition. In this game the teacher competes with the learners. Playful competition is good in the service of the players, but some adults cannot stop competing with each other or with children. They must win every time even if it is not in the interest of those who have come to learn how to identify, name and express their natural spirituality in religious language.

Only the winner has pleasure when pseudo-play dominates. One winner makes many losers. The false play's product is winning and not playing for play itself. Winning can only temporarily fill up an empty person, for this craving is never satisfied.

As said above, the four dangerous games are related. All are for the teacher's needs and all are compulsive. Pseudo-play takes many disguises. These are four examples from within the game of religious education to be alert for.

Teaching pseudo-play to children by nonverbal communication as the ground of Christian language teaches pseudo-play as normative and the use of religious language as dysfunctional. The resulting dysfunctional language gives rise to distorted relationships with the deep self, with God, with God's creation, and with all living creatures. The antidote to this tragedy is graceful teaching.

Grace – the combination of play and creation – is much more important to religious education than either science or theology have led us to believe. If it dies out among our kind, especially when we address our existential concerns, we will have no creature creative and spiritually motivated enough to counter the destructive tendencies of our species. Humankind will self-destruct and probably take life in the cosmos with it.

References

Berne, E. 1964: *Games People Play*. New York: Grove Press.
Brown, S. 1995: *Revision*. 17(4).

Deacon, T. 1997: *The Symbolic Species: The Co-Evolution of Language and the Brain.* New York: W. W. Norton.

Erricker, J., Ota, C. and Erricker, C. (eds) 2001: *Spiritual Education: Cultural, Religious and Social Differences, New Perspectives for the 21st Century.* Brighton & Portland: Sussex Academic Press.

Gardner, H. [1973] 1994: *The Arts and Human Development.* New York: Basic Books.

Gardner, H. 1993: *Creating Minds.* New York: Basic Books.

Garvey, C. 1977: *Play.* Cambridge, MA: Harvard University Press.

Golding, W. 1954: *Lord of the Flies.* New York: G. P. Putnam's Sons, Perigee Books.

Huizinga, J. 1955: *Homo Ludens.* Boston: Beacon Press.

Miller, D. 1973: *Gods and Games: Toward a Theology of Play.* New York: Harper and Row, Colophon Books.

Sutton-Smith, B. 1997: *The Ambiguity of Play.* Cambridge, MA: Harvard University Press.

Tolkien, J. R. R. 1966: *The Hobbit.* New York: Houghton Mifflin Company.

Tolkien, J. R. R. 1966: *The Lord of the Rings.* New York: Houghton Mifflin Company.

Chapter 6

Spirituality in Young Adolescents: Thinking Developmentally

DANIEL SCOTT

ALL THEORETICAL MODELS require a degree of flexibility and adaptability to be successful. It is also necessary to be critical of theories as they evolve in order to increase their range of potential application and to continually test them against existing knowledge to affirm their accuracy and viability. This chapter is concerned to stimulate a dialogue to assist in the elaboration of a stronger theoretical view of childhood and adolescent spiritual experience based on linking developmental insight and relational consciousness.

In this chapter, I will raise several questions about Hay and Nye's (1998) theory of relational consciousness, testing it against some insights from life-span developmental theory, and suggesting some cautions for claiming experience as particularly spiritual. At the same time, I will try to extend the core idea of relational consciousness into the early adolescent age group (10 to 14 years old) and explore some expressions of their spiritual sensitivities group and potential forms for spiritual experience and expression based on a developmental understanding of that early adolescent period.

My concern centers on a caution. In naming particular characteristics or qualities in children's life experience as spiritual development, it is important not to valorize the spiritual and ignore or downplay other areas of developmental insight. To consider the spiritual experience of children, it is necessary to locate their spirituality in the ecological perspective of development. Spirituality is nested among the other processes of human formation and maturation. The spiritual will be experienced through, shaped by and expressed with the skill, insights, and faculties available to children at the stage of their cognitive, emotional, social, moral and physical development. The insights that existing research and developmental knowledge offer must be considered. The spiritual will occur in a context of family and community influences, nested in the full range of eco-systems suggested by Bronfenbrenner (1979), and others (see Santrock 2002). Families exist in cultural systems, some near and immediate in their influence like schools, churches, and neighbourhood, some more distant, including various levels of government and social institutions, which in turn are shaped by policies, politics and beliefs at the cultural level. Any claims for the spiritual must be grounded in the full range of a child's experience and capacity, including the child's social systems and their interactions.

Life-Span Development and Relational Consciousness

Based on their observations of children ages six to eleven, Hay (1998: 59) proposes "three interrelated themes or categories of spiritual sensitivity or awareness" that he and Nye believe "must play a part in anyone's spiritual life." The categories are: awareness-sensing, mystery-sensing and value-sensing. Each of these, in turn, have characteristics that clarify how they see them occurring in children. *Awareness-sensing* is a form of giving attention: "being aware of one's awareness," or heightened awareness (1998: 62) that includes an ability to focus attention on the here-and-now; an ability to tune into the ebb and flow of experience (1998: 63); an ability to be caught up effortlessly in the flow of events, attuned only to them, and open to being moved by them (1998: 63–64); and an ability to focus on the "felt sense" or the bodily experience of events (1998: 65–66).

Mystery-sensing, as a spiritual sensitivity, is "closely associated with" the "notion of transcendence" (1998: 66). Hay is clear that there is difficulty in addressing mystery with children. Experiences of awe and wonder can be (mis-)understood as naiveté, not allowing children an acknowledged depth of experience. Explanations for events can blunt this potential in a child who may not separate "the common-place and the profound" (1998: 67) and so live in a state of wonder in which the transcendent is present in the everyday. Imagination and creativity are also claimed as expressions of, or forms of, mystery-sensing. Links are made between the symbolic, metaphoric and ritual practices of religion and children's attempts, in creative and imaginative forms, to express their sense of wonder or mystery. Hay suggests that such expressions provide a "window on this aspect of their spirituality" (1998: 70).

The third sensitivity is *value-sensing* and, according to Hay, it is based on affect: "Feeling is a measure of what we value" (1998: 70). There is a stress on children's ready expression of "their ideas of worth or value in the intensity of their everyday experience of delight or despair" (1998:

71). Hay notes links to religious traditions and expresses disquiet that children's concerns are dismissed or explained away, rather than being seen as spiritual sensitivity and of value in an orientation to life. Children are also credited with a sense of "ultimate goodness" (1998: 71) that allows them to have a basic "trust in being" (1998: 72). The last piece of value-sensing is "the endless curiosity and meaning-making of children" (1998: 73) that for Hay has both a cognitive and experiential aspect:

> The search for and discovery of meaning may directly form an aspect of developing spirituality. In childhood in particular, as a sense of identity is sought for, established and deepened, questions are raised which are essentially spiritual: Who am I? Where do I belong? What is my purpose? To whom or what am I connected or responsible? These apparently cognitive signs of spiritual activity are in many cases the secondary products of spiritual stirrings found in awareness-sensing, mystery-sensing and value-sensing. (1998: 74)

To his credit, Hay makes a significant effort to acknowledge psychological implications and raises questions about cognitive and emotional developmental factors. Initially, I think Hay and Nye underplay links to and the significance of life-span developmental knowledge and attempt to make the spiritual inclination the primary driver of perception. The three sensitivities may have spiritual implications and be significant in helping to formulate a clearer picture of childhood spiritual experience but all three sensitivities can also be expressed in terms of other developmental factors and so the specific quality of these sensitivities that makes them spiritual needs to be considered. It is possible to consider the spiritual as a part of the process of life-span development without giving it a special or primary status. The choice to reify the spiritual seems to be driven by an adult agenda, not by a careful consideration of the context and experience of children's lives.

I am concerned that the explanations of childhood spiritual experience offered use adult categories, insights or interests that are projected back onto childhood and read into the vocabulary and behaviours of children as spiritual. I will illustrate both of these concerns with examples.

Spirituality and Cognitive Development

In recent years there has been a significant re-thinking of the cognitive capacities of young children and their ability to be aware of the world and their relationship with it. For example, Gopnik, Metlzoff and Kuhl (1999) identify the child as a scientist (displaying a similar adult reverse projection onto children) who uses perceptual skills to test the world and its workings through careful observation. A child is alert, engaged and aware, exploring the world using cognitive capacity. An understanding of awareness-sensing as primarily a spiritual capacity is suspect if it ignores normal cognitive capacity. Does awareness-sensing, however, offer a special insight into the perceptual range of children?

The cognitive skills and learning capacities operative at birth may have significance for spiritual awareness. Heightened learning capacity may allow young children to perceive and know in ways that are spiritual. What they are seeing or knowing is less clear. The influence of increased skill and heightened perception on spiritual awareness and the process of spiritual awareness operating through cognitive capacities remains to be clarified. Levine (1999) makes a link between the concrete and imaginative cognitive skills of children, pointing out their ability to operate simultaneously in both modes. She sees cognitive capacity as part of the spirituality of children. Perhaps children are catching glimpses of what is beyond-the-self at an early age because of their cognitive abilities. Perhaps their lack of cognitive borders between modes of thinking and imagining liberates their perceptions giving them access to spiritual experience. There is need for more discussion and research to decide what may or may not be spiritual in the interplay of children's developmental processes to insure that claims for spiritual capacity include a consideration of other contributing developmental abilities.

Spiritual Development, Time and Culture

Hay (1998: 60) claims that children are focused on the here-and-now, because they have "no extended past stretched out behind them." The present is what they know and experience. As they grow older, their sense of time changes and both the past and the future become more imaginable as they develop personal history and anticipate events beyond tomorrow. The implication hidden here is that a changing sense of time is a loss of spiritual capacity. Yet it may only be a normative (and necessary) developmental process. If being present in the moment is based on the structure of experience, it is important to acknowledge the limits of that capacity but also to consider its circumstances. Cultural location and orientation become significant at this point. Do we know what cultural forces shape spiritual development?

In personal communications with several people from different aboriginal cultures, I have been assured that the development of spiritual awareness and voice is a central part of the work of the first seven to ten years of life. At that point spirituality moves from the foreground to the background and physical orientation takes over. Hay's concern that children in Western culture lose their spiritual voices around the age of ten raises questions about our knowledge of how spirituality moves and is expressed in human life. Perhaps it is natural for children to have their spiritual voice and interest fade at the onset of adolescence, becoming part of the background as attention turns to physical and sexual development. Perhaps spirituality takes a different form. I will explore this later in the chapter.

The spiritual may not develop in a linear fashion. It is possible that spiritual development is a process that includes a cycle of developmental loss and gain of capacity over the life-span in a seemingly discontinuous pattern. The sensitivities suggested by Hay and Nye (1998) may be erratic or non-linear in the sequence and timing of their occurrence, varied in their intensity and more evident in some people than others in human life-span development. Again, my concern for reverse projection surfaces. It is possible that adult spirituality, based on adult experience, is projected back onto children's lives and a gradual (linear) process of development throughout life is assumed and becomes the focus of study even though it may not represent how children experience the spiritual. The perceived absence of observable adult qualities in children may become a focus of concern misleading our understanding of the spiritual as it actually occurs in children.

The adult spiritual quest for living in the moment may be an attempt to recreate the simplicity and intensity of early life experience and cause adults to valorize the innocent quality of children's experience. At the same time, there may be an unconscious memory of an intense relationship with the world through childhood awareness/perception that becomes definitive of adult spiritual experience. The awareness-sensing capacity that Hay and Nye identify indicates that children have an open, broader perception that has a degree of spiritual insight but may be a necessary part of becoming a human child in all developmental aspects. So the question is whether the awareness capacity of a child defines spiritual experience or whether adult yearning for childhood innocence is projected onto natural perceptual and thinking capacities of children and gets called spirituality. The problematic, for me, is understanding both how a focused attention is specifically spiritual awareness and what it indicates about the formation and development of the spiritual in human experience.

A variety of spiritual traditions acknowledge that being attuned and aware offers a different sensitivity and responsiveness to life. This capacity may provide heightened spiritual perceptions to some individuals. The question remains whether the capacity for spirituality sensitivity is common to all children or only unevenly used or accessed by children? It is also not clear whether this capacity has different forms at different times during childhood and adolescent stages. Not all children have the same ability to concentrate, to be lost in flow, or to attune to events or experience. What form does the spiritual nature of children who are intellectually or emotionally challenged take? (See Morris 2001 for a consideration of autism and spirituality.)

There are many questions to be raised about normative spiritual process and development. I think it is necessary to study children's lives to see what of their experience may be a part of the formation of a spiritual identity or a spiritual awareness that will persist in them. Just as some children are more adept at physical or artistic activities, or are more competent intellectually or emotionally, so I would expect spirituality to be uneven in expression and ability. It will not always look the same or be expressed in the same forms.

If Hay and Nye are correct and the spiritual capacity that children are expressing is inherent, how experience, interest, inclination and maturation change is critical to discover. I believe it is necessary to consider what the capacity of awareness-sensing is permitting children to experience that *is* spiritual and to be thoughtful about the range of expressions available to children for their perceptions. It will also be important to consider what might impede or damage spiritual ability.

Spirituality, Curiosity, Imagination

I am similarly cautious in response to claims made about both mystery-sensing and value-sensing. My concern centers around acknowledging the full complexity of the role of cognitive and emotional developmental factors in what is being claimed as spiritual. I think the cognitive work of Gopnik *et al.* (1999), Harris (2000) and others makes interpretation of both the curiosity and imagination of children open to discussion. Children are curious and imaginative. For them, the world is new and mysterious, unfamiliar and unknown. But mystery and imagination are not exclusively spiritual.

Jane Goodall (1990) tells a story about her experience as a young child hiding for a long time in a hen house in order to see a chicken lay an egg. She was curious, wondering about the mystery of eggs (and birth), and wise enough to calculate a practice that would enable her to witness it. It is arguable that this was a formative moment in her pursuit of studying the life of creatures in their habitat. Is it a spiritual moment? If yes, how so? Because of the mystery and wonder? Because it has a vocational or visionary quality? Or was she being a naturally curious child and getting excited about and focused on learning and in doing so forming her life pattern? The defining borders are not clear and the lack of clarity may be important for grappling with what spirituality is and how it is experienced and expressed.

The spiritual may only be knowable in context, woven into other experiences. Relational consciousness may depend on context, culture,

perception, skill, degree of development and personality. I am
suggesting that the spiritual is part of many experiences and not necessarily distinct. The spiritual, as a quality threaded into other
experiences, may be more subtle than obvious in any study of children's
lives. Attempts to make spiritual experience objective and distinct will
tend to reify what may need to remain partial and ambiguous. As an
experience, and as part of a relational way in the world, spirituality may
be primarily a quality of experience, that is, an attitude in or to life. I am
purposing the idea that that the spiritual may have a necessary elusiveness to its nature in experience. It may be that the spiritual can only be
known in the midst of experience and cannot be independently
accessed. The energy and vitality it provides may be adaptive and
dependent on context, character and the range of human developmental
experience.

Before proceeding to early adolescent experience there are two other
points I want to highlight in my critique of the assumptions embedded
in relational consciousness. A central experience in many spiritual traditions that is reflected in Hay and Nye's framework is an intense
encounter with nature, or life, or a spirit or angel and sometimes with
the Divine that takes a person beyond themselves, often to feelings of
oneness or unity that may combine both a sense of uniqueness and a
complete loss of identity or ego boundaries. These encounters with
"mystery" are felt experiences and are reported in many different forms
in both children's lives (Coles 1990; Robinson 1983) and adult lives
(Hawker 2000; Miller and C'de Baca 2001).

Beyond-the-self Experience

Experiences beyond-the-self are often identified as experiences of
wonder or awe and are claimed to indicate a spiritual relational
moment. Again it is important to consider what aspects of that experience are spiritual. Is openness to experiencing the unknown or other
(Other) in children a sign of spiritual sensitivity? Do children, demonstrate a special capacity to go beyond themselves or be free to traverse
personal boundaries? It is possible that the personal boundaries of children are more porous and flexible than later in life, which leaves them
more accessible to beyond-the-self experiences? If this is the case, certain
emotional capacities and perceptual sensitivities may permit children a
degree of fluidity that may or may not have spiritual significance. They
are having these kinds of experiences; Robinson's (1983) research makes
that clear. It seems important to consider what their openness and
porosity is opening them to sense or know. Who or what are they
perceiving? And how do their perceptions reflect the assumptions of
their social, religious and familial context? I wonder also about the role

these experiences have in shaping a child's sense of self, their personal boundaries and the limits they will develop as they mature.

For example, in a conversation, Canadian poet Fred Cogswell assured me that he had childhood experiences of the world being infused with light that would last up to – in his case – two weeks. His poetry frequently plays with images of light and time as illustrated by the titles of several of his poetry volumes: With Vision Added (2000), The Trouble With Light (1996), As I See It (1994) and, When The Right Light Shines (1992). How much are his life vocation, perception, and imagery shaped by his early perceptions? And what of his childhood life gives rise to a spirituality that can write:

> . . . I live in a blind
> alley of time where senses
> sheltering behind
> frail protective skin
> make two worlds possible, one
> without, one within.
> (Cogswell 1994)

The beyond-the-self moment may be key in acknowledging spiritual experience in children. I think it is critical to consider what contributes to this potential in children in terms of their imaginative, cognitive, and emotional capacities. In my own work, I have heard a wide range of stories that identify awe and wonder-based experiences. Some seem to be emotionally triggered or based. Others seem to be more perceptual and imaginative. Some seem to arrive in complete surprise. They are often identified in retrospect by adults as spiritual moments. Such identification may be enculturation but there is some relational experience beyond-the-self that is being felt and remembered. They seem to have long-term impact in some lives. I hope there will be increasing dialogue between spiritual educators and developmental theorists to explore more carefully the complexity of these experiences and the spiritual component of them. It is not clear what is normative or possible nor what the implications are for working with children. Relational consciousness may be an appropriate descriptor to identify these experiences.

Valuing

My last comment concerns Hay's claim that children have a sense of ultimate goodness. From the earliest stages of life, children are aware of and responding to their care-givers. They are learning from and attuning to what matters in their social and emotional context. I believe caution is necessary in claiming for children an ultimate evaluative sense that may be developed as part of these early experiences of human perception. There are children who fail to develop values and connection to others. They may become sociopaths or psychopaths as adults. What may be more important than an in-built ultimate sense of value(s) is the need for and sensitivity to valuing as primary in human life. An in-built relational awareness and sensitivity may be an indicator of a primary potential for relations across a wide spectrum: to self, to others and Other, and to the rest of animate and inanimate nature that requires an attunement to valuing. The peak experiences of awe or wonder may underline this sensitivity as part of human reality.

If, as I am suggesting, the spiritual is woven in, and remains subtle in human experience, expressed through existing developmental capacities, it is important to consider what form spiritual experience might take for infants, toddlers, children and adolescents. Relational consciousness is a useful frame of reference but it is critical not to project adult assumptions and experience onto children's lives, nor to idealize or valorize particular kinds of experiences as especially or exclusively spiritual. It is necessary to continue to search for vocabulary and frameworks that help identify spiritual experience while acknowledging the role of developmental factors in spiritual expression.

Early Adolescent Experience

I want to turn now to a brief look at the spiritual potential and experiences of early adolescents (ages 10–14) to consider what aspects of their lives might display spiritual sensitivities or demonstrate spiritual awareness in keeping with early adolescent development processes. Relational consciousness will take shape and be expressed in ways that are shaped by the concurrent developmental capacities of these youth. Their experiences will include spiritual qualities woven into other developmental experiences.

Wonder and Inquiry

In much of the literature on spiritual formation wonder is presented, in an idealized way, as a quality of young children's lives. There is an implication that, at the onset of adolescence, wonder diminishes. I believe there are expressions of wonder in different forms that are part of the adolescent experience. One significant area of development in younger adolescents is cognitive. Their thinking skills change significantly as many early adolescents develop formal operational thinking and the ability to reason logically, employing abstractions and hypothetical examples. In using their new-found skills and testing them on ideas, beliefs and experiences, wonder can continue to have qualities of awe but may be expressed as inquiry. To wonder about something is a developmental shift from being in wonder of it. This occurs for many adolescents. Wonder, as inquiry, can include doubt, disbelief, critique, and even cynicism when claims are incongruent with practices. This must not be discounted as spiritual insight. The ability to question may reduce open, innocent responses to events and others but that may be necessary for developing a more mature and complex spirituality. There are many moral and justice issues available to be noticed by a newly developing, discerning mind. Educators may be missing a key piece of spiritual development by not acknowledging that the onset of adolescence brings a shifting spiritual sensibility that includes struggling with personal and social perceptions, based on developing cognitive, social and emotional factors.

There are several things to bear in mind. I have argued above that wonder in early childhood is a natural response to first-time experiences which must not be over-represented as spiritual. In the case of young adolescents, the cognitive, social, moral and emotional changes also produce first-time experiences: first understandings, first feelings, and first insights. Wonder may still be present and still have spiritual overtones. The form may be completely different.

Spirituality and Sexuality

Sexual awakening and first experiences of sexually informed affection may also include significant spiritual sensitivity. Relational consciousness may have a role in sexual awareness that includes a spiritual significance. Perhaps adolescence adds sexual-sensing to awareness-, meaning- and value-sensing. Perhaps sexual-sensing has a spiritual/relational component that is ignored because of cultural anxiety about adolescent sexuality. The dynamic tension between spirituality and sexuality is an issue that many spiritual and religious traditions have struggled with over the centuries. A serious study of how early adolescents work at making sense of sexuality may provide important insights about spiritual development and its connection to sexuality. How is sexuality a development of relational consciousness and an increasing awareness of the human condition?

The interplay between the spiritual and the sexual in adolescents may offer a very different sense of how the spiritual forms and is informed by life experiences: both successes and failures. Such a project may raise questions about the cultural stratagems for managing sexuality if there are spiritual consequences as well as psychological and emotional ones.

Vocation

In my critique of relational consciousness, I was concerned that there was a spiritualizing of the natural time sense of the here-and-now common to young children. In early adolescents the sense of time begins to shift. On one hand, there is an intensification of the significance of the present moment. Decisions and choices in the present can take on immense social and emotional weight. The intense self-consciousness of early adolescence means a decision to go to a social event or wear a certain outfit can seem over-wrought to adults. There are other ways to see these moments developmentally. They demonstrate a set of first-time experiences in social awareness. An adolescent is thinking of self from a new perspective and does not have a reservoir of experiences to measure the impact of self awareness. Their urgency and intensity echoes their child-like wonder at the natural world or the discovery of movement but now focused on social experience. Are there spiritual/relational qualities being shaped in this awareness?

On the other hand, young adolescents develop a growing sense of the future and its place in their lives. This produces an interest in life direction: what am I to become? Identity formation begins to be a major life issue, and it can have spiritual overtones. For adolescents, a future orientation can produce a sense of vocation: life is beckoning me to take up a particular task. Hillman's (1996) look at calling provides a number of examples of children who feel directed by forces outside themselves to a specific life-work. Although a sense of vocation may start earlier, the vocational force becomes active in adolescence when life-choices become a realistic cultural option. I see this as early adolescent spiritual experience that is another form of beyond-the-self experience. A particular child can feel that life or the Divine is calling him or her to a life task. This call is perceived as coming from beyond the self and across time. It may arise in dreams or as a consciousness of being impelled in a direction. (John Irving's 1989 *A Prayer for Owen Meany* is an exploration of this experience in fictional form.)

Vision

There is a third implication regarding time that links with developing critical and inquiry skills. Young adolescents sometimes use their critical abilities to see into or through circumstances in which they live. They begin to imagine the consequences of choices being made by adults in their social context. They test those imagined consequences against the existing social and cultural claims and then challenge the values, mores and prejudices of their family and community based on their observations. These young people take on visionary/prophetic roles asking for and expecting social changes based on their penetrating insights and their open, uncluttered first-time look at what is right or wrong in their context. Value- and meaning-sensing may thus be played out in their adolescent experience. Their visionary insights may be difficult and awkward for their friends and family while displaying a developing complex spiritual sensibility that includes a moral, justice orientation. Their concern is more than self-interest, based on a changing sense of self and others in relation to the world. The ability to begin to understand others in relation to the world is an important extension of a relational consciousness and the development of altruism and compassion. I believe that there is a spiritual significance to this process in adolescent development.

It is interesting to note how often, in the literature of religious traditions, children in this age group are credited with mystical visionary experiences. Such visionary experience may be examples of an intensively imaginative and highly critical spiritual sensibility. A question to consider is how this might be reflected in the day-to-day experiences of children who are less attuned or sensitive spiritually. In naming these two potential spiritual attributes of early adolescent experience as vocation and vision I have deliberately chosen words with roots in spiritual and religious traditions. Both demonstrate an increasing sense of relationship in and to the world and can be seen as part of spiritual development understood as relational consciousness.

Identity Formation

Nye's claim (Hay and Nye 1998) that relational consciousness includes a child-self consciousness is important at this stage of life when a child becomes deliberate about identity formation. Perhaps at no other point is the child's consciousness of self more extreme than during these early-to-middle adolescent years. In forming identity the child is creating and testing images of his or her self. This self-imagination (self-envisioning) will include not only the testing of emotional and social preferences, expression and levels of comfort but also the testing of values. What will matter in life? What will be important for me as an adult? Will I have the same or different values than my family? Will I resist prejudice or accept it? How will I treat others? How will I expect others to treat me? These are not simple questions and can take years to finalize.

Voice

Here, the spiritual is deeply entangled with moral development and it is important to pay attention to insights from the field of moral development. This includes the important identity work of the development of voice. How I speak of myself as an adolescent as I become adult does matter, as does giving voice to what matters to me. How can I claim what I know and see or speak of my insights and perceptions if I do not have a voice that I can use with confidence and assurance? Questions of voice and the ownership and authority of personal voice can be quite significant emotionally and spiritually in individual lives. It is critical to consider if the voice that a child develops as an adolescent allows the child to truly speak of him or her self. Is the voice congruent in representing her/his thoughts and feelings? Does the cultural context alter, subdue or favour his or her voice? As the person becomes adult is the voice used connected to inner awareness and sensitivity? Is the voice true or false? These questions are important in the adult life journey as relational ability and spiritual sensitivity may depend on how voice is developed, whether values and mattering are integrated, and whether there is a capacity to articulate experience and remain connected to it.

I want to be clear that voice is not necessarily expressed only in the spoken or written word. The imaginative and creative possibilities for voice are wide-ranging. I have known adolescents who have found their sense of self and voice through cooking, through handicrafts, music, visual art, dance, or sport. In each case I would argue that these forms express spiritual qualities when they include relational sensitivities and awareness. In expressing a sense of life and relations in whatever form it takes, a person is also expressing his or her way of being in the world, articulating some of what matters for him/her and demonstrating identity and value.

In adolescent experience, this includes the formation of adult character and may include both the claiming of and being claimed by a particular community. In becoming a part of a community the social development of an adolescent includes the absorption of communal beliefs and prejudices, social mores and the taking up of communal identity and purpose. Spiritual development is not solo work but ecologically embedded. It is relational and contextual.

For early adolescents, relational consciousness will be expressed in different forms than in younger children. Shifting developmental factors in adolescence will make for a different set of expressions. The spiritual might be noticeable and traceable in expressions of voice, in experiences of insight or vision, in an adolescent sense of vocation and life direction. There may also be signs of spiritual development arising in sexual awakening and awareness.

Conclusion

I intend these suggestions of the possible forms of spirituality as relational consciousness in early adolescents to be examples of how the spiritual may take shape in a non-linear fashion, with certain qualities being more in focus, and more critical, at different stages of the life journey. In adolescence innocence will be lost. That is necessary. Doubt will arise. That may be important. The spiritual may lose its central focus, for a time, as part of maturation.

It is also important that adults do not project images and needs from their middle and later years onto children or adolescents, searching for their own spirituality in juvenile form and making adult experience definitive spiritually. If the spiritual is natural and inherent, it will have as many variations in form and expression as the physical and emotional aspects of human experience. Researchers must be sensitive to the many forms of children's spirituality and not look for particular ones that assume adult expressions or cultural biases.

As well, it must be clear that the spiritual will not necessarily be marked by overt religious or identified spiritual practices. Looking only at large shifts – quantum changes (Miller & C'de Baca 2001), moments of awe or wonder, religious epiphanies, beyond-the-self experiences – may only portray the dramatic aspects of the spiritual and mask those aspects that are less evident. The spiritual may be woven into many forms of bodily, artistic, physical, emotional, social, and cognitive experiences. The degree of subtlety possible in spiritual expression may mean that many spiritual experiences are elusive. Their elusiveness may be a critical piece of how the spiritual occurs and is experienced by children.

The spiritual also may not always be positive in expression. It can include experiences of loss, difficulty, fear and sadness. It may be severely limited and constrained by a person's capacities or marked by their experiences of the darker aspects of human life. Violence, abuse, health problems, war, economic circumstances and developmental processes will shape the spiritual quality of a child's life and, consequently, their relational experience and capacity

If the spiritual is to be understood as relational consciousness, then I believe it is necessary to see it in the full range of human development and relationships, through expressions of life at every stage. A child's way is as spiritual as an adult's or an adolescent's. As relationships have many qualities, any study of them must acknowledge the possible variations of intensity, expression, affection, and form that are shaped by developmental capacity and human context. All these variations include the spiritual as they include other qualities of being human. To be alert to spirituality as relational consciousness requires skills of attention and listening, as well as a recognition that our own experiences are not definitive. It is necessary to respect the richness of human experience and the astonishing variety that life can take, staying open to the spiritual arising in others in unexpected ways, attuned to the widest range of possibility and difference in relational experience.

References

Bronfenbrenner, U. 1979: *The Ecology of Human Development: Experiments by Nature and Design*. Cambridge, MA: Harvard University Press.

Cogswell, F. 1992: *When The Right Light Shines*. Nepean, ON: Borealis Press.

Cogswell, F. 1994: *As I See It*, Nepean. ON: Borealis Press.

Cogswell, F. 1996; *The Trouble With Light*. Nepean, ON: Borealis Press.

Cogswell, F. 2000: *With Vision Added*. Nepean, ON: Borealis Press.

Coles, R. 1990: *The Spiritual Life of Children*. Boston: Houghton Mifflin Company.

Goodall, J. 1990: *My Life With the Chimpanzees*. Washington DC: National Geographic Society.

Gopnik, A., Meltzoff, A. N., and Kuhl, P. K. 1999: *The Scientist in the Crib: Minds, Brains, and How Children Learn*. New York: William Morrow and Company, Inc.

Harris, P. 2000: *The Work of the Imagination*. London: Blackwell Publishers.

Hawker, P. 2000: *Secret Affairs of the Soul: Ordinary People's Extraordinary Experiences of the Sacred*. Kelowna, BC: Northstone Publishing.

Hillman, J. 1996: *The Soul's Code: In Search of Character and Calling*. New York: Warner Books.

Irving, J. 1989: *A Prayer for Owen Meany*. New York: William Morrow.

Levine, S. 1999: Children's cognition as the foundation of spirituality. *International Journal of Children's Spirituality* 4(2), 121–40.

Miller, W. R., and C'de Baca, J. 2001: *Quantum Change: When Epiphanies and Sudden Insights Transform Ordinary Lives*. New York, London: The Guilford Press.

Morris, L. 2001: Autism and childhood spirituality. In J. Erricker, C. Ota, and C. Erricker (eds), *Spiritual Education, Cultural, Religious and Social Differences: New Perspectives for the 21st Century*. Brighton and Portland: Sussex Academic Press.

Robinson, E. 1983: *The Original Vision: A Study of the Religious Experience of Childhood*. New York: The Seabury Press.

Santrock, J. 2002: *Life Span Development* (8th edition). New York: McGraw-Hill Higher Education.

Chapter 7

The Spiritual and the Fantastical – George MacDonald's "Wise Woman"

JOHN PRIDMORE

T HE PURPOSE OF THIS CHAPTER is to call attention to one of the more remarkable figures in fantasy literature, to observe how her role in the stories in which she mysteriously comes and goes illustrates aspects of spiritual development and to suggest some implications of what we learn from her for the nurture of the spirit of the child. The hope is that by approaching familiar territory from a fresh – and possibly eccentric – direction new insights may appear. Needless to say the continuing debate about what the contentious term "spiritual development" means cannot be recapitulated here. The position assumed in this chapter is that it is a term we are not required to define. Our refusal to do so, as Jack Priestley has taught us, is on principle (Priestley 1996). To define is to destroy. It is to pin the butterfly to the board. But what we cannot define we can recognize and begin to describe. The broad-brush understanding which underpins what follows is that spiritual development is growth in the moral awareness of "the other and the beyond". The focus of this essay, however, is on the flight of the butterfly not on its anatomy, and in particular on one character created by a writer who succeeded in capturing – without arresting – something of the movement of the butterfly on the wing.

George MacDonald

If we wander upstream, seeking the spring from which flowed the river and, today, the flood of fantasy writing, we come eventually to George MacDonald (1824–1905). In his day MacDonald was honoured on both sides of the Atlantic as something of a sage and his prolific writings were much anthologized and extensively quarried for edifying quotations. After his death, however, his reputation suffered almost total eclipse. The revival of interest in MacDonald must be dated from the moment when a young student, one C. S. Lewis, chanced upon a copy of MacDonald's *Phantastes*, subtitled a "a faerie romance for men and women", on the bookstall of Leatherhead station. Lewis's comment on the impact of *Phantastes* on him is testimony to the formative power of fantasy. "It was as though the voice which had called me from the world's end", he later wrote, "were now speaking at my side" (Lewis 1959: 145).

Most of MacDonald's published writing was "realistic" fiction. He was the author of some two dozen novels. Many of these are implausible in their plots, stilted in style, and wooden in characterization. Moreover, fatally for the modern reader, they are heavily homiletic in tone. But in a series of far more interesting works MacDonald used an altogether different genre to explore the spiritual dimension of human experience, that of fantasy. In these works MacDonald abandons overt Christian terminology and it is in them that MacDonald's distinctive genius finds voice. The canon of MacDonald's fantasy consists of his fairy tales, such as *The Golden Key* or *The Light Princess*, his two adult fantasies, *Phantastes* and *Lilith*, and his children's books which are either set wholly in the realm of *faerie*, or in which the world as ordinarily experienced is invaded and subverted by the fantastic.

The Wise Woman

To convey the elusive character of the spiritual MacDonald introduces into a number of his fantasies the mysterious figure of "the Wise Woman". In this single figure, surely MacDonald's supreme imaginative creation, and in the myriad ways in which she relates to those whose lives she touches, MacDonald expresses all that he sees as shaping our highest good. The Wise Woman's concern – in his words, in her words – is that we "do better, and grow better, and be better" (MacDonald 1900: 39).

In attempting to separate out what the different strands in all this fecund figure suggests about spiritual formation we necessarily go against the grain of MacDonald's fantasy. The symbol of the Wise Woman, as is the case with any of the kaleidoscope of images MacDonald uses, will always suggest more than the artificial analyses we offer. But if we are to help the school down the road to formulate strategies to foster spiritual development a measure of systematization is inevitable, however clumsy the exercise.

I shall refer to five works in which the Wise Woman is a leading figure: *Phantastes* (1858), *At the Back of the North Wind* (1871), *The Princess and the Goblin* (1888 [1872]) and its sequel *The Princess and Curdie* (1900 [1883]), and the story entitled *The Wise Woman* (1875) – though, confusingly, this book has different titles in different editions. I shall suggest, with some hesitation, an interpretation of the figure of the Wise Woman. Whom or what does she stand for? The hesitation arises because there can be no one correct interpretation. Here as elsewhere in his fantasy MacDonald defers to his reader and we make of her what we will. Then I shall consider in turn five aspects of spiritual development and its promotion which we can identify in MacDonald's account of the Wise Woman and her ways, emphasising once again that by teasing apart strands intimately and subtly woven together we diminish the total impact of this singularly disturbing figure.

We do not know who the Wise Woman is. As the one who evokes what is beyond our rational grasp she cannot be captured in a net of words. This much may be suggested, that she can be seen as a personification of all that within a spiritually and morally ordered universe, as MacDonald holds it to be, is working for the well-being of its children. We meet her in different guises in the different texts. In *Phantastes* the hero Anodos wanders through "a fairy land afar", guided by the old woman sitting spinning in her cottage. In the two *Princess* books we have the great-great-grandmother figure, again sitting at her spinning-wheel, in a high turret of the castle which is home to the Princess Irene, a child who, like her young friend, the miner Curdie, has much to learn from her. We meet the mysterious woman, so old, so young, in *The Wise Woman*, the one who strives for the moral regeneration of the cosseted Princess Rosamond and the equally spoiled shepherd girl Agnes. Most memorably, perhaps, there is the mysterious, terrible, beautiful North Wind who, to the young boy Diamond, seems to act so arbitrarily and cruelly. In these tales the Wise Woman, whatever name she adopts, shapes the lives of the young protagonists.

The Wise Woman personifies all that nurtures the spirit. Whatever resistance she encounters, the Wise Woman ultimately works in harmony with the total universe of our experience which is purposed for our good. Yet the Wise Woman is not to be understood as the embodiment of an abstraction, as the anthropomorphizing of some impersonal process of cause and effect in a moral universe. She suggests that the providence shaping us for our good is personal. At the same time in the use of the image of the Wise Woman there is an avoidance of any confessional claims about the origin of any such benevolent pattern inhering in the scheme of things.

So much may be said. Yet we still sense that we have touched but the outskirts of her ways.

The role of the Wise Woman is to promote the well-being of those whose lives she touches. Different elements of the spiritual and its nurture are suggested by MacDonald's account of her. At least five such themes call for attention.

- The spiritual is to do with the mystery that surrounds us.
- The spiritual is manifested and experienced under many names and forms.
- Spiritual development proceeds and is promoted on the assumption that the universe is coherent and purposeful but there can be no final assurance that this assumption is not mistaken.
- Spiritual growth is at times painful.
- Spiritual development is never completed.

The Surrounding Mystery

The Wise Woman is a deeply mysterious figure. She appears in the tale that bears her name "muffled from head to foot in a cloak of black cloth" (1875: 13). So dark is North Wind's hair that it is scarcely to be distinguished from the darkness of the hayloft where the young boy Diamond sleeps and where she visits him (1871: 11). Princess Irene first discovers her in a room at the top of "a curious old stair of worm-eaten oak, which looks as if never any one had set foot upon it" (1888: 9). As elsewhere in MacDonald's work to climb a staircase is to explore beyond the familiar and commonplace. It is to ascend to the unknown.

There is much mystery about her age. She is "old and yet young" (1900: 67). To Curdie she is "a small withered creature, so old that no age would have seemed too great to write under her picture". He finds her a figure of fun – until, that is, he catches a glimpse of her eyes and then all laughter goes out of him (1900: 33–4). The uncertainty about the Wise Woman's age reflects MacDonald's conviction that age is not determined by date of birth. "The right old age", her great-great-grandmother tells Irene, "means strength and beauty and mirth and courage and strong painless limbs" (1888: 159). The Wise Woman appears as a little girl, her lap full of flowers, but she becomes "a woman perfectly beautiful, neither old nor young; for hers was the old age of everlasting youth" (1875: 195). Wisdom is not monopolised by the elderly any more than childhood is the privileged possession of the young.

So the Wise Woman is cloaked in mystery. The attempt to give conceptual clarity to the notion of spiritual development is laudable as is the concern to provide detailed maps to guide those charged with its promotion. Both philosophical foundations and curriculum strategies are necessary. But what must not be lost or diminished in the quest for clarity and a sense of pedagogical direction is the continuing sense of the mystery by which we are troubled, that aspect of our condition which both justifies and impels the nurture of the spirit as an essential educational goal. The interventions of the Wise Woman, visiting us from the "nameless region beyond all categories", at once dramatize and confirm a fundamental premise of spiritual education; that the mysterious, so far from being merely the term by which we dignify what we do not yet understand, refers on the contrary in Karl Rahner's words to "the primordial and permanent" (1966: 41–2).

A sense of mystery is educationally important as a spur to enquiry. For Roderick McGillis MacDonald's portrayal of the Wise Woman "dramatizes the efficacy of mystery in teaching" (1985: 147). "The efficacy of mystery in teaching" – it is as telling a phrase as we shall encounter in the literature, one to be written across much that has been published about spiritual development in the hope of making everything clear.

Truth's "Ten Thousand Changes of Raiment"

It belongs to the mystery of the Wise Woman that she bears many names. She has the same name as the girl who is the heroine of the two Princess stories, her granddaughter (or perhaps her great-great-granddaughter) Irene. She too is Irene. But she is also "North Wind" (1871 *passim*), "Old Mother Wotherwop" (1900: 52), "the Mother of Light" (1900: 65), "the lady of emeralds" (1900: 66), "the Lady of the Silver Moon" (1900: 70). The question "What *is* in a name?" is the title of a chapter containing perhaps MacDonald's most searching reflections on the identity of the mysterious grandmother figure, chapter seven of *The Princess and Curdie*. In a deep gallery of the mines the young Curdie, who so far has failed to recognize the Wise Woman, at last sees her, first only her face and then her radiant form. The encounter overwhelms him. "All the beauty of the cavern, yes, of all he knew of the whole creation, seemed gathered in one centre of harmony and loveliness in the person of the ancient lady who stood before him" (1900: 64). He learns that, although she has many names and fulfils multiple tasks, she herself is not many but one. "I could give you twenty names more to call me, Curdie, and not one of them would be a false one. What does it matter how many names if the person is one?"(1900: 71)

The Wise Woman adopts many guises. Her different names reflect her capacity to reveal herself – or to conceal herself – in many different forms. Diamond meets North Wind as a flower in the grass, as a small girl no taller than he is, as a wolf. "I have to shape myself", she tells Diamond, "in various ways to various people" (1871: 363). Curdie is bewildered that Irene's great-great grandmother can appear in so many different forms. She attempts to reassure him. "Shapes are only dresses, Curdie, and dresses are only names. That which is inside is the same all the time". Curdie is not satisfied. "But then how can all shapes speak the truth?" (1900: 71–2)

Curdie's question is crucially important. Curdie senses, as do we, that the Wise Woman's assertion that "shapes are only dresses", is an extremely bold assertion. But how bold? The sub-title of MacDonald's *The Wise Woman* is "A Parable". Is the claim being made, audacious enough, that the person and work of the Wise Woman is, as it were, an extra-canonical parable of the Christian gospel? Or is a much more radical claim being made, the claim that that Gospel, the Christian tradition itself, is also a "dress", a sequence of images, exchangeable with any number of others? Must the spiritual and its promotion be anchored, as David Carr (1995, 1996a, 1996b) has claimed, in the discourse of a specific religious tradition? Are the alternative spiritual discourses, the theistic and the non-theistic, incompatible as Andrew Wright (1998) has argued? Or does the haunting figure of the Wise Woman imply that no spiritual tradition has a primary and privileged status?

We have the cryptic texts and MacDonald leaves us to come to our own conclusions about them. I have argued more fully elsewhere for the view that in MacDonald's recourse to fantasy, not least in introducing us to the Wise Woman, there is tacit recognition that traditional religious signs and symbols are not the only images by which the spiritual may be evoked (Pridmore 2000).

At the end of the tale entitled *The Wise Woman* it at last dawns on the spoiled brat Princess Rosamond that all the different creatures which have hunted and chastised and comforted her throughout her adventures are all one.

> "It was you, then, after all!" (Rosamond) cried in delight . . .
> "It always is me, after all", said the wise woman, smiling.
> "And it was you all the time?"
> "It always is me all the time".
> "But which is the real you?"asked Rosamond; "this or that?"
> "Or a thousand others?" returned the wise woman.
> (MacDonald 1875: 1967)

It is a haunting exchange. We may never, it seems, speak univocally of that we long for – only analogically. But that reservoir of analogy is inexhaustible. "Fact", said MacDonald in one of his novels, "at best is but a garment of the truth, which has ten thousand changes of raiment woven in the same loom" (1886: 29).

We read about the Wise Woman in a culture that has largely abandoned traditional religious accounts of the human condition. In our contemporary schools it is perhaps only by one "dressed as the Wise Woman", shaped by images reaching beyond the grasp of traditional religious discourse, that the possibility of the transcendent may be made known.

Curdie's question, however, must still be pressed, "How can all the shapes speak the truth?" If the nurture of the spiritual is not to be confined to the patterns of traditional religious catechesis what safeguards are there against spiritualities – there is no shortage of them – that are mischievous or manipulative? By what criteria is one model of spiritual development preferred to another? The Wise Woman, Irene's grandmother, does not evade Curdie's question.

> It is one thing the shape I choose to put on, and quite another the shape that foolish talk and nursery tale may please to put upon me. Also it is one thing what you or your father may think about me, and quite another what a foolish or bad man may see in me. (1900: 72)

Not all the shapes speak the truth. But ultimately the criteria we must apply to judge between them are not metaphysical but moral. The realm of fantasy, with its constantly shifting images, is a world in flux, where nothing stays the same and little is as it seems. The paradox, the awareness of which underlies MacDonald's recourse to fantasy, is that such a world represents more accurately human experience than the apparently more stable world of purportedly "'realistic" fiction. Firm ground for MacDonald is found in the inexorability of the ethical, in the sovereign demands, not of religious truth-claims, but of the next thing to be done. Eventually the Wise Woman passes from Irene's life. But she remembers her, recalling the songs she sung sitting at her spinning-wheel. "And the very fancy would make her happier and abler to do her duty" (1900: 134).

The Acceptance of Uncertainty

In *Phantastes*, as in the *Princess* books, the Wise Woman sings as she spins. It is "a low strange song to which the hum of the wheel made a kind of infinite symphony" (1858: 234). In the Princess stories the thread she spins saves the children from perishing beneath the mountains. The message of Wise Woman's strange song, as is the sign of her wheel and its unbroken thread, is that in the end all holds together beautifully. She says to Anodos, who in *Phantastes* is each of us,

> In whatever sorrow you may be, however inconsolable and irremediable it may appear, believe me that the old woman in the cottage with the young eyes . . . knows something, though she must not always tell it, that

would quite satisfy you about it, even in the worst moments of your distress. (1858: 249–50)

And what of suffering? Diamond asks North Wind how she can bear to contemplate the suffering she has inflicted in causing a ship to sink in the storm she caused.

> I will tell you how I am able to bear it, Diamond: I am always hearing, through every noise, through all the noise I am making myself even, the sound of a far-off song. I do not exactly know where it is or what it means; and I don't hear much of it, only the odours of its music, as it were flitting across the great billows of the ocean . . . (1871: 76–7)

Spiritual development is the process of bringing the fragmentary and confused into some kind of concord. It is both the work of resolving the inner discords of our individual experience and also the endeavour to be part of a larger whole, to reconcile the alienation we experience and the contradictions we witness within a wider scheme of things. It is the quest for a pattern, for coherence. That pattern is "far-off", undisclosed, and far from realization, but for our flourishing we pursue it in hope.

But such "cosmic optimism" may be misplaced. We cannot be finally certain that the Wise Woman exists, that the notion of a transcendent purpose is more than wishful thinking. Its existence can never be proved to those who choose not to believe in it. Initially Curdie refuses to believe in Irene's grandmother and the thread she spins. Irene takes Curdie to meet her but he does not see her. For him her room with its burning roses, its lamp, its bed with its rich counterpane, is an empty garret (1900: 225–30).

Even Irene herself sometimes wonders if her meetings with this mysterious old lady are all a dream. Who knows whether the grandmother, North Wind, the Wise Woman, exist outside the imagination and the dreams of those who claim to have met her? There can be no conclusive certainty that she exists. There is only the choice, none more important, whether or not to act on the assumption that she does exist.

> The only question is whether you will believe that I am anywhere – whether you will believe that I am anything but a dream . . . It will rest with yourself after all. (1888: 120)

Diamond too in *At the Back of the North Wind* is tormented by the possibility that his experience of North Wind has been a sequence of dreams.

> "How am I to know that it's not a dream?"
> "What does it matter?" returned North Wind . . . "I'm either not a dream, or there's something better that's not a dream." (1871: 359–60)

But Diamond insists that it is North Wind herself he wants. Again he voices his fear that she is all a dream. And North Wind "shot herself into the air, as if uneasy because she could not answer him" (1871: 361).

There are a great many things I do not understand more than you do . . . Meantime you may be hopeful, and content not to be quite sure. (1871: 365)

We must rest content "not to be quite sure". The reality of the Wise Woman and of what she represents, the coherence and purpose of all that exists, is not beyond doubt. For those who question her existence nothing could count as irrefutable evidence that she is real. There are hints that towards the end of his life even MacDonald himself perhaps began to wonder whether the Wise Woman was there (MacDonald, Greville 1924: 559–60). What can be said is that MacDonald has forged a discourse that eschews dogmatic claims, that leaves open the issue of what are the referents, if there be any, of the multiplicity of symbols he uses, but which nevertheless asserts the urgency of entering into the same journey which the protagonists of his narratives undertake. While we cannot know for sure whether there is a pattern to our story, to take seriously the figure of Wise Woman – so reticent, so elusive, yet so purposeful – is to choose to act on the assumption that there is.

Spirituality and Pain

Irene, admitted for the first time to her grandmother's bedroom, sees that what she has taken for a bouquet of red rose is in fact a fire (MacDonald 1888: 145). We do not have to suppose that the incomparably greater poet was alluding directly to MacDonald to note that T. S. Eliot and MacDonald both recognized that "the fire and the rose are one" (Eliot 1944).

Irene's grandmother – our "Wise Woman" – tells Curdie to plunge his hands into the bowl of burning roses. He bears the terrible pain and only withdraws his hands when she tells him to do so. Then he sees "that her face looked as if she had been weeping" (MacDonald 1900: 89).

Spiritual growth, it is implied, entails suffering but such suffering can be purposeful. The principle that spiritual development is at times necessarily painful accounts for the Wise Woman's severe, even seemingly cruel methods. Rosamond is called "the lost princess" and she is lost because she is wholly self-centred. The Wise Woman has to subject her to a series of terrifying ordeals to shatter her self-regard, to bring her to some awareness of her moral and spiritual poverty, and to set her on the path of spiritual growth. When the Wise Woman carries Rosamond out of her father's palace the stubborn princess struggles and screams.

Set down on the road she rushes at the Wise Woman only to find that the cloak that had enfolded her was "hard as the cloak of a bronze statue" (1875: 21). Her guide allows her to be threatened by a pack of wolves (1875: 30–32). Rosamond's spiritual development cannot be advanced unless she attends to the next thing to be done. The Wise Woman insists that Rosamond keeps the cottage clean to which she has taken her and she resorts to severe measures when the princess refuses to obey. The love that shapes us, burns us.

MacDonald recognizes, as does every serious tradition of spirituality, that spiritual development is inescapably painful. This recognition is far from conspicuous in the literature about spiritual development in schools, whether we turn to the official or semi-official commentaries on the legislation or to the academic journals. Some proposals of how spiritual development might be promoted within the curriculum – the pause for thought in the chemistry lesson, the visit to the splendid view on the geography field-course, and the like – are hardly threatening.

To be sure the terrifying measures that the Wise Woman, North Wind, and Irene's grandmother adopt to bring their charges to their senses are not for introduction into the timetable of the common school. But this dimension of the Wise Woman's pedagogical strategy has to be admitted to the debate about spiritual development. Our becoming, our spiritual journey, is at times painful. Negative and contradictory experiences may be needed for the nurture of well-being and the educational project requires us to help pupils see that this is so.

The Mist of Unfulfilment

Towards the end of *The Princess and Curdie* Irene's great-great-grandmother, the Wise Woman, exchanges the guise of a housemaid for royal robes. And the narrator comments, "Her face was radiant with joy, the joy overshadowed by a faint mist as of unfulfilment" (1900: 299). The Wise Woman's work is never done. The story with the title *The Wise Woman* defers closure. Its "end" – though it is nothing of the sort – is enigmatic. The last paragraph reads:

> And that is all my double story. How double it is, if you care to know, you must find out. If you think that it is not finished – I never knew a story that was. I could tell you a great deal more concerning them all, but I have already told more than is good for those who read but with their foreheads, and enough for those whom it has made look a little solemn, and sigh as they close the book. (1875: 222)

We close the book but the story is unclosed. The Wise Woman's work, the task of spiritual development, is always unconcluded. The Wise woman's work is not done. Now she has entered my story, the life-story with which the tale I have been reading has merged. What she will be for me is for me to find out – though in my story too that ending is deferred, always "beyond".

Conclusion

George MacDonald's Wise Woman offers a "five-fold cord" to guide the process of spiritual development.

She teaches us that the natural concern to be clear about what is meant by spiritual development risks draining that process of its essential mystery. The fact that its promotion, along with other curriculum requirements, is subject to inspection means that schools must seek for criteria by which they can monitor and evaluate their success in this area. But there is a dimension to the spiritual that cannot be quantified. The Wise Woman will always escape the stern figures stumbling after her with clipboards. Spiritual education is a counterbalance to all within the curriculum which would rob life of its mystery.

The ways of the Wise Woman show, secondly, that maps may be drawn of the landscape of the spiritual life which use conventional signs other than the traditional religious ones. The Wise Woman has many names and adopts many guises. Spiritual development does not require, though neither of course does it exclude, assent to a particular religious tradition. It is not the case that spirituality without religion is merely a mood, the sentiment left when a religion is stripped of its specialized terminology and its metaphysical claims. The spiritual is a dimension of our becoming which alternative discourses, complementary to those of religious traditions but with their own autonomy, can both describe and promote.

Thirdly, our spiritual pedagogy proceeds on the premise that all ultimately coheres. The abiding image of the Wise Woman is of the woman, so old, so young, sitting at her spinning wheel in her loft at the top of a high staircase. Our well-being hangs by the thread she spins. The controlling idea behind this imagery is that there is a pattern, as yet undisclosed, to all that is random and contradictory in human experience. It follows that all that compartmentalizes human experience, not least in the curriculum, is hostile to her purposes of good.

There is a pattern, but spiritual development is promoted not by asserting what that pattern is. About such matters the teacher, as is the Wise Woman herself, must be reticent. The invitation is to live as if that pattern, albeit not yet disclosed, is no chimera. That invitation stands despite the fact that there can be no conclusive certainty that the universe of our experience is meaningful. That there is any overarching

order is beyond proof or disproof. The promotion of spiritual development does not depend on the certainty of such a premise being
demonstrated. More importantly, the task of spiritual education cannot
await such a demonstration. The total educational enterprise proceeds,
not from the certainty that everything makes sense, but from the adoption of a frame of reference which allows that possibility. It is scarcely
conceivable that schools should be organized on the contrary assumption, on the premise that values, spiritual or any other, can only be
explained as human constructs.

Fourthly, the process of spiritual development is arduous and often
painful. The nurture of the spiritual will meet with fierce resistance. The
scene of spiritual development is not always where there is a view of a
glorious sunset. Here is an aspect of the matter on which neither the
official publications nor the scholarly literature dwell. If the figure of the
Wise Woman and her sometimes harsh methods are taken seriously
then this omission, or at least the imbalance, needs to be addressed. The
implication is certainly not that edifying ordeals be introduced into the
curriculum. There is no place for a "cold showers spirituality".
Everyday experience, not least of children and young people, already
contains quite enough that is contradictory and tragic. Spiritual education does not mean facile moralizing about such experience but it does
require helping children to come to terms with it.

Finally we learn from the Wise Woman that her work is never done.
Spiritual development is essentially an unfinished process. About our
path is always the "faint mist as of unfulfilment". The stories in which
the Wise Woman figures so remarkably merge with my own. How far
her endeavours shape the lives of those she touches are finally effective
is for me to find out in my own continuing life-story.

Whether George MacDonald's quaint tales about the Wise Woman
are readable in today's classrooms is a moot point. What is certain is that
those classrooms will be impoverished places unless, in one or other of
her "ten thousand changes of raiment", she is admitted to them.

And how is she to gain entry to our classrooms? The Wise Woman is
a free spirit and her entrances will be unbidden and unpredictable. That
said, there are doors and windows that can be left open for her. Clearly
stories serve as such. Stories, subversive of our settled assumptions
about where worlds end, have the capacity to change us for good. The
kind of stories which will leave space for the Wise Woman to work will
be those which leave us wondering what happens next, stories, unbur-
dened by desiccating explanation or commentary, open-ended stories
whose sequel is absorbed into the unfinished business of one's own life.

Any classroom discussion, in any subject, about what we look
forward to will throw wide doors and windows for the Wise Woman.
The stories in which she appears, as are all George MacDonald's works,

are shot through by an intense longing for what lies beyond, both beyond present experience and beyond rational articulation. In *Phantastes* Anodos awaits the fulfilment of the promise breathed by the beech tree, "a great good is coming" (1858: 322). Children and young people are good at looking forward, a capacity on which spiritual education must capitalize. A spiritual pedagogy influenced by the Wise Woman will be "a pedagogy of hope". Curricular strategy – and those classroom discussions – will encourage the envisioning of the coming good, tempered always by the recognition that even our best plans can only be of the penultimate.

And here the Wise Woman's presence in the classroom will sometimes be subversive of the comfortable curricular consensus. Her work is promoted by awkward questions. A pedagogy influenced by the Wise Woman will be concerned about the societies we shape. It will, for example, support the place of "citizenship education" in the National Curriculum for England and Wales. But a caveat must be entered. The Wise Woman sees beyond the models of common order which the curricular proposals identify as propitious for the flourishing of citizenship. For example we may well proclaim the excellence of "our economy and our democratic institutions and values" (DfEE and QCA 1999: 183) but if there is a spiritual dimension to citizenship it will never allow us to settle for such objectives as the goal of our quest for meaning and fulfilment. Indeed a spirituality informed by the Wise Woman writings will forbid us taking our rest in any model of the social order, however essential it is to build such models and to try to make them work. The terrible climax of *The Princess and Curdie* – "let him that readeth understand" – stands as an abiding warning against seeing the achievement of social ends as the culmination of the spiritual journey.

References

Carr, D. 1995: Towards a Distinctive Conception of Spiritual Education. *Oxford Review of Education* 21(1), 83–98.

Carr, D. 1996a: Rival Conceptions of Spiritual Education. *Journal of the Philosophy of Education* 30 (2), 159–78.

Carr, D. 1996b: Songs of Innocence and Transcendence: a rejoinder to Blake. *Oxford Review of Education* 22 (4), 457–63.

DfEE and QCA. 1999: *The National Curriculum Handbook for Secondary Teachers in England*. London: DfEE.

Eliot, T. S. 1944: *The Four Quartets*. London: Faber and Faber.

Lewis, C. S. 1959: *Surprised by Joy*. London: Collins, Fontana Books.

MacDonald, G. 1858: *Phantastes: a Faerie Romance for Men and Women*. London: Smith, Elder and Co.

MacDonald, G. 1871: *At the Back of the North Wind*. London: Strahan.

MacDonald, G. 1875: *The Wise Woman: A Parable*. London: Strahan.

MacDonald, G. 1886: *What's Mine Mine*. London: Kegan Paul, Trench.

MacDonald, G. 1888 [1872]: *The Princess and the Goblin*. London: Blackie.

MacDonald, G. 1895: *Lilith: A Romance*. London: Chatto & Windus.

MacDonald, G. 1900: [1883] *The Princess and the Curdie*. London: Blackie & Son.

MacDonald, G. 1904: The Golden Key. In Greville MacDonald (ed.), *Fairy Tales*. London: Arthur C. Fifield.

MacDonald, Greville 1924: *George MacDonald and his Wife*. London: George Allen & Unwin.

McGillis, R. 1985: George MacDonald's *Princess* Books: High Seriousness. In Perry Nodelman (ed.), *Touchstones: Reflections on the Best in Children's Literature*, West Lafayette, IN: ChLA Publications, 146–62.

Pridmore, J. 2000: Talking of God and Talking of Fairies: discourses of spiritual development in the works of George MacDonald and in the curriculum. *International Journal of Children's Spirituality* 7 (1), 23–35.

Priestley, J. G. 1996: *Spirituality in the Curriculum*. Hockerill Educational Foundation.

Rahner, K. 1966: *Theological Investigations*, Vol. IV. London: Darton, Longman & Todd.

Wright, A. 1998: *Spiritual Pedagogy: A survey, critique and reconstruction of contemporary spiritual education in England and Wales*. Culham: Culham College Institute.

Chapter 8

Faith and Social Intimacy: Learning for Life

JOYCE E. BELLOUS

W HAT IS FAITH? The question invites a modern, conceptual focus on identity. A response marks off conceptual boundaries and distinguishes faith from semantically related terms. In carrying out an analysis, faith is named. Yet there is something static about asking identity questions and giving analytical answers. The question of faith's nature introduces and stipulates its identity and provides criteria for observing faith in the world. Unfortunately, faith may be trapped inside conceptual inquiry and domesticated beyond recognition. A second question is equally possible. We might ask: How does faith operate? The second question is post-modern so that the inquiry is dynamic and descriptive – faith is a moving target.

Suppose we ask the questions sequentially. Faith is depicted and dynamic. Yet a conflict remains. As we ask how faith operates, we contest its identity, challenging answers to the first question. Resolving the conflict allows our understanding of faith to move forward. Conflict is resolved by thinking. I will offer a conceptual analysis then speculate on how faith operates and finally link faith to intimacy. Exercising faith establishes groundwork for social intimacy to build its home. If we identify faith and ask how it works, we will see the bases for social intimacy. Faith builds toward intimacy because it holds confidence and vulnerability in tension. Faith opens up the possibility of hope. Intimacy likewise depends on hope. Intimacy is the developed capacity to be vulnerable and feel safe. Social intimacy adds to this definition the developed capacity for being near and different. Standing behind this inquiry, I would like the reader to imagine a relationship between an adult and a child – the adult desires to help the child discover and strengthen faith; the child longs for a spiritual friend. What may they hope? What might they learn together? Intimacy, hope and faith are not acquired apart from committed, constant, long-term relationships.

What is Faith?

Every human being requires an education in faith. Two of its aspects matter to education: the noun faith and the verb to believe. The noun and its adjective are expressed in the following sentences: The faith of her parents is Christianity. She is a faithful person. The second aspect in its religious sense is conveyed in the sentence: He believes in God. Under certain conditions, the second sense is an activity: we exercise faith. Faith as noun or adjective is the confidence, trust, reliance or conviction we place in someone or something. In its exercise, faith becomes a disposition. People who exercise faith can be counted on to act in certain ways because placing confidence in a person or thing alters thought and action with respect to that person or thing and to the world in general. Exercising faith is as changeful as is physical exercise.

Faith refers to content and to a way of life. As content, faith is intellectual assent, which implies affirming some content and suggests that a person holds consciously chosen statements about the world. These statements may be crass, for example: "Look out for yourself! No one else will do it for you." This belief is a barricade to social intimacy. In general, those who give assent feel bound to act according to the implications of statements they prize. I say generally because a dynamic of faith is caught in the relationship between what people say and what they actually rely on. There may be deep cleavages between what we say and what we count on when the going gets tough. Observing our own faithfulness (and its failures) requires seeing congruity between what is said and what is done, continuity that is more elusive than we like to admit, yet is core to the spiritual work of growing up.

There is a relationship between content and faith's exercise. When we ask what faith is we pose a question about human experience. While faith is essential to being human – everyone exercises faith – establishing a happy continuity between what we say and what we actually trust is difficult. When we ask how faith operates we observe particular traditions. Faith may be expressed in loyalty to a tradition that is consciously chosen as a way of life. Faith as an activity or way of life has to do with fidelity, with holding fast to one's integrity and keeping one's word; it is belief put to use. Faith's exercise implies a kind of attentiveness: we observe ourselves acting congruently with what we claim to believe. Faith as feeling is a way of loving the world. It is an attitude that opposes itself to fear and is forward-looking. Mature faith makes peace with uncertainty because it is a comfortably certain grip on the picture of the world a person holds.

Another dimension of faith is specifically religious. Faith is a comfortable grip on God. It is holding sure in God: confident reliance on God's own Self. From Christian perspectives, faith is not superstition but relies on Christ's "once-for-all" sacrifice on the cross at Calvary. It is based on a belief that the faithful are related to God *via* historical events of Christ's life, death and resurrection. Faith is grounded on God's initiatives. Faith as holding sure in God enables the faithful to enjoy the proffered resources of God's grace: forgiveness and a future. Our response to God's generosity expresses itself in worship, integrity and service – as a God-infused community, offering safety to those who suffer the realities of ordinary living. Faith is a way of hearing and seeing the world and perceiving ourselves in it. People see through eyes and hear through ears of faith, or else they perceive experience through a veil of despair. Believing is an outcome of faith: it is the action of faith – something like energy that affects ordinary experience. An essential human task is learning to use faith in the right way, whether or not people place faith in God.

Learning Faith

Faith is never far from us. Every human being has the capacity for exercising faith. There are three parts to the activity. There is the agent – a person exercising faith. There is the object of faith – something or someone the agent puts faith in. And there is the relation between the agent and object. Suppose a young child exercises faith in her mother. As they go for a walk, they come to a playground. The little girl indicates that she wants to play on the slide. She climbs up the steps. As she sits at the top her mother stands at the bottom of the slide. The mother looks steadily at her daughter and says she will catch her little girl. The child fixes her gaze on her mother's face. The little girl glances down the slide and is afraid but looks back to the familiar face and pushes away from her safe resting spot, keeping her eyes on her mother. Her mother catches her. The relation between mother and child is carried through their mutual gaze and expressed in their shared joy at success. Faith addresses fear; faith is the opposite of giving in to fear. Faith tries things out, and failing or succeeding, goes on trying. While it may be possible to avoid slides in a playground, every human being learns to exercise faith. We put faith in our trust or in our mistrust of other people. This girl is likely to put faith in trusting others.

We learn about faith as infants. Consider an infant who plays a game of peek-a-boo with his father. The father, the game and the baby constitute an activity in which the infant is learning that his father exists even though the baby can no longer see him. As they play the game the baby learns to have faith in things unseen. Faith is active when we cannot make use of our five senses. Faith is the consequence of experimenting with trust. We put faith in something or someone with the result that we acquire certain beliefs about the world. If conditions are *favorable*, beliefs form about the world encouraging us to exercise hopeful faith rather than succumbing to fear and refusing to put faith in anything that we cannot see, smell, hear, taste or touch.

People are compelled to put faith somewhere. Some put faith in the story that life will always disappoint them. Some put faith entirely in themselves, or more accurately in a snapshot of themselves – an image they make into an idol. But we all exercise faith. We have faith that the sun will come up tomorrow and that the sea will stay in place. We put faith in the roof over our heads and the weather that brings sun and rain to make our fields produce food. We put faith in other people. If we do not put faith in ordinary things we do not have sufficient energy to go on living. People who cannot put faith in the predictability and orderliness of the world are unwell. They become neurotic or psychotic. They are overwhelmed by anxiety and crushed by the demands of living. Faith speaks to anxiety. Faith is built into reality and confirms the wisdom of having faith in the predictable length of days and seasons, in rain falling to water the earth and in the sun shining to warm it.

In order to organize reality meaningfully, we need a story to shape our perspective. This perspective is also called faith. Faith is the story we tell ourselves about the world and

> does not create new things but it adds a new dimension to the basic realities of life. Faith brings our fragmented personality into a meaningful whole and unifies our divided self. It is the source of inspiration for a searching mind, the basis for a creative community and a constant incentive for an on-going renewal of life. (Nouwen 1969: 19)

The primary assumption then, is that every human being exercises faith to sustain life, as seems necessary. Faith cuts across secular and religious worldviews as an attitude that integrates the experience of a whole person – an entire self.

In its integrative role, faith influences human action due to the way it organizes our perception of experience. If human beings want to be well, they are compelled to make sense of life. Faith fills in gaps in our experience between what we sense and realities we cannot perceive or test empirically. Faith attends to depths that cannot be plumbed with a measuring stick. Faith organizes connections between what can be and what cannot be seen. This feature of faith is as true for scientists who study the atom as it is for those who trust an invisible God. Faith refers to a reality beyond mere seeing – a subject on which good science can only pay its humble respects.

A Metaphor for Faith

Modern science was consumed with division and order – a place for everything and everything in its place. But while modern order explained aspects of human experience, it could not account for its sum total. Human experience moves beyond our capacity for summing things up neatly. After modernity, our spiritual task is to disturb the order of things enough to let old ideas recover a rightful place in the human landscape and open up new ideas to the light of day. While we value the wealth modernity made in the world, it suffered poverty as well. An enormous loss to humankind was felt in the field of faith. Modern secular voices embarrassed the faithful into silence, leaving them with little to say in a marketplace tyrannized by empirical truth. Science believes it has the last word on experience and reality. In science, Reality is what is Measurable. Faith integrates experience but experience refers to more than what is measurable. Further, faith integrates the experience of a whole person – an entire self. Mature faith is flexible enough to integrate new knowledge within its frame of reference and keep pace with new discoveries of the human mind; it is essential for mature faith to be willing to shift gears, integrate new insights and to revise its positions (Nouwen 1969: 13).

In asking about faith, a prior question presents itself: how does human experience come to us? A useful image situates its integrative role and accounts for our need for faith as well. To say faith is an attitude of the heart is to say it is the responsive side of human consciousness; faith is found in mental states such as attention, interest, expectancy, feeling, imagination and reaction. Exercising faith is more than a mental state, it is expressed in action, but as an attitude, faith is "a subjective response to the power or powers that people conceive as having ultimate control over their interests and destinies"; it is an "attitude of a self toward an object in which the self genuinely believes" (Pratt 1956: 2–3), even if the 'object' is an object of thought, i.e., an idea, as it is in some faith traditions.

When we think of religion broadly, we can describe God as the Determiner of Destiny. Religious people attune themselves to the Determiner of Destiny – at the general and personal level. Destiny refers to what is going to happen to the world, humanity in general, as well as what is going to happen to you and me. We may agree with Immanuel Kant that while there is only one true religion, there can be several kinds of faith (Kant 1998: 118) e.g., Hindu, Christian, Jewish, Muslim; we might suggest further that there is faith that does not depend upon religious tradition, hence it is something we might call secular faith. Regardless of a particular tradition, faith integrates human experience with respect to the Determiner of Destiny – or as many young people say, with the impression that "Something is There". The vagueness of their description may arise from the absence of embodied religious knowledge.

An image that explains how faith integrates experience is an archipelago (Pratt 1956: 1–44). An archipelago is a landform in which islands are surrounded by an expanse of water. The island surfaces can be seen and explored but roots and connections between one island and another cannot be seen, they must be imagined. As people look at islands that can be seen and are close together, it is reasonable to suppose there are connections between them. Modern science focused on landforms; faith focuses on what lies between. Landforms can be charted and measured; their materials tested. Experience of landforms is repeatable and hence measurable – to a great extent. Maturing faith takes account of landforms but also imagines, speculates upon, believes in and narrates depths beyond sight. Faith makes sense of the geography of human experience and orients thinking about life as a whole (Kant 1998: 1–14).

The Structure of Faith

If it orients thinking, how is faith built up? Ludwig Wittgenstein (1889–1951) explored the idea of what we can know for sure. He suggested that everyone has a world-picture. We do not get pictures of the world by satisfying ourselves they are correct, nor retain them because we are satisfied they are correct. Rather the deepest layer of what we claim to know about the world is an inherited background against which we distinguish what is true from what is false (Wittgenstein 1979: #94). The propositions that structure our knowledge are part of a mythology. An analogy for the mythology of our mental life is that of a riverbed. Some inherited knowledge forms the bedrock of the river and is solid and firm, virtually unchanging, functioning as channels for other propositions that are not hardened; some propositions are fluid like the waters that flow over the river-bed, or else shift like sands that lie on the hard rock (Wittgenstein 1979: #96).

Wittgenstein acknowledged a change of state was possible between the waters and the river-bed (some ideas that were once solid may become fluid), but distinguished between water and river-bed in the following way: "the bank of the river consists partly of hard rock, subject to no alteration or only to an imperceptible one, partly of sand, which now in one place now in another gets washed away, or deposited"

(Wittgenstein 1979: #97). He later said, "when we first begin to believe anything, what we believe is not a single proposition, it is a whole system of propositions" (Wittgenstein 1979: #141), i.e., a mental system or a world-picture, such that, a

> child learns to believe a host of things; i.e. it learns to act according to these beliefs. Bit by bit there forms a system of what is believed, and in that system some things stand unshakeably fast and some are more or less liable to shift. What stands fast does so, not because it is intrinsically obvious or convincing; it is rather held fast by what lies around it. (Wittgenstein 1979: #144)

In making his case, he pursued this line of thought and observed that: "*Very* intelligent and well educated people believe in the story of creation in the Bible, while others hold it as proven false, and the grounds of the latter are well known to the former" (Wittgenstein 1979: #336). In addressing bedrock beliefs held by reasonable people, he implied that all thinking is grounded on believing, i.e., on holding assumptions (propositions) we seldom doubt. That is, thinking must rest on a solid foundation. Even for the most thoughtful, some ideas are steady and reliable like the hinges on a door that allow the door to open. As he put it: "One might say that, 'I know' expresses comfortable certainty, not certainty that is still struggling" (Wittgenstein 1979: #357). He spoke of comfortable certainty as neither hastiness nor superficiality, but as a form of life (Wittgenstein 1979: #358). Believing orients thinking, because, as he put it: "knowledge in the end is based on acknowledgement" (Wittgenstein 1979: #378). Further, "the rules of caution," so characteristic of skeptical moderns, "only make sense if they come to an end somewhere. A doubt without an end is not even a doubt" (Wittgenstein 1979: #625). Knowledge finds its resting place; it activates us according to a way of life that makes sense, so that we make sense to other people.

What do Wittgenstein's aphorisms contribute to our discussion? Believing is built up by layering assumptions begun in infancy. His insight is linked to Hebrew understanding of faith. The meaning of faith to ancient Hebrews was "Hold God" (Buttrick 1962: 222). What is a faithful grip on God like? Also for the Greeks, Philo in particular, faith was a kind of certainty (Buttrick 1962: 228). What sort of certainty is it? Wittgenstein's expression elaborates these ancient contexts. A grip of faith holds God with comfortable certainty – it has stopped struggling. It is a form of life designed as world-pictures reconfigured over time through personal and corporate experiences. Its exercise is shaped by the particular tradition we choose to take on.

An Aesthetics of Faith

Jesus of Nazareth observed faith. His attention was so persistent that his disciples asked him to increase their faith. In reply, he said faith the size of a mustard seed could move mountains. What was going on? I suggest Jesus used *complex irony* (Vlastos 1991: 1–44). Complex irony is a figure of speech in which what is said both is and is not meant. Complex irony moves people to contrast what is being said with current conceptions so that the concept shifts its shape. Complex irony is related to simple irony. Simple irony includes humour, mockery and riddle. When irony riddles, it risks being misunderstood (Vlastos 1991: 21). Complex irony riddles with a word's meaning, bracketing our understanding of it, so new meanings may emerge.

Simple irony works when what is said is not what is meant. Suppose a teacher is frustrated with a student's lack of progress, when the student is normally quite good. The teacher says: "You are being unusually clever today." If the statement were taken as it stands, the teacher's meaning would not break through. Further, if the teacher were trying to deceive, irony would not work. Simple irony works only if the hearer "gets it". Irony requires us to think for ourselves. Like all significant communication, irony puts the burden of communication on the hearer. Complex irony lays upon hearers an additional burden. Only those who have ears to hear, make sense of complex irony.

Jesus focused on faith as the centrepiece of relationship with God. Faith is complex irony. If we believe our actions save us, we place confidence in ourselves not in God. If we wait for God and do nothing, faith hibernates. If we place faith in God and act out believing, we move forward. Jesus seems to say that we must become aware of our faith; however much we have at the start, faith that is exercised will grow. Yet it is always God and not our faith that saves us, so even a little faith can move mountains. Jesus was doing two things at once: he was honouring a system already in place (Judaism) and bringing about significant changes. He said these changes were contiguous with the central and important message of the old system; others have disagreed. The point for a believer is to engage in self-observation. Self-observation is the root of a faithful life. Educational issues surrounding faith stem from self-observation. Christians do two things simultaneously: they observe themselves carefully; they keep their eyes on Jesus. In addition, faith comes by hearing. What does hearing suggest as a way of becoming a person of faith? How does hearing form faith on layers of assumption making from infancy onward that Wittgenstein described? Personal identity forms in association with a group; this identification is accomplished through oral, embodied interactions of the whole. Hearing is

personal: we hear what we *can* hear at any moment, given our history.
Hearing relates to seeing but faith is not sight. Seeing in a perceptual,
philosophical sense is more typical of Greek than Hebrew perspectives
(Boman 1960: 205–8). Seeing is linked to hope and hope is based on
seeing what cannot yet be seen with the eyes. Hope produces a certain
sort of person we might call as hopist. A hopist is neither an optimist
nor a pessimist. The pessimist sees that nothing can be done; the optimist sees that everything can be done. The hopist has courage to
perceive that some things can be done and sets about seeing what this
might be. The hopist says to the pessimist that if something is to be done,
we have to be attentive to the potential in things and not dismiss them
in advance. The hopist says to the optimist that life is complex: there
may be degrees of accomplishment in what we are trying to do. Faith
cannot exist without hope. Hope is rooted in our awareness of our
incompleteness (our knowing only in part). Hopelessness is a sorrowful
form of silence. Hope moves us beyond our settled opinions to search
for what is worthy. Hope amounts to expecting something good to come
from our efforts.

If faith is grounded on hope, what is seeing by faith? Seeing by faith
is an aesthetic skill in the same way that an artist can see a picture she
will paint and realize her vision in the final product. Faith's seeing is like
a gardener who observes his garden each year, confident that next year
this or that plant will be even more beautiful. Faith sees like an interior
designer who knows what a room will look like when he is done even
though the rough materials clutter the room at present, or are not even
purchased as yet. Seeing with the eyes of the heart is like a dress
designer who takes shapeless material and sews it into garments that fit
the body and soul of another woman. Faith's manner of seeing comes
through practice in the company of faithful people. Faith is the capacity
to see what is not yet visible and work for its realization with sustained
and sustaining passion. Faith allows the materials at hand, and people
close by, to be part of the fabric of the final product. Faithful seeing
brings a trustful intellect to bear on life's problems.

Faith and Trust

Believing is a form of trust. Faithfulness is related to and enhanced by
the growing skill children acquire to be socially intimate. Trust is an
ingredient in the process. Like faith, personal trust is based on deliberately cultivated, face-to-face relationships with friends and family
(Misztal 1996: 3). Conceptually, trust is related to confidence, as is faith;
both terms include a condition of dependence and uncertainty. Faithful,
trustful certainty is comfortable, not absolute; it is sure but not cocksure.

Faith as trust relies upon a vague and partial understanding of its object. It is not passive acceptance of the unknown but a strategic decision to take a risk under conditions of some uncertainty. Faith as trust has non-rational and incalculable elements. Faith by itself has an element of duty: we must keep the faith as the foundation of social life. Trust has the sense of promise attached to it; if we trust someone, perhaps they will trust us in return, although this aspect must not become manipulation. Some uncertainty is common to both trust and faith. In this way, trust is a form of faith in which confidence vested in probable outcomes expresses a commitment to something rather than just a cognitive understanding of it. Confidence is firm trust: it stops worrying.

The main difference between trust and confidence is the degree of certainty we attach to expectations. Trust involves judgment making: we trust the milkman to deliver milk tomorrow. We trust a colleague to reciprocate trustworthy communications. This second sense has more personal risk involved since we can go to the store if the milkman fails. Anything that facilitates accurate judgment about whom to trust has social value. Regardless of how hard we try to make good judgments, trust is a risky business. Time is always involved since we trust now something we must await. Trust is more than intellectual assent; it is to believe despite uncertainty. Trust involves action – like actually sitting in a chair we trust will hold us up. Risk is involved due to our inability to monitor the behavior of people or have complete knowledge of their motivation. Trust influences behavior on the basis of beliefs about the likelihood that others will behave or not behave in a certain way rather than by firm and certain calculation (Misztal 1996: 19). As we practice trust, we develop expectations. Expectations accumulate by learning what happens when we carry out mutual obligations (or fail to do so). In the social world there is always ambiguity: there are always those who act with integrity and those who ride for free. As a consequence, trust builds slowly from the ground up and can be destroyed easily and quickly.

Faith as trust learns to be discerning. It is also willing to accept disappointment as part of life rather than as evidence that we were wrong to trust. It is risky to put confidence in someone else, even ourselves (Misztal 1996: 101). But trust is essential for the growth of intimacy. People draw near to hear one another. As a result, members of a faith community learn to be near one another. But social intimacy requires that people learn more than how to be close, they must also sustain important personal differences. Social intimacy flourishes as the child of two kindly parents: neighborliness and authenticity.

What is Intimacy?

Intimacy has to do with the inner life. A careful balance between close-ness and distance is the most critical psychological task of people emerging from adolescence as they try to develop lasting and produc-tive relationships (Nouwen 1969: 2). Maturity comes when a growing intelligence is inspired by "a desire not to suffer arrested development, but to keep pace with the intake of relevant experience" (Nouwen 1969: 12). Interior lives are complex; life is complex, and this insight can be a source for maturity. Yet there is continual tension between experience and faith, tension that can shut down the progress of faith. Conflicts between formal theology and children's personal experience as well as their growing sense of morality and justice can be sources of doubt and disappointment (Pratt 1956: 101). Disappointment may produce rebel-lion against or rejection of a faith tradition. One way forward (out of the impasse of rebellion) is to integrate experience with the diversity inherent in the tradition itself. (Sometimes conversion to a different faith is the only option for a particular person.) People of faith can learn to have an optimum grip on religious tradition; they can search through its breadth to find an authentic location within it. Faith as trust creates the possibility of a religion of search (Nouwen 1996: 17).

On this quest, mature faith fulfils a creative function: it is a unifying power, bringing together isolated realities of life and casting them into one meaningful pattern. Faith as trust is a unifying perspective; giving meaning and direction to life, it reveals a goal and creates a task to be accomplished. On the basis of faith as trust, intimacy secures an optimum grip on the future. I agree with Harriet Lerner that intimacy is more than mere closeness. It is closeness balanced by distance to achieve optimum proximity between people that matter. Intimacy is true and enduring closeness balanced by appropriate distance; it is not just intensity. Some people confuse intimacy with intensity. But inti-macy implies both authenticity and vulnerability – it is both cool and intense, depending. With authenticity people are safe to be themselves, to talk openly and freely declare their limits. In intimacy, neither party silences the other; sacrifices are not total because the self is not betrayed; each person is strong and vulnerable, weak and competent. It is possible to define a whole and separate self as well as establish a more connected and gratified union. To be intimate is to have a relationship that does not operate at the expense of the self and does not operate at the expense of the other (Lerner 1989: 2).

Optimum proximity is captured in a familiar tale of two porcupines wintering in a cave. As they seek warmth yet avoid getting poked, the animals move backwards and forwards until they find the right spot –

one sufficiently close for warmth and reasonably distant to be safe from each other's quills. Optimum proximity is not static; conditions change. Shifting position *vis-à-vis* significant others is continual but is not betrayal. Faith as trust is an optimum grip on the future and prepares the ground for intimacy. We can confuse closeness and sameness. Closeness may reduce or eliminate differences between people: in order to feel safe, sometimes people think they must be the same as others, e.g., have the same opinions. But the presence of difference is the only way we learn. It is our difference from others that helps us acquire a sense of ourselves. In social intimacy, everyone needs to recognize a personal bottom line, a price that will not be paid for the sale of one's integrity. A bottom line position evolves from a focus on the self, from a deeply felt awareness (which cannot be faked, pretended or borrowed) of one's own needs and the limits of one's tolerance. An intimate relation with one's self is critical self-awareness through self-observation that produces self-knowledge (Lerner 1989: 70). When we focus on ourselves, in self-observation, we become less of an expert on other people and more of an expert on ourselves – which is not the same as being self-absorbed (Lerner 1989: 209). A self-absorbed person is not self-observant.

Intimacy is operative over time. Intimacy implies having deep knowledge of the other (Storkey 1995: 60). Only in long-term relationships are we called on to navigate the delicate balance between separateness and closeness, in which we address the challenge of sustaining both without losing either. The navigational challenge is to locate a connectedness that preserves the dignity of the self as well as other people (Lerner 1989: 214). As with porcupines, intimacy is threatening as well as desirable. Our need for others opens up the possibility of being hurt or not having important needs met by them. In social intimacy, we are comfortably certain that we are not alone in the universe, an awareness that becomes embodied knowledge so that we carry ourselves as those who are not alone. Intimacy involves reciprocal caring with people we recognize as being as significant as we are. In intimacy we want understanding to exist, hence we cannot hide behind a façade. As with faith, intimacy is inherently risky, especially at the beginning. Those who are intimate are open to committing themselves to and accepting others. Intimacy implies we are moved by other people's interests as well as our own. Intimacy recognizes that other people are deep: the surface we see does not capture their identity sufficiently. Over time, there is no longer fear of betrayal.

In short, intimacy is neither suffocating nor isolating but it is committed. Social intimacy calls forth commitment. Intimacy implies setting reasonable limits for reciprocation and obligation (Storkey 1995: 45). Social intimacy is a place of listening, recognizing, attending, smiling, greeting, waiting, respecting, helping, trying again, and ultimately feeling safe because we know we are valued. Hubert Dreyfus picked up Søren Kierkegaard's (1813–55) relevant observation as he witnessed the emergence of modernity. Kierkegaard thought the public sphere was destined to become a detached world in which everyone opined about and commented on public matters without any first-hand experience and without having or wanting any responsibility. In observing the times in which he lived, Kierkegaard said: "The public is not a people, a generation, one's era, not a community, an association, nor these particular persons, for all these are only what they are by virtue of what is concrete. Not a single one of those who belong to the public has an essential engagement in anything" (Dreyfus 2001: 77). But commitment and engagement are essential to the vitality of social intimacy.

The combination of effortlessly offered opinion and the lack of responsibility for the circumstances surrounding the subject of opinion, opens up the possibility of endless reflection. If there is no need for decision and action, and no actual experience with the complexity of the situation, mildly interested individuals can look at all things from all sides and always find some new perspective. As a result, action can always be postponed. Kierkegaard offered the following motto for the press because he felt that media was at the core of his criticism: "Here men [sic] are demoralized in the shortest possible time on the largest possible scale, at the cheapest possible price" (Dreyfus 2001: 78). People are demoralized in two senses: they lose their integrity to indifference and idleness and lose the passion to make a difference in the world – they become calloused to their own potential to make life meaningful. While endless reflection seems safe on the surface, anonymous spectators take no risks and have no fixed identity that threatens them with disappointment, humiliation or loss (Dreyfus 2001: 81); but faith remains uneducated. I agree with Kierkegaard; superficiality is not as safe as social intimacy. In social intimacy one is engrossed, engaged, identified, capable of working from the authenticity that identity signifies, yet safe to be different. In social intimacy, people learn to be near and different.

Conclusion

Under the conditions of optimum proximity beside people that exercise faith and social commitment, children learn what it means to be fully human, intimate people of faith. With intimacy, they become able to observe themselves while keeping their eyes on those who share enduring relationships with them. In order to be learned, intimacy must be incarnated – we must observe it active in a person we come to know: we need other people to see what we can become. Long-term relationships between adults and children allow the young to learn faith, authenticity and cultural know-how. The culture of the child is not the culture of the adult. Children must learn to negotiate their own landscape with wisdom and compassion. As adults take on the task of apprenticing the young, they move the future towards its brightest and most hopeful ends.

References

Boman, T. 1960: *Hebrew Thought Compared with Greek*. New York: W.W. Norton & Company.

Buttrick, G. A. (Ed.). 1962: *The Interpreter's Dictionary of the Bible*. New York: Abingdon Press.

Dreyfus, H. L. 2001: *On the Internet*. New York: Routledge.

Heidegger, M. 1969: *Identity and Difference*. New York: Harper & Row Publishers.

Kant, I. 1998: *Religion within the Boundaries of Mere Reason*. Cambridge: Cambridge University Press.

Lerner, H. G. 1989: *The Dance of Intimacy*. New York: Harper & Row, Publishers.

Misztal, B. A. 1996: *Trust in Modern Societies*. Cambridge, UK: Polity Press.

Nouwen, H. 1969: *Intimacy*. New York: Harper San Francisco.

Pratt, J. B. 1956: *The Religious Consciousness*. New York: Macmillan Company.

Rizzuto, A. 1979: *The Birth of the Living God*. Chicago: University of Chicago Press.

Storkey, E. 1995: *The Search for Intimacy*. Michigan: Eerdmans.

Vlastos, G. 1991: *Socrates: Ironist and Moral Philosopher*. Ithaca, New York: Cornell University Press.

Wittgenstein, L. 1979: *On Certainty*. Oxford, England: Basil Blackwell.

Chapter 9

How Metaphors Structure Our Spiritual Understanding

Mark Halstead

The Language of Spirituality

IN THE UPSURGE OF INTEREST in spiritual development in the United Kingdom and elsewhere over the last fifteen years, it is surprising that so little attention has been paid to the *language* of spirituality. Wittgenstein's notion of language games (1967) alerts us to the idea that just as mathematics education may be understood as initiation into the distinctive language of mathematics (square, multiply, quadratic equation . . .) and moral education as initiation into the distinctive language of ethics (ought, virtue, deontology . . .), so spiritual education may be thought of as initiation into the distinctive language of spirituality. In other words, if it is skill in language that empowers children to engage in thought, learning and communication, so children need to extend their understanding of the language of spirituality if they are to grow spiritually. But is there any such thing as the "distinctive language of spirituality"? And if so, does the term refer to the way that spirituality "speaks to us" (as the term "the language of music" refers to the way in which music can evoke particular responses from us), or does it refer to the specialist vocabulary which is needed before one can enter into specifically spiritual discourses? Neither of these seems to get at the heart of the issue.

In an earlier article (Halstead 2003), I argued that what distinguishes the language of spirituality from other languages is not a specialist vocabulary – indeed, the words used in spiritual discourse are generally commonplace ones, like journey, health, hunger, quest or struggle – but a powerful reliance on metaphor. Metaphor is used not simply as a way of clarifying meaning by providing a concise means of self-expression or by appealing to the imagination; rather, it is the main method by which meaning in the spiritual domain is constructed. Metaphor provides the normal way of exploring and talking about areas of life that are not open to scientific investigation through the use of the senses. The imagination uses readily understood social or physical experiences to explore more complex or abstract ideas. Our understanding of spiritual concepts and spiritual experiences is made possible through metaphor, and in this sense it may be claimed that metaphors actually structure the way that the spiritual domain is understood. All this is clearly in line with recent research on metaphor within the fields of linguistics, cognitive science and the philosophy of language.

I went on to suggest in the same article that metaphor in the spiritual domain sometimes takes a form rarely found elsewhere, in which a metaphor does not point ultimately to a literal statement, but points simply to another metaphor. Thus if we say, "Spiritual hunger is a desire for union with the infinite", or "I am my neighbour", it is not clear how to explain such statements at a literal level. They seem to trap us in a world of inescapable metaphor. The full implications of this were not explored at that time, and in particular, two issues relating to spiritual language, one theoretical and one practical, require further attention. The first is whether, if spiritual metaphors cannot be reduced to a literal equivalent, they actually have any meaning. If there is no anchor of rational understanding with which to attach them to the world of tangible experience or literal statement, are they anything more than a kind of free-floating, uncorroborated non-sense? The second is how, if they are found to have meaning, spiritual statements couched in this kind of metaphor can be taught to pupils in schools. Does learning in the spiritual domain not require that pupils are able to give an unambiguous account of what has been learned? Without the ability to articulate thoughts clearly, it is hard to know what evidence can be provided of pupils' understanding, yet the subject matter seems to defy articulation in literal rather than figurative language.

The present chapter is designed to explore these issues further. The first of the three sections examines the claim that metaphor is central to spiritual discourse and spiritual understanding, and relates this to recent research in cognitive science. The second explores the difficulty presented by metaphors that are not reducible to literal equivalents, and the sense in which it can be claimed that they have meaning. The third turns to the more practical problem of making the language of spirituality meaningful to children when it is so dependent on metaphorical expressions that are open to different interpretations and ways of understanding.

The Role of Metaphor in Spiritual Discourse

According to recent research in linguistics and the philosophy of language (see, for example, Johnson 1987, 1993, 1995; Lakoff 1987, 1993; Lakoff & Johnson 1980; Lakoff & Turner 1989; Leddy 1995; Sweetser 1990; Turner 1987, 1991; Winter 1995), a metaphor is much more than a simile with the term of comparison ("like" or "as") removed. Whereas the simile simply draws attention to a point of comparison between two different objects ("her eyes were like diamonds"), the metaphor can do much more than provide a new way of expressing a literal statement ("dollar signs lit up her eyes"). It can provide an effective way of exploring complex ideas, explaining abstractions, enriching and extending our understanding, and building up new conceptual systems. Metaphors do this by using the imagination to describe one concept (often a complex or abstract phenomenon) in terms of another (often shared a social or embodied experience). The outcome may be an open one, in which different audiences find different meanings. There are thus four key elements in the process we call metaphor:

- the exercise of the imagination;
- the grounding in bodily experience;
- the exploration of abstract ideas;
- the open outcome.

Each of these, as we shall see, is central to the use of metaphor in the spiritual domain.

The first element, the exercise of the imagination, is crucial. Recent work in the fields of morality, philosophy, therapy and other disciplines (cf. Burke 1999; Johnson 1993; Novitz 1987; Warnock 1994) suggests that human thought (unlike artificial intelligence) is essentially imaginative. However, the imagination does not operate as "a kind of cognitive wild card" (Winter 1995: 227), but rather in a regular, systematic fashion which is open to investigation and analysis (Johnson 1987; Lakoff 1987). The imagination can use the basic stock of root analogies to construct new ways of understanding the world or to explore deep, spiritual questions about the meaning and purpose of existence. Thus Hopkins takes a conventional conceptual metaphor from Psalm 23 ("The Lord is my shepherd") and weaves it imaginatively into his poem "The Wreck of the Deutschland" as he wrestles to find spiritual meaning in the apparently pointless death of a devout nun and others in a shipwreck. Stanza 31 opens with the comforting thought that the nun at least now has her reward for her patient suffering. But what of the rest of the passengers, who are like a helpless, comfortless flock (cf. Matthew 9: 36)? The second half of the stanza responds to this point:

No not uncomforted: lovely-felicitous Providence
Finger of a tender of, O of a feathery delicacy, the breast of the
    Maiden could obey so, be a bell to, ring of it, and
Startle the poor sheep back! Is the shipwrack then a harvest, does tempest
    carry the grain for thee? (Hopkins 1953: 22)

God's loving grace and care has used her obedience like a bell which
calls the other passengers ("the poor sheep") back to the safety of the
fold. What seems at first a cruel waste of human life turns out to be a
harvesting of souls for paradise (cf. Matthew 9: 38), and as in the
psalmist's original metaphor, the shepherd's care for his sheep is the
central point. It is Hopkins' imaginative reworking of a conventional
religious metaphor that points the reader away from the pointlessness
of the drowning to an underlying gracious divine purpose.

The second element, the use of embodied experience as a metaphor
for spiritual experience, has a long history. The Platonic tradition that
the physical world is a shadow of the spiritual has many parallels in
sacred texts (cf. Levine 1999: 134–7). In the New Testament, the human
body is "the temple of the Holy Spirit" (1 Cor. 6: 19). We are told that
Christ "is the head of the body, the church" (Col. 1: 18), that the church
is the bride of Christ (2 Cor. 11: 2; Rev. 19: 7), and that "we are members
of his body" (Eph. 5: 30). In the Jewish scriptures, the relationship
between Israel and God is described as that of an unfaithful wife and
her forgiving husband (Isa. 54: 1–10; Ezek. 16; Hos. 2: 2–3: 5), and the
Song of Solomon famously celebrates God's love for his people through
an extended metaphor of erotic love. It is as if metaphors drawn from
embodied experience are the only way of getting a grip on spiritual realities.

Otherwise, the spiritual concepts may be beyond our grasp. Our
understanding is led upwards from the familiar, the human, the
embodied, to the unfamiliar, the divine, the spiritual (Halstead 1999; cf.
Brunner 1952: 322). Understanding and loving God (whom we cannot
see) thus begins by understanding and loving our fellow human beings
(whom we can see, and who show in tangible form something of God's
nature). The conceptual systems through which we understand spirituality are constructed out of metaphors based on embodied experience,
and these conceptual systems in turn structure what we perceive, what
we experience, and the way we define spiritual reality.

Thirdly, what emerges from the fusion of the imagination and
embodied experience is new ways of structuring and understanding
abstract truths. Indeed, metaphors often appear to be the only way of
getting a handle on abstract spiritual ideas. For example, when Earl
(2001) writes an article entitled "Shadow and Spirituality", we understand what the article is likely to be about, though we might have

difficulty expressing it as a literal statement. It is not just that metaphors help us to understand things more clearly, but that in the spiritual domain at least the fundamental constituents of our experienced world are accessible to us only through metaphor. Certainly, seventeenth-century metaphysical poets use metaphor extensively to make the spiritual domain more accessible. In his collection of spiritual verse entitled "The Temple", George Herbert uses striking metaphors to reflect on rebellion, doubt and fear, a sense of being unworthy of God's love, the nature of spiritual conflicts, the serenity of worship and the meaning of prayerful devotion. In his hymn "The Elixer" for example, Herbert uses a wide range of metaphors to explore the concept of the sanctification of the mundane: when you look at a window you can fix your eye on the window itself, or look through it to heaven; the "tincture" of doing something "for Thy sake" brightens the most mundane action; the divine touch is the alchemical elixir which "turneth all to gold" (Herbert 1882: 178–9). Henry Vaughan calls the spiritual life "a quickness, which my God hath kist" (Gardner 1972: 283). In "Holy Sonnet XVII", John Donne describes God's love in a clever combination of the Old Testament picture of a jealous God and the New Testament picture of a God of love and self-sacrifice: the image is of a tenderly jealous lover willing to give everything for the one he loves but fearful that in the end he may lose out to a rival (the world, flesh or devil) (Donne 1996: 119). Andrew Marvell in "On a Drop of Dew" describes the soul"s longing to return to the spiritual reality of heaven in terms of a dewdrop delicately balancing on a leaf:

> Restless it roules, and unsecure,
> Trembling lest it grow impure,

until at last it evaporates and returns to heaven (Gardner 1972: 240–1). Richard Crashaw in his "Hymn to Sainte Teresa" uses sexual imagery to convey a compelling sense of the loss of self, of union with the transcendent and of the exultation which this sense of union brings (Gardner 1972: 208–13).

The fourth element, the open outcome, implies that the new meaning and new ways of looking at the world that emerge from the "deep conceptual metaphors" (Johnson 1995) or "cross-domain mappings" (Lakoff 1993) are not closed, but are constructed in such a way as to leave open the possibility that different interpretations and ways of thinking may emerge. Tensions occur, as Ricoeur points out (1977: 224), between the literal and metaphorical interpretation, and between the impulse to similarity and the impulse to difference, which may make interpretation difficult. This does not mean that the interpretation of metaphors is arbitrary or totally relative, but simply that they sometimes convey multiple meaning or that the insights they offer may be unexpected. Multiple meaning occurs either when the metaphor carries two or more different (sometimes even contradictory) meanings at the same time, or when a phrase carries equal significance both literally and metaphorically (for example, operating at a physical and spiritual level simultaneously). As an example of the former, Thomas Hardy's poem "He Never Expected Much" conveys both the poet's resignation and his resentment at the unfairness and mundaneness of life (Hardy 1976: 886). As an example of the latter, we have already mentioned *The Song of Solomon*, which is taken simultaneously as a love poem expressing Solomon's love for a Shulamite girl and as a sustained metaphor or allegory expressing God's love for Israel or Christ's love for the Church.

In John Donne's poetry, too, the sense often flows back and forth between the sexual and the spiritual, the human and the divine in a multi-directional way, and we need to be open to both. In "A Valediction: of weeping", Donne (1996: 23–4) suggests that when he weeps, it is the reflection of his mistress's face in his tears which gives them worth, just as it is the reflection of God's mercy which gives worth to his tears of repentance ("Holy Sonnet IX": Donne 1996: 113–14). Reflection is deep conceptual metaphor much loved of Donne (cf. Lacan 1977; Miller 1998). Woman is often presented as a mirror in which the male poet sees himself reflected. She is the "glorious nothing" (as opposed to the male "thing": cf. DiPasquale 2001: 211), an empty space which acquires meaning through the projection of the speaker's masculinity into her, just as the church acquires meaning through the action of her bridegroom, Christ. In "A Valediction: of my name in the window" (Donne 1996: 15–17) the poet's mistress can see both her own reflection (" . . . and cleare reflects thee to thine eye") and his name engraved in the window ("here see you mee"): the result is both self-knowledge and knowledge of the other, and at the same time a merging of the two ("I am you") (cf. Davies 1994: 13–16). Such merging is the goal of the spiritual life too. And just as human love needs to "put on" corporeality in order to express itself (according to Donne's argument in "Aire and Angels": 1996: 13–14), so God's love needs to "take a body too" if it is to be understood and experienced. The Word must become flesh and dwell among us. I have argued elsewhere (Halstead 1999) that for Donne the physical world is more than a symbol of the spiritual world, and sexual relationships are more than symbols of spiritual relationships: incarnation – the embodied world – is the *only way* in which the spiritual dimension to life can be understood. Spiritual love is a mystery and can only be explained (perhaps even experienced) through physical images and symbols. The sexual and spiritual are thus kept in balance; sometimes sexual metaphors illuminate spirituality, sometimes spiritual metaphors illuminate sexuality, and sometimes a single metaphor illuminates both areas of experience at the same time.

So far I have suggested that the recent analysis of metaphor provided by the cognitive scientists and philosophers of language mentioned earlier is a helpful way of understanding spiritual discourse. In brief, it involves the claim that all metaphor is the product of a more general framework of correspondences or core metaphors, which Lakoff (1993) calls "cross-domain mappings", Johnson (1995) "deep conceptual metaphors" and Goatly (1997) "root analogies". Whatever their name, they take the form *x is y*, where *x* is a conceptual domain in need of description or clarification, and *y* is the thing to which it is compared. For example, we may say, "Spirituality is the search for the infinite", or "The spiritual life is a journey". In fact, there is a limited number of core metaphors in the spiritual domain, but it is possible to elaborate on them in a wide variety of ways. Metaphor, of course, is only one of a number of cognitive mechanisms, and in some areas its impact in terms of transforming our understanding might be modest (for a discussion of metaphor in science, see Kuhn 1993; in law, Winter 1995; in social policy, Schon 1993; in morality, Rethorst 1997; in warfare, Lakoff 1991). In spirituality, however, as in the arts, metaphor may be a key to the very conceptualization of the topic, such that understanding is impossible without it.

In the third section of this chapter I shall stress the centrality of metaphor in the task of promoting children's spiritual development. Before proceeding to this point, however, there is another issue that must be discussed, one that threatens everything that has so far been said: whether spiritual metaphors that cannot be reduced to a literal equivalent can be said to be intelligible at all. If they are irreducible, does this not make them self-enclosed, idiosyncratic, devoid of cognitive meaning and unteachable?

The Problem of Irreducible Spiritual Metaphors

From time to time, theologians have been criticized for using language that is irreducibly metaphorical, i.e. using metaphors that cannot be paraphrased in literal language (Black 1962; Burgess 1972; MacCormac 1975). The claim is that if metaphors cannot be reduced to literal expressions, they cannot be said to have any cognitive meaning or truth value (cf. Edwards 1965: 199–200). The problem can be illustrated by comparing an everyday metaphor like "the moon is a peeled banana" (where we have sufficient knowledge of the shape of the crescent moon and the shape of a peeled banana to compare the two), with a religious metaphor like "God is our father". Although it is commonplace to refer to God in terms of human experiences and human qualities (merciful, jealous, gracious, angry) and in terms of human relationships (father, king, master, judge), these metaphors give at best an imprecise, and at worst a misleading, sense of what God is like. My own father (and indeed all the fathers I know) may be mean, irresponsible, over-indulgent, cruel or dead, but these are clearly inappropriate points of comparison in our understanding of the metaphor "God is our father". How do we know? Presumably because of what we already know about God. But how do we know these other things about God? Either from other metaphors, in which case the whole argument is circular and we are trapped in a world of inescapable metaphor, or from belief, in which case it is clear that religious metaphors are only intelligible to those prepared to take a certain leap of faith. In any case, the metaphor may be context-bound: the connotations of "father" in Victorian times, let alone biblical times, may be very different from its connotations today.

If irreducible metaphors are a problem in the language of theology, they are even more so in the language of spirituality. The common metaphor of "spiritual health", for example, only makes sense to those who already have some understanding of what the domain of the spiritual is, but that understanding can only be gained from other metaphors. It is this use of double metaphors in the spiritual domain that distinguishes it most clearly from other domains. As we have seen, most core metaphors take the form x is y, where x is a literal object in need of description or clarification, and y is the metaphor which conveys the description. Thus we say "She is an angel" or "Marriage is a trap into which only those blinded by love will fall." Spiritual metaphors, on the other hand, often take the form $y1$ is $y2$, where both $y1$ and $y2$ are conceptual metaphors, as in the sentences, "The quest for enlightenment is a constant battle", or "My spiritual transformation was the first step on a painful journey." This is not just an expansion of a core metaphor, as occurs, for example, when Jesus says "[The sheep] shall hear my voice" (John 10: 16), which is just part of the conceptual mapping of the root analogy "I am the good shepherd" (John 10: 11). On the contrary, the topic and the comparison are separate spiritual metaphors. It is no longer a matter of a literal expression being explained by means of a metaphor, but of one metaphor being explained in terms of another. It is rather like saying, instead of "my feet are lumps of lead", "my lumps of lead are an insoluble problem", except that the underlying topic is abstract and intangible, not physical like feet.

So are spiritual metaphors just an elaborate form of nonsense, perhaps meaningful and enriching to those on the inside of a complex language game, but gibberish to those on the outside? Are there any objective measures by which we can distinguish the meaningful from the meaningless in the spiritual domain? I have suggested elsewhere

(Halstead 2003) that it "may be through the accumulation of metaphors that spiritual truth is to be found." But if each individual metaphor is not open to literal paraphrase, how can it be claimed that the cluster of metaphors together represent something that is meaningful and true? Several answers are possible:

1. It is possible to claim that metaphors perform "the task of saying the unsayable" (Martin 1981: 63) – in other words, the things that they say cannot be said any other way. This may well be true, but it does not in itself help us to distinguish sense from non-sense.

2. Gualtieri (1966: 153–4, drawing on Evans 1963) chooses to define religious language (and particularly religious metaphor) as "metaphysical parabolic onlook". "Onlook" is a coined word used here to express the adoption of an attitude to something. Thus "God is our father" is best understood as "We look on God as we would look on a father", and understanding it in this way confirms that the comparison implicit in the metaphor is one of attitude, not of content. As we have seen, the resemblances between God and a human father are elusive and undefinable, but it is our attitude to God that is at the heart of this metaphor. The central claim of the Gaia hypothesis, that the earth is a single living organism, provides an effective non-religious example of the same point. To take it as a claim about a state of affairs in the world raises all sorts of problems, such as whether it has a brain, or any kind of moral dimension, or whether it is a god (Allaby 1989; Lovelock 1995, 2000). But to take it to mean "We look on the earth as a single living organism" opens up all kinds of positive responses based on ideas to do with human responsibility, spiritual awareness, the interconnectedness of all life and the need to rethink our understanding of the natural environment. It is very hard to assess the truth of this kind of metaphor, but as an expression of an attitude it can influence our actions in many positive ways. It is this which leads Gualtieri to conclude on a pragmatic note: even if the ultimate convictions encapsulated in the metaphor are undemonstrable, adopting this attitude and basing our behaviour on it leads to desirable ends. Thus, he claims, "the image is verified pragmatically" (1966: 162).

3. MacCormac (1975) argues that religious and spiritual metaphors are essentially the same as scientific ones. It is the nature of all metaphors to be irreducible, he says, but "the fact that a metaphor cannot be reduced to ordinary sensible discourse does not of necessity justify its condemnation as meaningless" (1975: 402). Even if no definitive paraphrase is possible for the metaphor – as in the metaphor "I am my neighbour", for example – a partial understanding or interpretation may still be worth pursuing (1975: 405). What we should be aiming for is not to reduce a metaphor to a literal equivalent, but to understand its connotations. This involves a consideration of how the words "interact", "co-operate" and "illuminate" each other (Burgess 1972: 356). For example, the significance of the choice of the name "Gaia" for James Lovelock's earth metaphor is its wealth of connotation. It calls to mind the ancient goddess of that name, the mother earth, and all the myths and images that have enriched our understanding of our relationship to the earth over many centuries.

4. It is sometimes claimed that special qualities are needed to understand spiritual metaphor, or indeed any metaphor. Perhaps this is what William Blake means when he writes in "Auguries of Innocence":

> To see a world in a grain of sand,
> And a Heaven in a wild flower,
> Hold infinity in the palm of your hand,
> And eternity in an hour. (Blake 1970: 134–7)

According to Burgess, understanding metaphor may be a matter of discernment, insight and maturity beyond the capacity of many individuals, and in any case an explanation which works for one person may not work for another. People must be willing to make a leap of imagination in trying to understand spiritual metaphors, and still "some poetic images may yield us a mere glimmer of insight" (1972: 364). Responses to metaphor may not come intuitively, but may have to be learned, and successful teaching will need to take account of the "particular capacities, community traditions and experiences" of the learners (1972: 366).

5. Wheelwright (1962) and MacCormac (1975) suggest that there are two types of metaphor, which they call "epiphor" and "diaphor". The "epiphor" has as its main purpose the expression of experience, and therefore its value depends ultimately on its capacity to be paraphrased in ordinary language. The "diaphor", on the other hand, is more concerned with imaginative suggestion than expression. We can illustrate the difference by reference to the statement "God is Love". Believers will take this as an epiphor which expresses their experience (though of course the statement still retains a degree of suggestiveness and mystery for them as well), but unbelievers are more likely to take it as a diaphor, suggestive of imaginative and poetic ways of looking at life which should not be interpreted literally. For unbelievers, the metaphor is thus irreducible, but not devoid of meaning. This distinction helps us to understand the problem of spiritual metaphor as well. For those for whom "spiritual experience" is an unproblematic, literal concept (see, for example, Hay 1990), spiritual metaphors may be epiphors for which a literal equivalent can be found; but for the many people who are agnostic about spiritual experience, spiritual metaphors can still provide imaginative and stimulating insights into life, so long as no attempt is made to impose too specific an interpretation on them.

To claim that it is the nature of spiritual metaphor to be "more suggestive than expressive" (MacCormac 1975: 407, 409) does not mean that it has no serious purpose, or that it gets in the way of serious thought. On the contrary, once one is free from the constraint of having to look for literal equivalents, one can see in spiritual metaphors attempts to explore the profoundest questions about life, death and the human condition. In this respect, spirituality has much in common with aesthetics. As Peter Hall wrote recently, for Beckett "theatre is metaphor, about life itself" (2003). Those critics who try to impose too rigid an interpretation on *Endgame* (1958), for example, by saying that it is a reworking of the story of the Flood, or a post-nuclear holocaust play, or the conclusion to a game of chess, or a representation of the inside of a skull (cf. Kenner 1988: 41), are trying to provide too rigid a paraphrase of Beckett's life-metaphor; Schwab says that such critics fall into the trap of "closure" (1992: 88). Still worse would be an attempt to impose conventional moral judgments on visual features like keeping disabled parents in ashbins and feeding them dog-biscuits. The life-metaphor intentionally shatters our familiar world so that we can approach profound human experiences like suffering, attachment and despair without preconceptions. Beckett forces us to think deeply, but also to question the desire for meaning, the nature of rationality, and the very meaning of meaning. At their best, spiritual metaphors can do the same.

These points, taken together, suggest that there are good reasons to try to initiate children into understanding the distinctive world of spiritual metaphor, but they also warn us that there is no point in doing so unless we are sure that we can help children to make progress. If they end up perceiving spiritual metaphor as nonsense, or jargon, or of interest to only a small section of society, we shall have done them no service.

Helping Children to Understand Spiritual Discourse

If metaphors are the mirrors through which people see and come to understand spiritual ideas, does this suggest ways to approach the task of spiritual development in schools? Are there ways we can help children to move forward in their spiritual thinking? There is comparatively little research in this area, but two projects have come up with relevant findings.

Goldman's research in the 1960s into the psychological bases of children's religious development accepts as one of its starting points the fact that religious language "is almost entirely based upon analogy and metaphor, inferring from other non-religious experience the nature of the divine and supporting such concepts upon previously acquired concepts" (Goldman 1964: 14). He also draws attention to the large number of abstract concepts that feature in religious discourse, including concepts such as "love, goodness, holiness, spirit" (Goldman 1965: 30). His research suggests that both of these facts create difficulties for children in what he calls the "concrete operational" stage of religious thinking. The first difficulty is that without guidance young children will tend to take religious metaphors as literal statements. God is not thought of *as* a shepherd, but he *is* a shepherd; thus one child in infant school describes God as follows:

> God is in the sky and you can't see him. He flies around. Sometimes he stops behind a cloud to have something to eat. He goes down to land at night to see shepherds and to talk to them. (1965: 80)

As Goldman points out, children's "imprisonment within concrete concepts and their frequent literalisms make it difficult for them to step forward into a more spiritual understanding of religious truth" (1965: 30). A second, related difficulty is that as children are conditioned into the use of abstract religious language and religious metaphor they may learn to use it correctly, but without necessarily understanding it (1965: 32, 81). When twelve year-old Martha describes God as "standing in the clouds, with lots of glory round" (Goldman 1964: 90), one cannot help wondering what sense out of the vast array of possible meanings she gives to the word "glory" (cf. Boyle 1960: 47ff).

However, Goldman's proposed solution to these difficulties is surprising to say the least. He argues that to understand religious and spiritual metaphor, "we must first be able to comprehend the experience upon which the . . . metaphor is based" (1965: 33). On this basis, he argues that in order to understand a sentence like "The Lord is my shepherd", children need to know "something of the conditions of the Palestinian sheep-farmer" (1964: 14), including "the helplessness of sheep" and "what it feels like to be a sheep" (1965: 33, 112). He therefore recommends a major curriculum project on "Shepherds and Sheep", with sub-topics entitled: finding out about a sheep farm; dipping and shearing; wool and its uses; shepherds and sheepdogs; shepherds in Palestine; sheep in Palestine; a sheep's day – morning; and a sheep's day – evening (1965: 113). The main problem with this approach is that it seeks to impose a spiritual straightjacket on children (albeit a woollen-lined one), restricting their spiritual thinking to conventional metaphors rather than liberating it. I shall argue shortly that we need to start where the children are, encourage them to engage directly in the imaginative use and exploration of metaphors drawn from their own everyday experience, and respect their developing spiritual understanding.

The Religious Experience and Education Project directed by David Hay in the 1980s identifies the following as among the particular core concerns of the teacher of religious education:

- Raising and deepening awareness of the spiritual.
- Appreciating how symbols, images and metaphors are used to express or convey the meaning of difficult and otherwise inexpressible thoughts and feelings, especially the religious and spiritual. (Hammond *et al.* 1990: 23)

The major outcome of the research is a handbook of new methods for RE teaching, which includes a large number of exercises carefully designed to raise children's awareness of metaphor as an essential component of spiritual and religious discourse (Hammond *et al.* 1990: 93–168). The exercises approach metaphor from lots of different angles: they develop children's imagination by encouraging the use of fantasy, they explore the way that symbols create meaning, they help children to think of life as a journey, to see themselves as a flower, an animal, a color, a food, a building, a matrioshka doll, and to construct metaphors for friendship, life and death. Underpinning the project is a coherent view of the place of metaphor in spiritual understanding, and a profound belief that educating children in this area must start with what the children understand, and that we must provide them with the tools to explore and understand and extend their own developing spiritual experience.

What the two projects have in common is the belief that children have two natural qualities which contribute to their spiritual development – strong imaginations, and a natural spirituality – which schools can either develop or discourage. What the present chapter has attempted to provide is a stronger philosophical grounding for the practical teaching approaches which Hammond *et al.* (1990) recommend. Once children are comfortable with the concept of metaphor and have learned to devise their own metaphors drawn from their own personal experience, they can be introduced to some of the core metaphors that are found within spiritual discourse, such as going home, rebirth at Springtime, the search for the infinite, hunger and thirst for goodness, and spiritual healing. One of the most widely used core analogies takes the form "the spiritual life is a journey." The journey may involve planning an itinerary, checking which direction to go, acclimatization, following in someone else's footsteps, persevering in the face of difficulties and temptations, overcoming obstacles, following the right signposts, accepting diversions where necessary, discarding unnecessary baggage, passing through a particular landscape, focusing on the destination, helping others along the way, refusing to turn back. The core metaphor thus finds expression in very many variations on the theme. Scott Peck uses a quotation from Robert Frost as the title of his six million copy best seller on the spiritual life, *The Road Less Traveled* (1978). The seventeenth century best seller, Bunyan's *Pilgrim's Progress* (1984) builds the same core metaphor into a thorough going allegory of the spiritual life, in which Christian makes his way towards the Celestial City, passing through many places including the Slough of Despond, the Valley of the Shadow of Death and Vanity Fair *en route*. Hammond *et al.* include several exercises on the "journey of life" (1990: 93–6), "walk my walk" (1990: 113–15), "lifelines" (1990: 126–9), "pilgrimage" (1990: 155–7) and "journey to the stars" (1990: 164–8), all of which introduce children to this core metaphor and help them to understand its spiritual significance

At the start of this chapter it was suggested that spiritual education may be thought of as initiation into the distinctive language of spirituality. Such initiation does not involve learning a specialist vocabulary, but coming to understand the way that metaphors, symbols and analogy are used to explore the most profound questions about life. As we have seen, spiritual metaphors typically express complex, abstract ideas in terms of shared social or embodied experience. The concept of metaphor is not itself difficult for children to grasp; indeed, their strong capacity for imagination facilitates their understanding of metaphorical expression, and the fact that the metaphors are grounded in shared experience makes them generally accessible to children. Where children do need help, however, is in recognizing the spiritual significance of metaphors. They need guidance away from their natural tendency to look for closed, literal meanings, and towards more open interpretations, greater awareness of the richness of connotation and more symbolic ways of thinking about life. This is precisely the guidance that Hammond *et al.* (1990) seek to provide. The ultimate aim is for children to come to understand that profound human experiences of love, wonder, suffering, attachment and despair can be explored only through metaphor and symbol. The development of spiritual understanding is not easily assessable (because it is not measurable or quantifiable), but this does not undermine its importance. On the contrary, extending children's awareness of the deep spiritual significance to be found in metaphor and symbol contributes both to their personal development and to their understanding of the human predicament, and is arguably one of the most important things a teacher can do.

References

All biblical references are from the Authorized Version.

Allaby, M. 1989: *Guide to Gaia*. London: Macdonald Optima.

Beckett, S. 1958: *Endgame*. London: Faber and Faber.

Black, M. 1962: *Models and Metaphors*. Ithaca, NY: Cornell University Press.

Blake, W. 1970: *Songs of Innocence and of Experience and other works*. London: Collins.

Boyle, R. 1960: *Metaphor in Hopkins*. Chapel Hill: University of North Carolina Press.

Brunner, E. 1952: *Dogmatics II: The Christian doctrine of creation and redemption* . London: Lutterworth Press.

Bunyan, J. 1984: *The Pilgrim's Progress* (first published 1678). Oxford: Oxford University Press.

Burgess, A. J. 1972: Irreducible Religious Metaphors. *Religious Studies* 8 (4), 355–66.

Burke, P. A. 1999: The Healing Power of the Imagination. *International Journal of Children's Spirituality* 4 (1), 9–18.

Davies, S. 1994: *John Donne*. Plymouth: Northcote House.

DiPasquale, T. M. 2001: *Literature and Sacrament: The sacred and the secular in John Donne*. Cambridge: James Clarke.

Donne, J. 1996: *John Donne's Poetry* (ed. A. L. Clements). New York: W. W. Norton and Co.

Earl, M. 2001: Shadow and Spirituality. *International Journal of Children's Spirituality* 6 (3), 277–88.

Edwards, P. 1965: Professor Tillich's Confusions. *Mind* 74, 192–214.

Evans, D. 1963: *The Logic of Self-Involvement*. London: SCM Press.

Gardner, H. (ed.) 1972: *The Metaphysical Poets*. Harmondsworth: Penguin.

Goatly, A. 1997: *The Language of Metaphors*. London: Routledge.

Goldman, R. 1964: *Religious Thinking from Childhood to Adolescence*. London: Routledge and Kegan Paul.

Goldman. R. 1965: *Readiness for Religion*. London: Routledge and Kegan Paul.

Gualtieri, A. R. 1966: Truth Claims for Religious Images. *Religious Studies* 1 (2), 151–62.

Hall, P. 2003: Godotmania. *Guardian Review*, 4 January, 16–17.

Halstead, J. M. 1999: John Donne and the Theology of Incarnation. In L. Gearon (ed.), *English Literature, Theology and the Curriculum*. London: Cassell, 149–72.

Halstead, J. M. 2003: Metaphor, Cognition and Spiritual Reality. In D. Carr and J. Haldane (eds), *Spirituality, Philosophy and Education*. London: Routledge Falmer.

Hammond, J., Hay, D., Moxon, J., Netto, B., Raban, K., Straugheir, G. & Williams, C. 1990: *New Methods in RE Teaching: An experiential approach*. Harlow: Oliver & Boyd.

Hardy, T. 1976: *The Complete Poems*. London: Macmillan.

Hay, D. 1990: *Religious Experience Today: Studying the Facts*. London: Mowbray.

Herbert, G. 1882: *The Temple: A facsimile reprint of the first edition, 1633*. London: Fisher Unwin.

Hopkins, G. M. 1953: *Poems and Prose* (ed. W. H. Gardner). Harmondsworth: Penguin.

Johnson, M. 1987: *The Body in the Mind: The bodily basis of meaning, reason and imagination.* Chicago: University of Chicago Press.

Johnson, M. 1993: *Moral Imagination: implications of cognitive science for ethics.* Chicago: University of Chicago Press.

Johnson, M. 1995: Why Metaphor Matters to Philosophy. *Metaphor and Symbolic Activity* 10 (3), 157–62.

Kenner, H. 1988: Life in the Box. In H. Bloom (ed.), *Samuel Beckett's Endgame.* New York: Chelsea House, 41–48.

Kuhn, T. S. 1993: Metaphor in Science. In A. Ortony (ed.), *Metaphor and Thought.* (2nd edition). Cambridge: Cambridge University Press.

Lacan, J. 1977: The Mirror Stage. In *Ecrits: a selection* (trans. A. Sheridan). London: Tavistock Publications.

Lakoff, G. 1987: *Women, Fire and Dangerous Things: what categories reveal about the mind.* Chicago: University of Chicago Press.

Lakoff, G. 1991: *Metaphor in Politics: An open letter to the Internet.* Available at <lakoff@cogsci.berkeley.edu>.

Lakoff, G. 1993: The Contemporary Theory of Metaphor. In A. Ortony (ed.), *Metaphor and Thought* (2nd edition). Cambridge: Cambridge University Press.

Lakoff, G. and Johnson, M. 1980: *Metaphors We Live By.* Chicago: University of Chicago Press.

Lakoff, G. & Turner, M. 1989: *More than Cool Reason: A field guide to poetic metaphor.* Chicago: University of Chicago Press.

Leddy, T. 1995: Metaphor and Metaphysics. *Metaphor and Symbolic Activity* 10 (3), 205–22.

Levine, S. 1999: Children's Cognition as the Foundation of Spirituality. *International Journal of Children's Spirituality* 4 (2), 121–40.

Lovelock, J. 1995: *Gaia: A new look at life on earth* (new edition). Oxford: Oxford University Press.

Lovelock, J. 2000: *The Ages of Gaia: a biography of our living earth* (new edition). Oxford: Oxford University Press.

MacCormac, E. R. 1975: Scientific and Religious Metaphors. *Religious Studies* 11 (4), 401–9.

Martin , J. 1981: Metaphor amongst Tropes. *Religious Studies* 17 (1), 55–66.

Miller, J. 1998: *On Reflection.* London: National Gallery Publications.

Novitz, D. 1987: *Knowledge, Fiction and Imagination.* Philadelphia, PA: Temple University Press.

Peck, M. S. 1978: *The Road Less Traveled.* New York: Simon & Schuster.

Rethorst, J. 1997: *Art and Imagination: implications of cognitive science for moral education.* Available at <http: //www.ed.uiuc.edu/EPS/PES-year-book/97_docs>.

Ricoeur, P. 1977: *The Rule of Metaphor: Multidisciplinary studies in the creation of meaning in language.* Toronto: University of Toronto Press.

Schon, D. A. 1993: Generative Metaphor: a perspective on problem-setting in social policy. In A. Ortony (ed.) *Metaphor and Thought* (2nd edition). Cambridge: Cambridge University Press.

Schwab, G. 1992: On the Dialectic of Closing and Opening in *Endgame*. In S. Connor (ed.), *Waiting for Godot and Endgame*. London: Macmillan, 87–99.

Sweetser, E. 1990: *From Etymology to Pragmatics: Metaphorical and cultural aspects of semantic structure*. Cambridge: Cambridge University Press.

Turner, M. 1987: *Death is the Mother of Beauty: Mind, metaphor, criticism*. Chicago: University of Chicago Press.

Turner, M. 1991: *Reading Minds: The study of English in the age of cognitive science*. Princeton, NJ: Princeton University Press.

Warnock, M. 1994: *Imagination and Time*. Oxford: Blackwell.

Wheelwright, P. 1962: *Metaphor and Reality*. Bloomington: Indiana University Press.

Winter, S. L. 1995: A Clearing in the Forest. *Metaphor and Symbolic Activity* 10 (3), 223–45.

Wittgenstein, L. 1967: *Philosophical Investigations* (3rd edition). Oxford: Blackwell.

Chapter 10

The Chinese Approach to Learning: The Paradigmatic Case of Chinese Calligraphy

WONG PING HO

Air in Movement: Spririt and *Qi*

W HAT, IF ANY, are the equivalent Chinese terms for "spirit" and "spirituality"? A brief consideration of this question provides some helpful background for understanding how the spiritual dimension of human life is conceptualized and expressed by the Chinese.

Etymologically, in Chinese "it is probably *qi*[1] that bears the closest resemblance to 'spirit'" (Adler 1997). A simple comparison shows the basis for this judgement. According to Barnhart, "The original English uses of *spirit* are mainly derived from passages in the Vulgate, in which Latin *spiritus* is used to translate Greek *pneuma* and Hebrew *ruah*" (1999: 1047). Holl gives the original meaning of *ruah* as "air in movement" (1999: 8), while Adler highlights "the analogous words in Hebrew, classical Greek, and Sanskrit (*ruach, pneuma,* and *prana*) that similarly cover the range of meanings from wind and breath to spirit" (1997).

The original pictograph for the Chinese character *qi* consists of three roughly horizontal strokes representing parallel layers of clouds arising from the condensation of moisture. It thus denotes "air, vapour, gas" (Lindqvist 1991: 172). Later, the pictograph for rice was inserted under the original strokes,[2] probably to show "the 'vapors' rising out of a saucepan of boiling grain" (172). This composite pictograph became the present character for *qi*. Pas and Leung speculated that, in a natural extension of meaning, *qi* as vapours "came to mean 'breath' (which in winter is very similar to steam). Because in many cultures 'breath' signifies 'life,' a further extension became understandable: 'vital spirit, vitality, vital breath, life energy, vital force'" (1998: 78). They stress the parallels *qi* has in other traditions, particularly regarding the fact that the same vital principle or energy that *qi* represents is supposed to course through both the cosmos and individual beings, quoting Mair's judgement that "The same concept exists in the Indian tradition as *prana*, in the Greek tradition as *pneuma*, in the Latin tradition as *spiritus*, and in the Hebrew tradition as *ruah*" (Mair, quoted in Pas and Leung 1998: 78).

Qi is a central term in both Daoism and Confucianism, the two dominant Chinese intellectual traditions influencing all aspects of life, from health and medicine, martial arts, *fengshui* (geomancy), to literature and the various fine arts. A multiplicity of terms have been used for translating *qi* into English, including "ether, *élan vitale* or vital force, humour, breath or psychosomatic force" (Lai 2001: 446), but often it is simply left untranslated. Interestingly, *qi* is seldom translated as spirit, suggesting that, despite the commonalities, there are also important differences between the two.

In its most generalized sense, *qi* denotes "the primal stuff out of which everything else in the universe condenses" (Van Norden 1996: 227). Its all-encompassing nature is exemplified by the following extracts from the ancient classic *Guanzi*:

> "the *qi* of all things changes and thus becomes life"; "when *qi* goes to the ground, grains grow; when it goes into the heavens, there emerge the constellations; when it floats in the air, it becomes ghosts and spirits; when it goes into man's chest, the man becomes a sage," and ... "therefore when there is *qi*, there is life; when there is no *qi*, there is death." (quoted in Tang, 1991: 21)

It is tempting to apply the Western philosophical categories of "matter" and "spirit" to *qi*, a point that Kalton seems to have both made and himself exemplified when he remarked that the role of *qi*, "as the concretizing and energizing component", is one which "thinkers East and West have intuitively equated with the 'matter' side of Western thought. In effect, much of what went into 'spirit' in the West went into the physical in East Asia" (1998: 88). Tu cautions that with *qi*, "the dichotomy of spirit and matter is not at all applicable. ... The most basic stuff that makes the cosmos is neither solely spiritual nor material but both. It is a vital force. This vital force must not be conceived of either as disembodied spirit or as pure matter" (1998: 106–7).[3] Tu is aware of the possible denigration of this conception of *qi* as symptomatic of "a sort of pre-Cartesian naïveté lacking differentiation between mind and matter". However, he rather believes that it:

> signifies a conscious refusal to abandon a mode of thought that synthesizes spirit and matter as an undifferentiated whole. The loss of analytical

clarity is compensated by the reward of imaginative richness. The fruitful ambiguity of *ch'i* [*qi*] allows philosophers to explore the realms of being which are inconceivable to people constricted by a Cartesian dichotomy. (Tu 1998: 108)

Qi and Self-cultivation

The cultivation of *qi* (*yangqi* – *yang* literally means nourish) is an important theme in Chinese culture. One famous remark on the topic was by Mencius, who said that he was proficient in cultivating his *haoran zhi qi*, which has variously been translated as a "flood-like *ch'i*" (Tucker 1998: 191), "*qi* of vastness" (Tang 1991: 23), the "vast, flowing passion-nature" (Legge 1992: 311), and the "Great Morale" (Fung 1997: 78). He explained that this *qi* is:

> in the highest degree, vast and unyielding. Nourish it with integrity and place no obstacle in its path and it will fill the space between Heaven and Earth. It is a *ch'i* which unites rightness and the Way. Deprive it of these and it will collapse. It is born of accumulated rightness and cannot be appropriated by anyone through a sparodic show of rightness. Whenever one acts in a way that falls below the standard set in one's heart, it will collapse. (translation in Tucker 1998: 191)

Two points about the remark are worth noting. First, this is Mencius' description of "the development of his own spiritual cultivation" (Fung 1997: 78). Judging from the context of this passage, which "includes a preliminary discussion about two warriors and their method of cultivating their valor", Fung infers that Mencius' *qi* "is the same *ch'i* as occurs in such terms as *yung ch'i* [*yongqi*] (courage, valor) and *shih ch'i* [*shiqi*] (morale of an army)" (1997: 78), and translates *haoran zhi qi* as the "Great Morale". This brings to mind Neville's characterization of the soldier as one of the three ancient models of spiritual perfection, who "must have psychic integrity to such a high degree as to be able wholly to devote himself or herself to life-threatening tasks", and as such provides an "archetype for the development of the spirited part of the soul" (Neville 1978: 1, 7) as described by Plato. This brings out another semantic connection between *qi* and spirit, the latter represented by its derivative "spirited", meaning "full of energy, enthusiasm and determination" (Pearsall 1998: 1794).

Secondly, this flood-like *qi* (to adopt Tucker's translation), when nourished properly, will fill the space between Heaven and Earth. This is "an example of that 'non-separation' between human and external nature" (Richards 1932: 34), often considered a distinctive hallmark of the Chinese mentality. In Tucker's words:

It is clear that this psychophysical energy must be cultivated carefully, for it is that which links us to all other living things. In other words, in humans *ch'i* is a special form of material energy which can be nurtured by self-cultivation. This contributes to our moral and physical well-being and provides a basis for respecting other humans. The whole universe is, likewise, filled with matter-energy of *ch'i*. By nourishing not only our own *ch'i* but also the consciousness of our connection to this energy in nature, we become full participants in the dynamic, transformative processes of the universe. That is because *ch'i* is the underlying unity of life that is simultaneously moral and physical, spiritual and material. (1998: 191)

This reminds one of the idea of relationality, a central concept in some approaches to spirituality. (See, for example, Hay with Nye 1998.) What is distinctive about the relationality underpinned by *qi* is its mutually-transformative quality.

Jing and *Shen*

Although *qi* is probably the Chinese word most closely related to "spirit" etymologically, in modern Chinese the most widely adopted translation for "spirit" or "spirituality" is *jingshen*, which has two characters, *jing* and *shen*. The written character of *jing* includes two components, the character for "rice", and the character *qing* (included to indicate the pronunciation). It originally meant "selected rice", that is, very fine rice (*Comprehensive Dictionary of Chinese Characters*, Vol. 5: 3150), and its present-day meanings, for example, "essence",[4] are all related to the generalized meanings of "selected" and "fine". In Daoism, *jing* is a concentrated form of *qi*, as illustrated by the following quotation from *Guanzi* translated by Roth, who renders *qi* as "vital energy", and *jing* as "vital essence": "The vital essence is the essence of the vital energy" (Roth 1991: 614). As refined *qi*, *jing* is "the vitalizing energy that suffuses and animates our bodies" (Weller and Bol 1998: 316). Based on another ancient compendium, *Lüshi Chunqiu*, Weller and Bol add that:

> Human vitality and consciousness are merely two of the more important consequences of its activities. Vital Essence [*jing*], the most rarefied and quintessential form of *ch'i*, was thought to pervade the universe, occasionally coalescing within objects and giving rise to marvellous properties. The vitality of animals was also attributed to Vital Essence, as was the growth of plants and trees and the luster of jade. (1998: 339)

Note the reference to the coalescence of *jing* (and therefore *qi* refined to a second-degree). Humans are privileged in that our:

> mind is naturally filled with the vital essence [*jing*] and naturally tends to

generate and develop it. Yet the mind inevitably loses this essence, due to emotions, desires, and selfishness. But if the mind can discard such disturbances, it will follow its natural tendency towards equanimity and harmony. (Roth 1991: 614)

Hence the necessity of self-cultivation, which of course requires "concentration" and "devotion" – two other common meanings of *jing* probably derived metaphorically from "selected", "fine" and "essence".

Yet another common meaning of *jing* also echoes "spirit" as "a supernatural, incorporeal, rational being or personality" (*Oxford Dictionary Online* 2000). What is special about those Chinese spirits designated as *jing* is that they were all initially normal entities, such as a hill or a fox, and have achieved their state of being as *jing* through self-cultivation, building up their *jing* (vital essence).[5] This in its own way illustrates the interrelations among the various meanings of *jing* and their importance in the Chinese conception of self-cultivation.

The other character in the word often used for translating spirituality, *jingshen*, is *shen*. One prevalent meaning of *shen* is "deity". The written character consists of two parts, the pictograph depicting an altar, and another pictograph showing "'lightning', which was supposed to represent god" (Yip 2000: 302). Therefore *shen* is employed as a translation for "spirit" in the sense of "supernatural being".

Shen is also a central concept in Daoism, forming a triad with *qi* and *jing*. Weller and Bol (1998) interpret the Daoistic *shen* as denoting the entity within the body that is made up of *jing* and responsible for consciousness. Roth goes further by translating *shen* as numen, and describes it as "the numinous power present within the mind", citing *Guanzi*: "By concentrating your vital energy [*qi*] as if numinous [*shen*], / The myriad things will all be contained within you" (Roth 1991: 616). This is reminiscent of descriptions of numinous states offered by the mystics. This numinous state enables precognition (Roth 1991: 617). Thus it is unsurprising that *shen* also means "miraculous", overlapping the sense of "spiritual" as "supernatural". And by virtue of its intimate relationship with *qi* and *jing*, *shen* also means "vitality/energy", again one of the meanings of "spirit". And of course in Daoism, these two are related: precognition is enabled by a concentration of vital energy.

Learning as Penetration into *Dao*

I previously mentioned that *qi* and related Chinese words are important concepts in diverse areas, including the arts. For example, Su Dongpo, a Song dynasty literati-official, had this to say about calligraphy (writing with brush and ink): "Learning calligraphy is similar to practising

'Tao' [*Dao*, The Way], the supreme practice is pursuing *divinity* [*shen*, which in this context might more properly be translated as "spirit" without necessarily carrying the religious connotations of "divinity"], the secondary is pursuing Chi (life energy or vigour), and then comes pursuing the forms" (quoted in Lee 1996: 63; italics in original; remarks in square brackets added). But what does that mean? And is there a contradiction between this emphasis on *shen* and *qi*, which connote freedom and creativity, and the traditional practice of calligraphy education? For, as Lee notes, "In the conventional training of a Chinese calligrapher, not only the way of holding a brush has been taught strictly, copying Masterworks has been highly promoted as a single learning method" (Lee 1996: 38), which she thinks is detrimental to originality.

The case of Chinese calligraphy is representative, for "the tracing of characters is often described as if it were the definitive act of Chinese learning" (Stafford 1995: 8).[6] (Note also that in the past, learning to write was simply the initial stage in the learning of calligraphy.) We would therefore take a look at the learning of Chinese calligraphy, see how its seemingly mechanical learning methods are in fact necessary for the achievement of the states alluded to by *qi* and *shen*, and how it provides a paradigm for interpreting the point of learning in Chinese culture, at least as understood by the sages. That point is summed up by Mencius:

> The superior man makes his advances *in what he is learning* with deep earnestness and by the proper course, wishing to get hold of it as in himself. Having got hold of it in himself, he abides in it calmly and firmly. Abiding in it calmly and firmly, he reposes reliance on it. Reposing a deep reliance on it, he seizes it on the left and right, meeting everywhere with it as a fountain *from which things flow*. It is on this account that the superior man wishes to get hold of what he is learning as in himself. (Legge 1992: 414; italics in original)

Richards describes this passage as an "account of deep penetration into *tao*" (1932: 36) that lends itself better to meditation than exposition, but he immediately offers his exposition:

> What is studied, when we attain it " for ourselves" (or in ourselves), is no longer something over against us to be examined, but a guiding source of ability in us. This, however, reverses the metaphor – *we rather dwell in it than it in us*. Everywhere, to left and to right, we meet instances contributing to (flowing into) this ability. The contrast behind the passage is that between mere information about a state of affairs and the power of understanding. *For Mencius, as for other Chinese philosophers, wisdom is very much what we should describe as a skill*. (1932: 36; italics added)

I would caution that we should not take Richards' second last sentence to mean that what is at stake here is only intellectual learning.

We might as well add "mere skill in carrying out a certain task", for example, to "mere information about a state of affairs"; and "understanding", which is offered as a contrast, should not be confined to intellectual understanding. Furthermore, I would add to the last sentence its "mirror image", that "a skill is very much what we should describe as wisdom". With this in mind, let us return to the learning of Chinese calligraphy.

Learning to Practice Calligraphy: Mechanical Yet Joyful?

It is true that to the novices, the learning of Chinese calligraphy is very mechanical. The following exhortation from a *Qing* dynasty literacy primer is representative: "the brush must be held properly, and cleanliness must be kept when preparing the ink by grinding the ink bar in water" (Wan 1993: 1379). And these are only the preliminaries. The really hard work consists in practising strokes and characters in copybooks with model characters, and in the correct way:

> A teacher at any Chinese primary school often says to his pupils that they must try to write characters, not describe them. When a young pupil learns to write Chinese characters from a copybook, he may choose between "to write" [*xie*] and "to describe." [*miao*] "To describe" means to trace the characters in the copybook without being concerned with the way the hand moves . . . "To write," on the other hand, means to do as the writer of the copybook did, thus following more the calligrapher's *way* of writing than merely the *traces* he made. The right way is "to write." (Gao 1996: 57; italics in original)

That is, the basic techniques of writing are acquired through following the calligrapher's way of writing. Even when copybooks are later replaced by reproductions of masterworks, students of calligraphy still "trace and imitate the calligraphy of a master, down to every stroke and nuance, in order to achieve mastery" (Stafford 1995: 61). They "are not expected to discover how to use the brush to create various effects, but rather to learn what the masters have already discovered" (Winner 1989: 47). Does this not kill enjoyment and creativity? To begin to answer this question, we should note that whereas the initial means is imitation, the ultimate goal is not. Lee cites Billiter's observation that:

> great calligraphy masters tell us of "three initial phases that *necessarily follow in the same order*":
> acquiring of technique
> the study of past works
> the emergence of the personal style. (1996: 39; emphasis in original)

Admittedly, "the teaching rarely reaches the final stage of 'emergence of personal style' and concentrates instead on the first two stages" (Lee 1996: 39). This is to be expected, because some students are more gifted than others in calligraphy, unless by "personal style" we wish to mean any style regardless of artistic merit. However, even the achievement of the first two stages is valuable in itself, as I will show in due course.

What are the appropriate methods for mastering a practice? The following remark by MacIntyre on teaching might have come from a Chinese calligraphy teacher:

> Characteristically each teacher is engaged in initiating her or his students into some practice, generally in the elementary stages by teaching them skills, the use for which and the point of which the student cannot yet know. What the student can do is twofold: first, learn to care about "getting it right", and, second, learn to feel a sense of his or her own powers, of achievement in getting it right. (MacIntyre and Dunne 2002: 5)

Of course, in a sense students know the point of learning to write, but it is natural for students nowadays not to grasp the point of imitating studiously characters in copybooks. Why can they not write the character any way they like so long as it is recognizably that character? It is because calligraphy has its own intrinsic good (in MacIntyre's sense), the appreciation and achievement of which requires being initiated into the tradition that defines the practice.

But then why can students not be introduced to the principles of calligraphy rather than being required to copy mechanically? As it is, "Both in the field of calligraphy and in that of painting, a beginner need not think about the general principle of sequence, but he simply follows it under the guidance of his teacher" (Gao 1996: 73). Regarding this question, the following observation by Dreyfus *et al.* is instructive:

> Even if there are rules underlying expertise, the rules to which the expert has access are not the rules that generate his expertise, and so learning and acting on the rules the expert can formulate will not improve performance. Moreover, trying to find rules or procedures in a domain often stands in the way of learning even at the earliest stages. (1986: 152)[7]

And Davidson remarks in a discussion of the teaching of Chinese musical instruments that imitation "is often the only means of instruction, at least if one is to develop a vehicle with which to express musical thoughts." He further stresses that in fact "imitation requires active and creative participation on the part of the student and the teacher", referring to Polanyi's observation that "Even mastery of seemingly intellectual pursuits like chemistry relies on the tacit knowledge gained through observation and imitation of expert models" (Davidson 1989: 94). Even in the case of a child mastering basic calligraphic techniques through copying, the copying requires active participation, as demonstrated by the above reference to following the calligrapher's *way* of writing rather than the *traces*. To be able to do this, the child must observe each stroke of the model characters carefully. And as the appropriate perceptual and kinesthetic schemas are gradually constructed through repeated copying, the child will actively grasp the calligrapher's body movements hidden behind the traces with the help of these schemas, and inform his or her copying with these movements grasped through "kinesthetic empathy".

But surely a method relying so heavily on sitting and holding the brush properly and on meticulous copying is no fun to young children? The answer lies in whether, to repeat MacIntyre, the child is able to "feel a sense of his or her own powers, of achievement in getting it right" (MacIntyre and Dunne 2002: 5). And the answer seems to be "yes". Winner observes in relation to Chinese children's learning of painting that "the method used . . . is to teach in incremental and imitative fashion, so that even the ordinary or slow child will succeed" (1989: 51). The children were absorbed in their exercises because they could actually master the skill. Winner contrasts the learning of Chinese calligraphy and painting with the approach in American art lessons. Although the latter can better encourage students' explorations and problem-solving, very often the lack of structure and training in basic skills leads to disaffected students (Winner 1989: 62). I would conjecture, from my own experience, that the Chinese children Winner observed were absorbed in the calligraphy exercises because of the pleasant bodily feelings accompanying the calligraphic movements, the joy derived from the exercise of mastered skills, and the sense of achievement upon producing an acceptably nice piece of calligraphy.

Winner's observation that the method employed to teach Chinese calligraphy and painting ensures that even the ordinary or slow child will succeed is a crucial point. While the traditional method of learning Chinese calligraphy is open to diverse interpretations, including the charge that it represents violence done to children and serves to train domicile subjects, which I do not deny may well be among its outcomes, I would like to focus on the fact that it provides an almost foolproof means to initiate Chinese children into the practice of calligraphy. In Mainland China today, although brush calligraphy is now taught separately as a traditional art, learning to write (with everyday writing instruments) still follows the traditional pattern. This in effect creates and perpetuates a mass art form out of an everyday necessary activity engaged in by almost everyone. The effect can be seen in the contrast between the handwriting of Mainlanders and that of the people of Hong Kong, where the teaching of writing with regard at least to handwriting has been much more lax: almost every literate Mainlander has nice handwriting, while Hong Kong people's handwriting is on the whole awful. This is not to deny that the traditional learning method has serious drawbacks. No method is perfect. If I seem to be partial to the traditional method, it is only because its shortcomings have long been the centre of attention and I would like to redress the balance somewhat by dwelling on its possible strengths.

Calligraphic Appreciation: Practising Calligraphy Vicariously

It is true that, despite the rigorous calligraphic education to which children are traditionally subjected (literally), inevitably only a minority will become calligraphy masters. However, even to the majority whose mastery of calligraphy is mediocre, that level of mastery already enables them to appreciate the art of the calligraphy masters by being an active viewer. Lee likens a Chinese calligrapher's hand in the act of writing to the hands of a music conductor. "The trace of the 'conducting movements' of the [calligraphic] artist are recorded on the paper waiting for the sensitive viewers to respond to such recorded conduct and play the music in their own '*mind*'" (Lee 1996: 30; italics in original). She refers to Tsukamoto's observation that "it is the actual process of performance that is appreciated in *calligraphy*, though not directly as in musical or theatrical performance but through 'retracing' the dynamic of its lines" (quoted in Lee 1996: 30). And Bryson reports his experience of appreciating a Chinese painting:

> Looking at the Chu Jan scroll . . . , I can imagine all of these gestures; no film is necessary for me to locate these movements, for the silk is itself a film that has recorded them already; I cannot conceive of the image except as a trace of a performance. (quoted in Gao 1996: 86)

Chinese literati painting is inspired by Chinese calligraphy and based on its principles. What Bryson says of Chinese painting applies equally, if not more, to Chinese calligraphy. What makes such appreciation possible is the viewer's own experience with, and competence in, calligraphy. To use psychological jargon, the viewer possesses the perceptual-kinesthetic calligraphy schemas that allow him to resonate with the brush strokes by seeing the movements that led to the strokes and re-creating them in his imagination. As mentioned above, the copying that calligraphy novices undertake requires them to observe and follow closely the way of writing leading to the model characters. This habit must have contributed to the "retracing" that is an integral part of calligraphy appreciation. And simply by viewing good calligraphy, one's own calligraphic competence will likely improve. As psychologists have shown, mental practice, defined as "the cognitive rehearsal of a physical skill in the absence of overt physical movements" (Schmidt and Wrisberg 2000: 261), in itself aids both skill acquisition and performance, and the appreciation of calligraphy involves the viewer in actively "shadowing" the stroke movements, a kind of mental practice.

Meditation through Everyday Practice

What is the relevance of all this to spirituality? The characteristic Chinese emphasis on emulation and learning by heart, despite its commonly noted shortcomings, is based on an I–thou relationship between the learner and what is learned. The aforementioned quotation from Mencius (see above) shows that the goal of learning is to dwell in what is learned, in a sense becoming one with it. To use an example outside calligraphy, the Chinese approach to language learning requires:

> frequent reading and writing, reading the same pieces over and over and reflecting on them in depth, and revisiting previous learning. Zhu Xi wrote in *Crucial Points about Study* that "frequent practice enables one to master the language, since all strengths and weaknesses will then be felt directly." The strengths and weaknesses of a written piece will be appreciated only after repeated recitations. Yao Nai said . . . , "Studying a book requires first reading it over and over until it feels as if the words had come directly from one's own mouth." Natural and fluent language comes with repeated readings. (Zhang 1997: 84)

This respect for, and dedication to, what is being learned is spiritual. What is learnt merits respect and cannot be bent to one's will at whim, and that includes what is valuable in the tradition. The novice's meticulous imitation of the master calligrapher's stroke execution is an expression of this respect and dedication.

For an example of how dwelling in what one studies may feel, consider this description by a mathematician:

> [L]*earning* new mathematics is like constructing a mental house in my mind; *understanding* that new mathematics is like becoming familiar with the interior of my mental house; and *working on a mathematical problem* is like arranging the furniture. *Thinking* mathematics is like *living* in the house. As a mathematician, I create a symbolic world in my mind and then enter that world. (Devlin 2000: 124; italics in original)

The symbolic house requires much effort to build. However, if people "could only get beyond the plans and enter the house, they would find it as easy to wander around that mathematical house as an ordinary house" (Devlin 2000: 125). Devlin sees the place and its beauty, which a non-mathematician is unable to see.

Let us now return to the question about the pursuit of *shen* (spirit) and *qi* (vital energy) in calligraphy (or for that matter, other Chinese art forms). We have noted that traditionally one necessary phase of calligraphy learning is to study past masters' works. What is equally, if not more, important is learning from nature and the other arts. The following is Master Li Yang Bing's description of how he found his inspiration:

> From Heaven and Earth, mountains and rivers, I learned the permanent concepts of squares and circles. From sun, moon and stars, I learned the varied methods of repeating. From clouds, trees and grasses, I learned the capacity of the nature. From clothing, craft and culture, I learned notions of bowing, yielding and turning in the composition. From the emotional changes appearing on the eyebrow, hair, mouth and nose, I learned to distinguish between happy, angry, sad and comfortable sensations. From the worms, fishes, birds, and beasts, I learned the ground of the twisting, stretching, flying movements. (quoted in Lee 1996: 64)

It is not that nature offers a visual model for the calligrapher or painter to emulate. Learning from nature rather involves an intuitive grasp of, for want of a better expression, the essence or spirit of what is observed, which the Chinese call *shen*. This essence is not to be grasped by the senses, but by the spirit (*shen* again) of the observer, so that there is mutual indwelling of the observer and the observed, in the state of *shen yu* (meeting by, or of, spirit). In this state, the practitioner grasps, and is being grasped, by *Dao*. Hence in the practice of his art, he is not exactly himself. Arnheim calls this "the artist's selfless immergence in the objects he represented" (1997: 156), as described in Su Dongpo's poem on his artist friend Wen Yuke: "When Yu-k'o painted bamboo, / He saw bamboo, not himself. / Nor was he simply unconscious of himself: / Trance-like, he left his body. / His body was transformed into bamboo" (quoted in Arnheim 1997: 157).

According to Arnheim, "this behavior is reflected in the Taoistic harmony of man and world in their productive interaction" (1997: 157). The artist identifies with his object and merges with it. Gao quotes Wang Yu to make the same point:

> The mind is in emptiness, without even a single piece of dust. The mountains and valleys directly flow out from the mental faculty. Some of them are simple (solemn); some fluent (lively); some vigorous (high and steep); and some scattered. When [the painter] contemplates (*guanxiang*) the true visage of the mountains and forests, showing it from the point of the brush, how can he not be outstanding? (1996: 138)

The two characters in the term *guanxiang* above mean "to penetrate" (*guan*) and "to think" (*xiang*). The term therefore means "to penetrate through the surface of the objective world" (Gao 1996: 138). This state is also called *shen* (spiritual state). With the spirit (*shen*) thus in command, the artist is infused with *qi* which guides the execution of actions in a state of flow, and this *qi* is embodied in the work.

This returns us to the quotation from Mengzi (above). The goal of learning is the attainment of *Dao* through dwelling in a practice, a view held by the founders of both Confucianism and Daoism. Confucius believed that the dedicated pursuit of a practice (vocation), even such a far-from prestigious practice as charioting, leads to *Dao* (Wu 1999: 28). Zhuangzi put it nicely:

> Cook Ting . . . said, "What your servant loves best is the Tao, which is better than any art. When I started to cut up oxen, what I saw was just a complete ox. After three years, I had learnt not to see the ox as a whole. Now I practise with my mind [*shen*], not with my eyes. I ignore my sense and follow my spirit [*shen*]. I see the natural lines and my knife slides through the great hollows, follows the great cavities, using that which is already there to my advantage . . . "

> "Splendid!" said Lord Wen Hui. "'[From cook Ting's] words I have learned how to live life fully.'" (Chuang Tzu 1996: 23)

The dedicated pursuit of one's practice is a form of meditation. This spiritual (*shen*) state of penetrating *Dao* through one's practice requires the initial mastery of correct skills, often fine-tuned through countless generations of trial and error. Thus without the perceptual-kinesthetic schemas developed through skill practices, one will not be able to learn much from nature that would benefit one's art, much less penetrate *Dao*. This is not to say that *Dao* cannot be penetrated, or oneness achieved, through other paths, perhaps not requiring any dedicated practice. However, I suspect that for the majority of people, the dedicated pursuit of a practice provides a path that is a bit more reliable.

Demise of Dedicated Practice?

Let me make the following points by way of conclusion. First, in such a practice as Chinese calligraphy, even the initial stages of seemingly mechanical copying requires engaging the model characters to be copied and the copying itself with the spirit (*shen*), as alluded to by the Chinese terms for paying attention, such as *liushen* ("to retain the spirit") and *quanshen guanzhu* ("filled with the whole spirit").

Second, calligraphy provides a very popular artistic practice in the form of an everyday pragmatic activity. When I write Chinese, even only with a pencil, I feel a connectedness with my body, the meaning I am expressing, and the marks on the paper, a watered-down version of flow perhaps. It is meditation through everyday activity. Recently there has been some interest among educators in the place of meditation in education. I would suggest that meditation can also be achieved through the performance of a skilful activity. It is thus a pity that calligraphy is now given a very low priority in Hong Kong schools, and the art is being lost to both pupils and teachers alike. New technology may soon render even ballpens obsolete. It is unfortunate that hitherto the replacement of menial activities by technology often seems to rob the resultant activity of the ability to involve and express one's whole being and promote a holistic relationality to different levels of one's engagements. For example, with word processing (what I am now doing) I am unable to experience any degree of the pleasure coming with writing in my own hand (although during word processing I may still enjoy expressing the ideas). Maybe the problem lies with the fact that I did not learn word processing as a child, and thus cannot master it to an extent that would allow someone with a fine mastery of the art of word processing since childhood to experience the bodily-spiritual pleasure of word processing. But I am not sure.[8] Furthermore, nowadays with the rapid obsolescence of all technology, no everyday activity may be performed in the same way long enough to allow the emergence of such pleasure concomitant with a sufficient level of mastery.

This leads to the last point. As Sennett describes the change in the nature of work "in the new capitalism":

> The most tangible sign of that change might be the motto "No long term." In work, the traditional career progressing step by step through the corridors of one or two institutions is withering; so is the deployment of a single set of skills through the course of a working life . . . [The market] is too dynamic to permit doing things the same way year after year, or doing the same thing. The economist Bennett Harrison believes the source of this hunger for change is "impatient capital," the desire for rapid return . . . he market believes rapid market return is best generated by rapid institutional change. (1998: 22–3)

This is unconducive to the dedicated pursuit of a practice, in terms both of the necessary "reverence" for one's practice emphasized by Confucians, and of the time and effort available for the pursuit. It remains to be seen whether the dedicated pursuit of one's practice, which I have argued enhances one's spiritual development, will successfully reassert itself, a possibility raised by Himanen in his exploration of the "hacker ethic" that is held to "have had a significant role in the formation of our new society and that represent[s] a challenging alternative spirit to informationalism" (2001: 130).

Notes

1 There are two commonly used systems for the transliteration of Chinese: *Pinyin* and Wade-Giles. Here I will use *Pinyin* except when the source I quote uses Wade-Giles. In such cases I will add the *Pinyin* transliterations in square bracket when a term transliterated according to Wade-Giles first appears.

2 A Chinese character often includes within itself other simpler characters.

3 I do not wish to overstate the contrast between the Chinese and the Western traditions. As Jeeves shows by analyzing the Hebrew words *nephesh* (soul) and *ruagh* (spirit) and the corresponding Greek words *psyche* and *pneuma*, the Cartesian, strong dualism of matter and spirit may be largely absent in the Bible (1997: 98–126).

4 Note the parallel with "spirit", one of whose meanings is "a liquid of the nature of an essence or extract from some substance, esp. one obtained by distillation; a solution in alcohol of some essential or volatile principle" (*Oxford Dictionary Online* 2000).

5 Chinese folktales and traditional popular literature abound with fox spirits and the like. Probably the most popular *jing* is the Monkey King in the novel *Journey to the West* (*Xiyou Ji*).

6 Speaking only about the fine arts, Winner observes that "The age-old method for teaching calligraphy provides the standard; teaching methods in the various art forms are slight modifications of the techniques used to teach calligraphy" (1989: 47).

7 The quintessential example is "language acquisition", to use the term psycholinguists adopt to highlight the priority of language use over the explicit learning of grammar in infants' acquisition of the mother tongue.

8 I am aware that the ink-brush (and all other writing instruments), like the word processor, is a piece of technology. The difference between the two lies in the degree and the extent to which various body parts are involved in their use, the nature of that involvement, and the responsiveness of the outcome to how the person-tool composite performs. The issue merits a detailed analysis, which is beyond the scope of this chapter.

References

Adler, J. A. 1997. Varieties of Spiritual Experience: *Shen* in Neo-Confucian discourse. Paper presented at *Conference on Confucian Spirituality*, The Harvard University Centre for the Study of World Religions, July 30–August 3, 1997; accessed at <http: //www2.kenyon.edu/depts/religion/fac/adler/Reln471/Spirit.htm> on 2 July 2001.

Arnheim, R. 1997: Ancient Chinese Aesthetics and its Modernity. *The British Journal of Aesthetics* 37(2), 155–7.

Barnhart, R. K. (ed.) 1999: *Chambers Dictionary of Etymology*. Edinburgh: Chambers.

Chuang Tzu 1996: *The Book of Chuang Tzu*, translated by M. Palmer with E. Breuilly. London: Arkana.

Davidson, L. 1989: Observing a Yang Ch'in Lesson: learning by modeling and metaphor. *Journal of Aesthetic Education* 23(1), 86–99.

Devlin, K. 2000: *The Maths Gene: Why everyone has it, but most people don't use it.* London: Weidenfeld & Nicolson.

Dreyfus, H. L., Dreyfus, S. E. and Athanasiou, T. 1986: *Mind Over Machine: The power of human intuition and expertise in the era of the computer.* New York, NY: The Free Press.

Editorial Board of *Comprehensive Dictionary of Chinese Characters* (ed.) 1986–1990: *Comprehensive Dictionary of Chinese Characters*, 8 volumes. Wuhan: Hubei Dictionary Publishing House and Sichuan Dictionary Publishing House. (Chinese) (*Hanyu Da Zidian* Bianji Weiyuanhui (ed.) 1986–1990: *Hanyu Da Zidian*, 8 volumes. Wuhan: Hubei Zidian Chubanshe and Sichuan Zidian Chubanshe.)

Fung, Y.L. 1997: *A Short History of Chinese Philosophy: A systematic account of Chinese thought from its origins to the present day*, edited by D. Bodde. New York, NY: The Free Press.

Gao, J. 1996: *The Expressive Act in Chinese Art: From calligraphy to painting.* Stockholm: Almqvist & Wiksell International.

Hay, D. with Nye, R. 1998: *The Spirit of the Child.* London: Harper CollinsReligious.

Himanen, P. 2001: *The Hacker Ethic and the Spirit of the Information Age.* London: Vintage.

Holl, A. 1999: *The Left Hand of God: A biography of the Holy Spirit*, translated by J. Cullen. London: Bantam Books.

Kalton, M. C. 1998: Extending the Neo-Confucian Tradition: questions and reconceptualization for the Twenty-first Century. In M. E. Tucker and J. Berthrong (eds.), *Confucianism and Ecology: The interrelation of heaven, earth, and humans*, Cambridge, MA: The Harvard University Center for the Study of World Religions, 77–101.

Lai, W. 2001: *Qi.* In O. Leaman (ed.), *Encyclopedia of Asian Philosophy.* London: Routledge, 446–7.

Legge, J. (trans.) 1992: *The Four Books.* Changsha: Hunan Publishing House.

Lee, A. G. F. 1996: *The Spirit of Chinese Brush Lines and Its Application to Creativity in UK Art & Design Education.* Ph.D. dissertation, Manchester Metropolitan University.

Lindqvist, C. 1991: *China: empire of living symbols*, translated by J. Tate. New York, NY: Addison-Wesley.

MacIntyre, A. and Dunne, D. 2002: Alasdair MacIntyre on Education: in dialogue with Joseph Dunne. *Journal of Philosophy of Education* 36(1), 1–19.

Neville, R.C. 1978: *Soldier, Sage, Saint.* New York, NY: Fordham University Press.

Oxford Dictionary Online. Oxford University Press, 2000.

Pas, J.F. and Leung, M.K. 1998: *Historical Dictionary of Taoism.* Lanham, MD: Scarecrow Press, Inc.

Pearsall, J. 1998 (ed.): *The New Oxford Dictionary of English.* Oxford: Oxford University Press.

Richards, I.A. 1932: *Mencius on the Mind: experiments in multiple definition.* London: Kegan Paul, Trench, Trubner & Co., Ltd.

Roth, H.D. 1991: Psychology and Self-Cultivation in Early Taoistic Thought. *Harvard Journal of Asiatic Studies* 51(2), 599–650.

Sennett, R. 1998: *The Corrosion of Character: the personal consequences of work in the new capitalism*. New York, NY: W.W. Norton & Company.

Schmidt, R. A. and Wrisberg C. A. 2000: *Motor Learning and Performance*, 2nd edn. Champaign, IL: Human Kinetics.

Stafford, C. 1995: *The Roads of Chinese Childhood: Learning and identification in Angang*. Cambridge: Cambridge University Press.

Tang, Y. 1991: *Confucianism, Buddhism, Daoism, Christianity and Chinese Culture*. Washington, DC: The Council for Research in Values and Philosophy.

Tu, W. 1998: The Continuity of Being: Chinese visions of nature. In M. E. Tucker and J. Berthrong (eds.), *Confucianism and Ecology: The interrelation betweenof Heaven, Earth, and Humans*. Cambridge, MA: The Harvard University Center for the Study of World Religions, 105–21.

Tucker, M. E. 1998: The Philosophy of *Ch'i* as an Ecological Cosmology. In M. E. Tucker, M. E. and J. Berthrong (eds.), *Confucianism and Ecology: The interrelation between of Heaven, Earth, and Humans*. Cambridge, MA: The Harvard University Center for the Study of World Religions, 186–207.

Van Norden, B.W. 1996: What Should Western Philosophy Learn From Chinese Philosophy? In P.J. Ivanhoe (ed.), *Chinese Language, Thought and Culture*. La Salle, IL: Open Court, 224–49.

Wan, D. 1993: Rhymed Verses on What Children Must Know. In X. Han (ed.), *A Comprehensive Collection of Classical Chinese Children's Readers*, Shenyang: Liaoning Educational Publishing House, 1376–82. (Chinese) (Wan Douquan 1993: Tongmeng Xuzhi Yunyu. In Han Xiduo (ed.), *Zhonghua Mengxue Jicheng*. Shenyang: Liaoning Jiaoyu Chubanshe, 1376–82.)

Weller, R. P. and Bol, P. K. 1998: From Heaven-and-Earth to Nature: Chinese concepts of the environment and their influence on policy implementation. In M. E . Tucker and J. Berthrong (eds.), *Confucianism and Ecology: The interrelation of heaven, earth, and humans*. Cambridge, MA: The Harvard University Center for the Study of World Religions, 313–41.

Winner, E. 1989: How Can Chinese Children Draw So Well? *Journal of Aesthetic Education* 23(1), 41–63.

Wu, B. 1999: Word Into Stone and Spirit Wandering Beyond Material Constraints: Phenomenological observations on the religiosity of Chinese art. *Christian Culture Review* 10, 1–31. (Chinese) (Wu Bofan 1999: Roushen Cheng Shi yu Shenyou Wuwai – dui Zhongguo yishu zhong zhi zhongjiao xing de xianxiangxue guancha. *Jidujiao Wenhua Pinglun* 10, 1–31.)

Yip, P. 2000: *The Chinese Lexicon: A comprehensive survey*. London: Routledge.

Zhang, L. 1997: *Studies in Quality Language Education*. Changsha: Hunan Educational Publishing House. (Chinese) (Zhang Lunghua 1997: *Yuwen Suzhi Jiaoyu Yanjiu*. Changsha: Hunan Jiaoyu Chubanshe.)

Pedagogical Approaches

P ART III consists of a further six studies that are based on consideration of pedagogical processes. They are different in location,
covering university education in Tacey's, Chater's and Azvedo's
and Gil Costa's contributions, English schooling in Pike's and
Priestley's, and faith education in Erricker's. However, there are similar
issues that cross-reference within the different contributions, identi-
fying significant tensions involved in considering how attending to
spirituality in education is intimately linked to a consideration of pedagogical process and the particular vision of education that is entailed. In
turn, these tensions raise issues focusing on the agency of teachers and
students in relation to both the institutionalisation of education and religious faith and how that affects pedagogy's capacity to attend to the
spiritual.

David Tacey's "Encountering Tradition in a Postmodern Context"
contends that traditional religious forms are anachronistic within a time
within which established forms are crumbling; and yet spirituality is
emerging within this postmodern context. Tacey reflects on his students
views within his spirituality course and their tendency to engage with
the spiritual but be wary of the religious, often seeing it as an obstacle
to spirituality and a mode of conformity and authority that they need to
be released from in order to thrive spiritually. However, the more
mature students often come to realise, within the context of encounter
his course provides, that there are paradoxes to be encountered in trying
to separate religion from spirituality. Tacey uses his students written
reflections to reveal the difficulties and the spiritual possibilities they
encounter. Tacey concludes that religions themselves need to reflect on
and change their own forms in order to be receptive of a burgeoning
spiritual need amongst the young. Tacey reflects a critical approach to
modernist institutional life that he discerns within religion and
especially the Christian Church. Criticism of the shallow, soulless and

controlling character of such forms is also central to Priestley's and Chater's studies, but directed at education. Here we find a significant critique of modernism emerging by those who contend that post-modernity is a condition within which there is spiritual opportunity.

Mark Pike's "Reading and Responding to Biblical Texts: Aesthetic Distance and the Spiritual Journey" also engages with the postmodern theme introduced by Tacey. The openness of Tacey's pedagogical approach is reflected in Pike's approach to the reading of biblical texts. Recognising these texts as works of art they have the capacity to cause profound spiritual change, but how is their power to do so to be released? Pike turns to Heidegger's reading of Van Gogh's painting of "Old Shoes" to demonstrate the method of reading required, that fore-fronts our encounter with the text and the open and transforming possibilities that can arise from that. Shifting his focus to the bible itself he argues that we should introduce students to reading its text in the same way to "foster the spiritual, aesthetic, imaginative and creative lives of students". There is a strong connecting between Tacey's re-forming of religion and Pike's re-reading of biblical texts. They both suggest that approaches informed by the postmodern can spiritually revitalize religion and education. Pike's contention is that religious education should positively seek to transform students through aesthetic encounter and its application to their lives.

Jack Priestley's "The Spiritual Dimension of the Curriculum: What are school inspectors looking for and how can we help them to find it?" presents both a critique of common assumptions as to what the term spiritual refers to and of the way in which the English education system fails to engage with it effectively. The problem lies in thinking that we have to define the spiritual and add it on to what is then addressed by teachers in schools. For Priestley the spiritual is a dimension of educa-tion that is addressed within pedagogy as a whole. Engaging with the term development Priestley argues that it can be understood in two very different ways. Within our modern education system it refers to constant and measurable improvement, but it can also be understood as "to show what is there or hidden" suggesting "growth from below, not fashioned from without". In effect, Priestley is criticizing both the peda-gogical aims and methods of the education system and its lack of vision. His argument resonates with Tacey's in many respects. But one of the difficulties Priestley poses is how teachers are to engage with the spiri-tual dimension in an education system that is not designed to accommodate it, despite the fact that teachers have to make provision for it. This, Priestley notes, has caused confusion and anxiety, which, we might say, is not a very spiritual state of affairs.

Mark Chater's "Teacher's Values and Spiritualities: From Private to Public" is based upon a study of his own students and how they see themselves and their work. He distinguishes their attitudes as broadly falling into two different categories: a private spirituality of vocation and a public spirituality of profession. He contends that there needs to be an evolution from a privatised to a public space spirituality but that the present bureaucratic nature of the education system and its inspection regime inhibits this evolution because it limits empowerment and trust. For Chater the emphasis focused on school improvement, whilst potentially supporting a public space spirituality of profession, nevertheless, acts contrarily by privileging "the value of effectiveness, in ways that are morally questionable and which teachers...appear to find oppressive". For Chater, at the same time as the English education system has encouraged a greater sense of professionalism it has also despiritualized the profession, thus making the improvement it seeks impossible. The resonance with Priestley's critique is very clear and reinforces the sense of pedagogical dilemma that educators within the English system are confronted with.

Clive Erricker's "Faith Education of Children in the Context of Adult Migration and Conversion: The Discontinuities of Tradition" enquires into the extent to which adaptation occurs within religious communities and how that affects pedagogy in faith education. Just as Tacey's study is concerned with the relation between religious tradition, spirituality and the possibilities of change within the tensions of modernity and postmodernity, this study investigates the tensions between change and stasis in the context of cultural relocation. Erricker detects a significant difference occurring dependent upon whether such relocation is brought about by conversion or migration. Nevertheless, in the context of the faith education of the next generation similar issues emerge. In investigating these issues, with regard to Buddhism and Shia Islam, Erricker divides pedagogical models into two categories: wisdom and doctrinal. He suggests that the balancing of these two different models is a significant factor in how successfully the religious communities can embrace change and nurture a new generation in the community and related this to teaching observed within a Buddhist Dhamma school and a Shia medrassa. Erricker also points to the tensions this raises between authoritarian discourse and pupils' agency that were evident in empirical studies in **Part I**.

Maria Azvedo's and Helen Gil Costa's "Metaphors of Spiritual Education: Fight and Blessing" pursues themes that connect with Halstead's contribution in Part II and Pike's above in terms of metaphor and textual reading respectively. Starting from an inclusive anthropological definition of spirituality and an understanding of education informed by Friere's concept of *conscientization* they speak of teacher's spiritual education as enabling teachers to help themselves and their learners toward a self-knowledge and a creative life. On this pedagogical basis the authors then illustrate what this would mean in practice using the biblical text of Jacob fighting with the Angel as an exemplar. The textual reading is similar to Pike's method in that it is existential and intends to apply itself to transformation in self-understanding and action. The text used acts as a metaphor for the relationship between teacher and learner and the potentially creative process of education that occurs within the dynamics of this relationship. The authors present their students' evaluations of their education programme. In particular, these reveal changes in perception relating to risk-taking and more confidence in being open to possibilities in life situations. In this respect, this study, conducted in Portugal, makes an interesting comparison with the observations of Priestley and Chater.

Within **Part III**, we can identify an extension of the critiques made in **Part II** with regard to present educational and religious institutions and systems. Contributors have identified that attention to pedagogy and the agency of students is a key factor to be addressed in attending to spirituality and that the latter cannot simply be accommodated without revisiting the question of what educational vision such institutions and systems have. In doing this there needs to be an openness to change and a recognition of the possibilities of postmodernity.

Chapter 11

Encountering Tradition in a Postmodern Context

DAVID TACEY

Our Present Dilemma: The urge to change, the need to belong

THE CONTEMPORARY SPIRITUAL LANDSCAPE is fraught with contra-dictions and tensions. Our success as spiritual educators ought to be judged in part by how we deal with these contradictions and how we maintain the tension between opposite points of view. For instance, religious identity is hugely about belonging to a religious tradition or community, yet how do we entertain our need to belong when the tradition itself is so out of step with the times and urgently in need of repair? The tension between the urge to change and the need to belong is one that effects many of us, students and teachers alike. To emphasize change only is often to find ourselves "outside" the tradition and caught up in increasing levels of alienation and isolation. However, to capitulate to the instinct to belong is to appear "compliant" with a tradition that ignores or represses the urgency of change.

The philosopher Gadamer expresses the postmodern dilemma succinctly: "Today the world needs, but cannot have, religion" (in Derrida and Vattimo 1998: 204). We need religion to orientate ourselves to the world and to ultimate questions of meaning, but we cannot have religion because it asks us to subscribe to dogmatic beliefs and propo-sitions that we cannot support. Out of this contradiction, this tension between opposites, something new can be born, if we have the capacity to endure the pain this generates within ourselves and in society. Spiritual education must, I believe, situate itself at the core of this contra-diction, and make something useful of it. I get worried when our thinking about spiritual education becomes narrowly "religious", because then it seems to me that the complexity and opportunity of the postmodern moment has been obliterated. I would call myself a religious person, but hasten to add that I subscribe to a revisionist project, and that religiosity without a consciousness of change is oppressive and reactionary. I think spiritual education should offer a dual perspective: respect for religious traditions, along with a constructive critique of traditions. Without such a critique, spiritual education might become yet another opportunity for devotionalism or for coercion into a particular faith community.

We live in a time in which established forms are crumbling, for a whole host of reasons to do with a lack of fit between religion and society (Tacey 2003). With anachronistic forms collapsing, often for good reason, we cannot expect children or young adults to support those forms. Young people are growing through and beyond religious forms; their spirituality is being built upon the rubble of old religions. Our students are reaching out to the future, which is still largely unknown. After expressing the spiritual contradiction of our time, Gadamer follows with this important question: "Will the world, perhaps, be able to discover an answer which, as yet, can only be guessed at?" (in Derrida and Vattimo 1998: 204). The task of the spiritual educator is not only to teach students what we know, but to confess to what we do not know, and there is an enormous amount that remains unclear and unknown to us. In part, there is often a reversal of roles in this historical moment: the students may well be giving birth to the future world to which Gadamer points. If this is the case, the task of the spiritual educator is to listen deeply and intently to what our students are saying. Their voices contain the seeds of a future which we as yet cannot know.

Spirituality Studies: drawing from religion, keeping faith with the secular

But to build our spiritual future, religious tradition will be needed, but not in the old way. Whereas in the past "spirituality" was the intense inner life "inside" religion, today, with the crumbling of forms, spirituality is newly exposed, naked to the world, unclothed. Spirituality is welling up from our postmodern and post-religious society, and is the intense inner life of the secular world. In the past, spirituality was attributed to those who were "very" religious, while today it often describes those who are "not very" religious. Spirituality is now much larger than religion itself, and looking back into the past we see that this was always so, but it has been newly revealed to our sight. As one of my students said, "the spirituality of the people had been hijacked by the church; now we are reclaiming what is rightfully ours". This is an ironic reversal of a complaint made by those inside religious traditions, who remark that spirituality is being hijacked from religion, and that its proper location is, and remains, inside the institutions of faith.

I would argue that Spirituality Studies, as an academic discipline, has to be given a life of its own, rather than be seen as a part of theology. All the world over, theologians are complaining that spirituality must not develop as a separate discipline, but must be returned to their fold. But the spiritual horse has bolted from the old stable, and since spirituality has now shot out into the secular world, it takes many secular disciplines and intellectual perspectives to track its course and analyze its development. To understand spirituality today, we need at least sociology, history, psychology, psychoanalysis, feminism, political science, philosophy, and cultural studies. Theology cannot be stretched to include all these new knowledges and perspectives. Spirituality has become worldly, and this means we have to "keep faith" with the secular world and study the socio-cultural, political, philosophical and psychological disciplines in order to understand spirituality.

Staying in the difficult present or the flight into fundamentalism

This new situation creates freedom, diversity, individuality, and adventure such as we have never seen before. It is an exciting time for spirituality, but it is also a dangerous time, and here we remember the ancient Chinese curse: "May you be born in interesting times". Spirituality, naked in the world, in the hands of everyone, is exposed and vulnerable. Some say it does not even exist: that it is nothing, unless it is expressed in traditional forms. It is hard to live with "something" when it is described as "nothing"; similarly, it is hard to bring a new discipline to birth when others deny its very existence.

The escape from the "nothingness" of spirituality can lead to a flight into the "something" of religious fundamentalism. I think we can expect large numbers running into fundamentalism, fleeing from the postmodern rubble and the uncertainty of a collapsed religious landscape. But such activity is a reaction-formation to the anxiety and fear of the present: it is not of the time, but reactionary to the time. I think the new spirit will eventually find its own legitimate form. Spirit cannot exist for long without form, but struggles to create a vessel or container in which it can flourish. As William Blake writes: "Eternity is in love with the productions of time" (1793: 151). When the productions of time are no longer useful to the spirit, then eternity, through its love for time and embodiment, will inspire new religious forms.

Tradition Needs Prophetic Imagination Not Empty Repetition

In critical times, we have to distinguish between the *spirit* of tradition and the *forms* of tradition. Those who cling to and prop up the old forms call themselves traditionalists, but they may be betraying their tradition if the spirit of their tradition is finished with the old forms and prophetically calls us to create new ones. This is precisely the dilemma in which both Jesus and the Buddha found themselves: facing a tradition that had lost credibility and spiritual vitality, and having to denounce that tradition in order to bring its authentic spirit to a new fulfillment and realization. In this sense, contemporary spirituality, which so often moves outside or beyond religious form, is perhaps the spirit of tradition itself, searching for new and legitimate forms. It is natural that the spirit of tradition would not wish to die with the collapsing forms; it would want to move ahead, to develop a new covenant with the people, a new pact with secular society. This is not an organizational task but a prophetic task: it takes prophetic imagination and courage to see and identify the spirit as it moves forward in its history-making journey (Brueggemann 1978).

My sense is that many of our young people are forced to become prophetic by the peculiar nature of the times. They appear to be dishonouring tradition, but at another level they may be helping to create a new dispensation that will legitimize tradition in a new way. The so-called traditionalists view the honouring of tradition in an opposite sense: by doing more of the same, by repeating acts and rituals, they see themselves keeping the spirit of tradition alive. Picasso once said in an interview: Tradition is having a baby, not wearing your father's hat. Those who call themselves conservatives are proudly wearing the old hat, but the spirit of tradition is only "conserved" by making it relevant to the present. There is an important mystical dimension of tradition: it is not about repetition, but re-creation. The Jewish tradition has recognized the need for "making new", which is honoured in the art of *midrash*, where truths are revived by linking them with new understandings. The Christian West must not allow the reactionaries to see themselves as the sole bearers of tradition, but on the contrary, following the examples of Christ and Buddha, we have to see the new prophetic spirit as the necessary development of tradition itself.

The rising generations feel the need to break away from the past, but religious leaders tell them this is the wrong way to move. Leaders call youth to return to the fold, and the carrot dangled before them is the promise of "belonging" to something old and wise, to something greater than themselves. But as the leaders call "belong, belong,

belong", the majority of youth hear this differently, as "conform, conform, conform". Youth believe, with Gadamer, that they need but cannot have religion. Religion offers youth three important elements: a language to express the spirit; a history to inform the spirit, and a community to support the spirit. But youth might reply: that is all very well, but we will go about finding these three elements in our own way, and not in accordance with the dictates of established religious authority. Hence we find that youth frequently go in search of their own language of the spirit, they comb through numerous and unorthodox histories of the spirit, and often they create or invent their own communities of the spirit. There is more than one way of doing things, and youth culture seems to thrive on the diversity of expressions offered by the postmodern culture.

Problems Besetting the New Spirituality and Spiritual Education

But it is of course difficult to invent new communities of the spirit, or to produce overnight what has taken hundreds of years to develop and evolve. When young people say they are doing fine in their spiritual journeys, and that they have dropped religion as excess baggage on the spiritual way, this optimism is often boastful and unfounded in their actual experience. I often find that students are repressing the shadow side of their experience, that their spirituality is lonely, isolating, alienating them from others. But they won't admit this, because it is too depressing and their spirituality is supposed to produce connectedness and relatedness. But because their spirituality is mostly private and inward, a product of modern individualism, the pursuit of connectedness can lead to increased loneliness.

Moreover, since spirit is felt to emerge from the inner self, and is experienced as intensely personal, it tends to produce a self-reinforcing inwardness that can disturb one's relationship to social reality and the wider world. When this happens, it is doubtful that we have contacted the living spirit at all, for the true spirit is universal and always strives toward full expression in the world around us. Although spirit is experienced as personal today, its true nature is universal: it cannot be confined to privatized, hemmed-in space. Therefore, those of us who strive to keep our spirituality private are pushing against spirit itself, which is communal, social, shared. It is important to ensure that our personal spiritual journey is not a parody of spirituality, a "pretend" spirituality which can justly be criticized as narcissistic by those with a more traditional religious view. We have to learn to be discriminating, and to practice spiritual discernment, which means not only being critical of established religion but also being critical of our own spiritual practice.

The postmodern spiritual experience is full of twists and surprises. What is called "religion" is often thrown out, but it is needed as resource and as a counterpoint to our personal experience. Individual self-expression is initially viewed as freedom, but it can end up being stifling if we are unable to experience the spirit in others or the world around us. Thus, in my spirituality course, I strive to get the students to be critical of their own assumptions, to think again about what they may have thrown out or rejected. Nevertheless, I do not encourage uncritical fusion with religious tradition. This makes me hard to read by some students, who cannot quite ascertain my real agenda. Fundamentalists see me as free-thinking and radical, while the radical and atheist students see me as intensely conservative and too concerned with the past. My own position, which is to hold the tension between the need to belong and the urge to change, is apparently too complex for some students to grasp. Explosions of temper occur, and sometimes students withdraw from the course for opposite reasons: a few withdraw because it is too religious, and some others have withdrawn because it is not religious enough. The majority understand my motives and appreciate what I am doing, but I have come to accept that it is not possible to impress all parties when one is trying to discover an "in-between" place that is neither unconditional acceptance of tradition nor full-blown rejection.

Drawing Out What Is Within: "Educare"

In my spirituality course, I attempt to contact the spiritual element in students' lives, and lead this out into a wider cultural sphere. I do not focus on scripture or theology, but urge students to study inspirational poetry, mysticism, ecology, and art, in a quest for spiritual understanding. As we look at culture and nature, I urge them to explore their deepest feelings and emotions, and especially to explore the place inside where something is missing. Drawing out what is within, what is inside each one of them, is the first task of a spirituality course, and it should be the first task of all good education, since the word education comes from the Latin "educare", meaning to lead or draw out. Good religion, like good education, must also attempt to lead out the spiritual elements in people's lives, and get over its obsession with pouring religious facts and ideas into people's lives. Tradition, if founded on the living spirit, is not wholly reliant upon external factors or influences, but must have its own internal resonance in the souls and hearts of ordinary people.

In effect, good spiritual education means going back behind religious or creedal lines, and asking primary questions about human life and existence. Do we find materialism satisfying or not? Most will agree that it is not satisfying. Can man or woman live by bread alone? Most will agree that we cannot. Do we hunger for the water of the spirit and the bread of the holy? Most will agree that we do hunger for something more, although many will stop short of applying religious terms to this "More". To be effective at this level, the spiritual educator must not force the students to make leaps and bounds they do not want to make. "Less is more" should be our slogan, and it is often enough to identify spiritual hunger and yearning, and allow the student to discover how that hunger will then seek to be satisfied.

This is not evangelism, but it can indeed lead to revivalist kinds of feelings in students. Once the student is put in touch with his or her spiritual hunger, the results can be surprising, and these results should make religious organizations think again about the best way to evangelize or spread the word. Here, for instance, are two responses to the spirituality course, both of which have led the students to think again about the religions that they had previously dismissed as irrelevant:

> It is hard to sway a convinced materialist like myself from his constant scepticism about religious matters, at least I thought it was before this course. But it is terribly hard to continue to oppose the idea of "spirit" when it is presented in poetry and inspirational writings. Before the course, I blocked out religion as irrelevant to my life, it made no sense to me at all in its conventional, archaic and drab form. But when spirituality is expressed in poetry, passion, and subjectivity, I have to take another look, as these expressions are inspirational and move me in an unexpected way. I now see that emotion and spirit can be included in my world, and I can have such elements without straying from reality. (Steven, 18 years of age, in 2002)

> Before I started this subject, I was confident in "bagging" Christianity for the way in which it had failed me. Empty rituals, outmoded morality, and corrupt institutions, etc. Yet as the weeks have passed, I have come to realize that a more sophisticated dialogue is at my disposal. I have discovered that my childish repudiation of the Christian Church revealed a lack of knowledge into the nature, depth and multi-layered appearance of spirituality within religion. I come away with greater respect for my religion of origin, and for the presence of spirituality in what I had thought was a dead and moribund institution. (Jenny, 19, 2002)

I must emphasize that I have not tried to impose religion upon these students, I have tried to draw their innate spirituality out of them, and to give expression to areas of their life that are rarely expressed. Religion is first seen as incomprehensible or irrelevant, and most students write in the first few weeks that religion is an obstacle to their spirituality. By the end of the course, they begin to shift their perception: religion gets a second viewing, no longer purely an obstacle, it can become a resource for spirituality. When people go in search of spiritual meaning, it is then that the lost inheritance of childhood often comes to the fore. It is often the more mature student who realizes the benefit of childhood exposure to religious education:

> Secular people are looking for spiritual renewal but don't know where to look. I think that people who have been given the opportunity to grow up with some connection with a faith have more of a starting point to explore their own spiritual beliefs. (Beth, 26, 2000)

Spirituality needs language, symbol, myth, and metaphor: we can't just have religious feelings (or spirituality) without religious forms (or tradition) to contain and nurture those feelings. The present war between religious feeling and form is a phony war, but, paradoxically, it is also a real one, and it is intensified in our time by the prevailing sense that the forms are collapsing.

What delights me about my course is that, by working behind religious lines, I am seeing similar processes operating in different faith traditions. For instance, a Jewish student of mine said she had been in Jewish schools as a child, and afterwards she went to live in Israel. But the spirituality course had been most powerful in linking her with her native Judaism. Although the course was not about Judaism, she said it had done most to connect her to her religious heritage. I found this astonishing, and she wrote two essays on this theme.

Islamic students have said the same thing: "my Islamic teachers taught me about religion, but not about spirituality", wrote Fatima (18, 2002), an Australian student who was born in Turkey. "I have seen how Allah speaks to me from within, and he is not confined to the outside religion or the Koran". The spirituality course creates a climate of validity in which faith positions can be re-experienced and affirmed, and this process, if sensitively handled, can operate in a truly post-modern and multifaith context. If I came across as more overtly religious, using language that constrained and limited the spirit, less religious experience would happen.

A Case Study: Losing My Religion, Recovering My Faith

I want to conclude with a case study. This is the story of a student called Elizabeth, and she has given me permission to use her work. Elizabeth indicated that she had come from a religious family and her early experience of religion had been essentially positive. Elizabeth wrote that she had been born into the Catholic faith, and she had followed the faith of her family in childhood. But by the arrival of adolescence, she had adopted a "secular" identity as a way of distancing herself from the family, and as a way of staking out her own relationship to the world:

> I suppose I was attracted to things outside the church and outside my religious family. New interests and experimentations led me to put religion on hold and to live a secular kind of life, along with most of my friends. Despite having a strong religious presence in my early life, I entered adulthood as a non-Christian, although I don't think I ever lost the sense that there was a God. (Elizabeth, 19, 2000)

The pattern that I find operating in Elizabeth's story, as with stories like hers, seems to include five stages or elements: (1) Natal faith; (2) Adolescent separation; (3) Identification with the secular; (4) Disillusionment with the secular; and (5) The quest for a personal spirituality. In this process, religious tradition is at first adopted as one's own religious life, then it is set aside or "put on the back burner", as so many young adults put it. Then there is the surprising shift, where tradition rises again from within, as a personal inner resource, as a companion to the individual search for spiritual meaning.

On this point about initial repudiation and later recovery of religion, Sandra Schneiders can be illuminating:

> The justification of intense interest in spirituality and alienation from religion is often expressed in a statement such as, "I am a spiritual person, but I am not very religious". Interestingly enough, and especially among the young, this religionless spirituality often freely avails itself of the accoutrements of religion. Invocation of angels, practices such as meditation or fasting, personal and communal rituals, the use of symbols and sacramentals from various traditions . . . are common. Indeed, even the most secular types of spirituality seem bound to borrow some of their resources from the religious traditions they repudiate. (Schneiders 2000: 2)

It is this "rebuilding" of religion from the inside that interests me, and I suppose this is an extension of the work begun by William James (1902) a hundred years ago. "Losing my religion" and "recovering my faith" are happening simultaneously in our postmodern society. The only problem is: who is watching this, monitoring, recognizing it? Religious organization is not interested because it is not propping up the organization or increasing the membership.

I now pick up Elizabeth's story again at the fourth stage. The secular person often pretends to be happy and adjusted to the norms of society, but inwardly, if he or she dares to look, there is a deep unhappiness and a lack of fulfillment. The heart is broken and the psyche is at war with itself.

> From the age of eleven to the present day (nineteen), I have been divided. I have been a different person to different people, never quite knowing who I really am nor what I really believe. I adopted a position of almost total ignorance toward the sacred. This position is almost entirely viable in our materialistic society. But hidden within the recesses of my life was another life, that I secretly wanted to be connected to, but was scared to acknowledge very often, if at all.

In "normal" conditions, the secular person has to stage-manage and control this inner fragmentation and make the best of it. If the ego is resilient, the person may convince herself that nothing is wrong, that there is no second life "hidden within the recesses of my life". The secular ego can work hard to deny this inner life, because it brings such unpleasantness, brokenness, and incompletion. However, if the person is sensitive to truth, and has a genuine longing for wholeness, then she may seek out this buried or hidden self, even though it will come at incredible cost. Students often talk in up-beat and positive ways about their search for spirituality, but a few recognize that if their spirituality is to be genuine it will challenge them to the ground of their being, and they may have to make a new adaptation to self, reality, and world.

Elizabeth is one of those who recognize that spirituality is not just another game we play, but a challenge to break the old and to create a new personality:

> I was scared to acknowledge the sacred in case it meant the ultimate death of the subtle underlying apathy that protected myself, and all of us, from the shocking reality of the presence of mystery in our lives.

This made me sit up and take notice. Rudolf Otto (1923) wrote that spirituality is paradoxical and double-sided. On the one hand we are "fascinated" by its mystery; on the other hand we live in "dread" and may even be "appalled" at the reality of the sacred. The modern mind rejects religion not simply because it fails to square with commonsense, but because our mind is terrified of the existence of a reality greater than itself. The modern person likes to imagine that he or she is in control, that we are masters of the universe, but that is an illusion protecting us from the shocking fact that something greater is in control. The reality of the sacred shatters, as she says, the "subtle underlying apathy" that protects us from the admission that there is something other. With spirituality becoming more popular and fashionable, the foreboding or shocking aspect of the sacred is frequently repressed, or is projected outside us onto others.

Elizabeth has the emotional maturity to realize that it is partly the emptiness of the secular life that has driven her to seek out a more profound reality beneath her secular existence. She is impelled to a sense of the sacred not out of fun or excitement, but out of the sense of imperfection in her existence. She is driven to a deeper realization by an admission of poverty and lostness:

> Why did my life feel so empty? Perhaps, for me, spirituality is an essence noticed more easily in the absence. Was this absence a holy thing? I mean, was the absence a prelude to a deeper sense of presence? Realizing your own emptiness, and thinking about its possible meaning, is scary and hard. I had to confront this unknown quality, let it change my life, and this is pretty scary, pretty hard.

I was arrested by the honesty and integrity of this disclosure. The facing of our emptiness is not easy, and most of us will do anything to avoid it. As she writes, this work is scary and hard, but if we are able to endure it, it will change our lives.

Metanoia: A Life Turned Around

At this point in her writing, she takes stock of her situation, and reflects on the life-changing implications of what she has just revealed:

> In these sentences I have revealed something which is extremely difficult and confronting to admit. I realize I do believe in an Other, in a Sacred Other. If I analyze my feelings thoroughly, I would probably conclude that it was God. The reason I put God on hold was because it is easier to live in the distractions of the secular without commitment or responsibility to the sacred. To make that conscious choice is to admit my own weaknesses and frailty as a human being amid other human beings like me. It is to admit my dependence on a mystery and a beauty greater than myself.

The term "Sacred Other" was introduced in my lectures and I often use it as an umbrella term, inviting students to use their own more specific term where appropriate. Elizabeth has been able to lift her self-imposed bans on the idea of a sacred presence. It is almost as if the idea of the Sacred Other was a necessary middle term or transitional idea, which acted as a bridge between her secularism and her new position of recovered faith.

We notice that the achievement of faith is not a blind leap into the dark, but a position involving "conscious choice", "commitment" and "responsibility". The religious awareness is *relational*, an admission that we live our lives in relationship with a mystery which is greater than ourselves. The secular ego blocks out this relationality, and assumes that we live as free agents. The secular state appeals to our egocentricity, but ironically, such selfishness is unrewarding and the self is not fulfilled by it. Elizabeth reflects on these problems in personal and philosophical terms:

> It seems desirable to believe in "modern" man and his secular utopia without the gods. But when you think about this at some length, and realize the beauty and mystery around us, you realize how ridiculous this secular belief is. We have to let go of this idea of our autonomy from the Sacred Other. It is easier to delude oneself, to be false, than it is to face the truth. Easy, but without satisfaction.

She considers the possibility of adopting a "secular" spirituality, like so many of her fellow students, but she rejects this option:

> The problem of "secular" spirituality is that it is full of holes. We want it all. We want the conviction that we are masters of our own destiny, and we want a sense of mystery without God and without ethical responsibility.

Secular spirituality is having our cake and eating it too; or wanting the sense of mystery without the embarrassment of God. It is, she argues, an easy option, where we benefit from the sense that the world is enchanted, but we are not answerable to a greater moral force. This is tough reasoning, and she realizes the isolating implications of what she is saying. Her new position will alienate her from some other students in the class who say they are "spiritual but not religious".

At this moment she senses the possibility of a new wholeness, and this is worth risk and sacrifice:

> I don't want to be all these different people any more. I want to be the same person to everyone. To be real. And so the struggle begins to keep your soul. To have soul is to dedicate your life to others, and to pursue the truth, while some others live in "blessed" ignorance, and feel no sense of responsibility either to God or to fellow humans.

She senses the possibility of a breakthrough, and if she has the courage of her convictions she could experience much joy and celebration:

> But my sense is that if I take a step further along this path, after what I have seen and revealed, there is the potential for great joy, wholeness, purpose, and worth.

Her problems with her social identity will probably remain for some time. Is she religious? Is she a born again Christian? Will her secular brothers chastise and mock her for recognizing God? What will her religious parents think after putting up with her teenage years in which religion was put "on hold"? How will she manage this transition without alienating others?

I want to open up the possibility of a spirituality which is not alienating to the people I love, that could possibly unite them, and in doing so, unite me too, body, soul, spirit, as one person to everyone. I have to take the leap. I still don't know in what direction to jump. But I feel I'll actually come to something, find what I'm looking for.

The Spiritual Life Beneath Our Secular Mask

The postmodern world in which we live is challenging and confusing. The confusion is clearly apparent, but the challenge is that we take possession of the situation, and refuse to become a victim of fragmentation, chaos, and stress. In the shadow of a great deal of cultural collapse, individual lives are finding their own meaning, and discovering new ways to achieve wholeness, integrity, and spiritual worth. On the large, macro level there is incredible confusion, anguish, and disruption, and if we focus on that level alone, we often end up terribly depressed and disheartened. Too many people are looking at the externals, the emptying churches, the breakdown of traditions, and are drawing bleak and often terrifying conclusions about the end of God and civilization.

But at the micro level, which is the level at which spirituality operates, the situation is quite different. As David Hay and Kate Hunt said in a recent report on adult spirituality in Britain, "at the surface, the situation looks bleak for religion in this country, but underneath a very different picture emerges" (2000: 7). The question then arises: who is looking at the different picture underneath? There is no institution prepared to do this, yet the life beneath the surface is thriving, growing, and full of hope. It is the site in which tradition is being rediscovered.

The truths of religion are newly apprehended through spiritual experience, which is, as it were, the back door into religion. I say "back door" because Western religion has yet to figure out how to make such an entrance into a dignified or front-door entry. Western religion has not encouraged spirituality, because it is too hard to manufacture on a mass scale, and because personal experience of the sacred would be divisive and schismatic, giving rise to too many variants of the sacred. By restricting people to communal worship, rather than encouraging individual exploration, tradition maintained its internal unity, and its authority over the community. Personal experience could be risky, dangerous, threatening, and such experience was often stigmatized as gnosticism or esotericism, which was labeled heretical. Today we are in a different situation, and the religion of the future must encourage individual exploration, because the communal dimension of faith will have collapsed, and we will need to work in an entirely different way. The spiritual ground of our being is the site in which tradition can be rediscovered and reborn.

References

Blake, W. 1793: "The Marriage of Heaven and Hell". In G. Keynes (ed.), *The Complete Writings of William Blake*. Oxford University Press, 1972.

Brueggemann, W. 1978: *The Prophetic Imagination*. New York: Fortress.

Derrida, J. and Vattimo, G. (eds.) 1998: *Religion*. Stanford University Press.

Hay, D. and Hunt, K. 2000: *Understanding the Spirituality of People who don't go to Church*. Research Report, Centre for the Study of Human Relations, Univeristy. of Nottingham.

James, W. 1902: *The Varieties of Religious Experience*. London: Penguin Books, 1990.

Otto, R. 1923: *The Idea of the Holy*. Oxford: Oxford University Press, 1980.

Schneiders, S. 2000: Religion and Spirituality: Strangers, Rivals, or Partners? In *The Santa Clara Lectures* (California), 6 (2).

Tacey, D. 2003: *The Spirituality Revolution: The Emergence of Contemporary Spirituality*. Sydney: HarperCollins.

Chapter 12

Reading and Responding to Biblical Texts: Aesthetic Distance and the Spiritual Journey

MIKE A. PIKE

IN THIS CHAPTER I suggest that the "aesthetic distance" between the world of the literary text and that of the reader maps out the landscape across which a reader's unique and intensely personal spiritual journey can be made. The relation between aesthetic response and spiritual experience is explored with reference to the theoretical perspectives of Wolfgang Iser (1971), Louise Rosenblatt (1978), Hans Robert Jauss (1982) and Martin Heidegger (1936/1977). The implications for spiritual education of the National Literacy Strategy, a powerful influence across the curriculum in state schools in the UK, is evaluated. Specific examples of fifteen and sixteen year old readers' reading of biblical texts, in a school that has a distinct sense of itself as a spiritual community, are given to illustrate how perspectives from reader response criticism and aesthetic theory can inform a pedagogy for reading as spiritual experience. I conclude that the approach described here can be employed in a range of contexts with readers who possess heterogenous beliefs and have diverse spiritual commitments and orientations because it respects the individuality and identity of the reader, does not enforce conformity, and fosters genuinely personal response.

Aesthetic Distance and "Horizonal" Change

Great works of literature possess "aesthetic distance" and for Hans Robert Jauss, it is the disparity between the reader's "horizon of expectation" and the text which can bring about a "change of horizons" either "through the negation of familiar experiences or through raising newly articulated experiences to the level of consciousness" (Jauss 1982: 25). Works of art, whether literary or visual, have the capacity to cause profound "horizonal change" and reorientation. Literary texts and particular pedagogic approaches to them (derived from reader-response theory) have previously been seen to foster spiritual and moral development (Pike 2000c; 2002a) but here, the potential of certain biblical texts to bring about such development is considered. Employing pedagogy that promotes active reading (Pike 2001) and nurtures aesthetic response (Pike 2003d) so that spiritual and moral development can thrive is essential as readers need to be enabled to immerse themselves in the text and bring themselves before it. The most complete understanding and, therefore, the aim of interpretation, according to Gadamer and Ricoeur, requires a "fusion of horizons" where the "world horizon of the reader fuses with the horizon of the world projected by the text" so that the "reader enters into and is transformed by the text" (Schneiders 1991: 172). How such '"fusion" can occur when readers read the Bible is an important issue for spiritual education.

Lectio Divina as Aesthetic Reading

It is important to consider reading as a spiritual activity. Indeed, reading is one of the daily disciplines practised by spiritual communities and is so important in schools because it can enable us to "recover a sense of education as a process of spiritual formation" (Palmer 1993: 17). Clearly, students are "formed by the reading they do" and also by the "views of self and world such reading presents" (Palmer 1993: 19). Texts "contain clues about our view of ultimate reality" and hold "the images of self and world in which our students are formed"; consequently, reading and other daily practices are the "disciplines" to which our students are asked to "disciple" themselves (Palmer 1993: 19). Yet the contrast between reading for comprehension, a discipline often practised in schools, where the objective is to extract information, and the more personally responsive and meditative reading of spiritual communities is marked. In most schools, children are urged to engage in rapid, businesslike reading whereas monks, "dwell on a page or a passage or a line for hours and days at a time" and engage in *lectio divina*, sacred reading, which is taken at a more contemplative pace as the "purpose of this slow meditative reading is to create a certain sort of space that allows readers to enter and occupy the text" (Palmer 1993: 76). Indeed, a feature of very high quality literary texts, such as the Bible, is that they possess "indeterminacy" or "gaps", that the reader fills (Iser 1971). In a sense, the reader completes or even co-creates the text with the author. One way we can foster the "postcritical encounter of reader and biblical text that results in what Ricoeur calls appropriation – that is, making one's own that which is other" is through "aesthetic surrender" because the relation of "reader to text" is, in fact, the "relation of participant to work of art" (Schneiders 1991: 173).

The Spiritual Significance of the Aesthetic Encounter

Aesthetic surrender is modelled for us by Heidegger and can help us to understand the nature of spiritual response (Pike 2003f). In Amsterdam in 1930 Heidegger had seen one of Van Gogh's eight paintings of shoes. It might well have been "Old Shoes". In attending to this painting, according to Heidegger, we might at first just see a pair of shoes and no more:

> From Van Gogh's painting we cannot even tell where these shoes stand. There is nothing surrounding this pair of peasant shoes in or to which they might belong – only an undefined space. There are not even clods of soil from the field or the field-path sticking to them which would at least hint at their use. A pair of peasant shoes and nothing more. And yet. (Heidegger 1936/1977: 159)

At this point, Heidegger brings himself before the work and models the aesthetic encounter for us. By bringing ourselves before the work and living through an encounter we are able to apprehend it:

> From the dark opening of the worn insides of the shoes the toilsome tread of the worker stares forth. In the stiffly rugged heaviness of the shoes there is the accumulated tenacity of her slow trudge through the far-spreading and ever-uniform furrows of the field swept by a raw wind. On the leather lie the dampness and richness of the soil. Under the soles stretches the loneliness of the field-path as evening falls . . . (Heidegger 1936/1977: 159)

For Heidegger the true nature (or being) of what was depicted could not be perceived through comprehension or the "delivery" of information:

> Not by a description and explanation of a pair of shoes actually present; not by a report about the process of making shoes; and also not by the observation of the actual use of shoes occurring here and there; but only by bringing ourselves before Van Gogh's painting. This painting spoke...The artwork lets us know what shoes are in truth . . . The Greeks called the unconcealment of beings aleithia. We say "truth" and think little enough in using this word. (Heidegger 1936/1977: 161)

Neither science nor experience can reveal the shoes to us. Science might proceed with "the relevant chemistry of leather" but the result is "a dead abstraction" and equally inadequate is experience that "uses the object of its insight"; arguably, then "only art lets – be" for it is only "in and through the painting (that) the pair of shoes achieve a total, autonomous being per se" (Steiner 1987: 134). If Heidegger's reading of the work of art is applied to the reading of the sacred text it is clear that "experiencing the text" is utterly "integral to the work of biblical interpretation" for unless our response "ends in appropriation it remains peculiarly sterile and lifeless" (Schneiders 1991: 173). The reader needs to allow the text to "project a new world in which a greater fullness of being is possible for the one who comes to inhabit it" so that his or her own "horizon of existence is expanded by merging with that of the text" (Schneiders 1991: 172).

The Redefinition of Reading and its Spiritual Consequences

Regrettably, the reading currently promoted by the UK government is far from the sort that constitutes the *lectio divina* described by Palmer or that which might evoke the aesthetic response depicted by Heidegger. The National Literacy Strategy (NLS / DfEE, 1998) is transforming reading across the curriculum in both primary and secondary schools and is founded upon the "functional grammar", expounded by linguists such as Halliday (1978), Kress (1989), Littlefair (1991; 1992) and Derewianka (1990). The simplicity (and attraction to managerialists) of the model of language underpinning the NLS is that a text is as it is because of what it has to do. There is consequently a heavy emphasis upon knowing the conventions of certain non-fiction text-types and on reading with a text's function and purpose in mind. All this is rather utilitarian and simply misses the point when it comes to aesthetic response and spiritual development, which is individual and idiosyncratic and cannot be precisely planned.

Such an approach is not only prevalent in the UK where teachers want to foster "personal growth" (Pike 2002b) but also prevalent in other nations such as South Africa where there is an inherent tension between teachers' desires to foster aesthetic response, what might be described as a spirituality of reading, and the need to teach towards "pre-determined outcomes...to pinpoint the exact nature and parameters of a particular response" and to "fragment it into a discrete unit of competence or knowledge" (van Renen 2003: ii). Evidently, there are "aspects of the spiritual that cannot be 'managed'" (Langford 2001: 6) and defy measurement. The reason for this shift away from the sort of literary reading, that has the potential to foster personal and aesthetic response as well as spiritual and moral development, is worth considering; one view, shared by many, is that it is "to enhance our economic perfor- mance" (Marshall 1998: 109). As well as transforming reading, this ideology is altering the nature of literature teaching (Pike 2003g).

Explicitness in teaching is now often seen as a panacea for all perceived pedagogic ills but the government's prescribed treatment may have very grave side effects upon children's aesthetic and spiritual response. Heavy doses of explicitness, regularly administered, can deprive children of the "gaps" and "indeterminacy" in which they can spiritually flourish. Robbing children of such gaps in lessons could well result in their failure to thrive spiritually.

The National Literacy Strategy in England, in the form of the *Framework for teaching English: Years 7, 8 and 9* promotes teaching that is "direct and explicit" (DfEE 2001: 16) and the simplicity of this ideology is apparent in the admission that the "implications…for lesson organ- ization are few, but very significant: more explicit teaching" (DfEE 2001: 17). We are told that "explicit attention to language learning" (DfEE 2001: 66) will be of great benefit and the "transfer of skills from one lesson to another" must be "part of the explicit teaching agenda in all lessons" (DfEE 2001: 15) as objectives "benefit from being explicitly taught and from being identified" (DfEE 2001: 11). The whole emphasis on the explicit is problematic from the standpoint of spiritual education and we need to ensure that its converse, the implicit, is not marginal- ized (Pike, 2003c).

If a distinctive feature of any literary text is that it has gaps in it we need to realize that lessons are texts that children read too. By increasing the degree of explicitness in the lesson, and focussing on knowing and applying the conventions of different text-types rather than what a poem makes a reader feel, the nature of the space inhabited by learners is radically altered. The fewer the gaps the lesson supplies, or the more routinized they are, the less personally involved and spiritually respon- sive the learner may become. Having the right sort of gaps or spaces in lessons is a precondition for spiritual response. Like the literary text, the lesson needs to provide a degree of implicitness that allows the reader to make it his or her own.

Belief as an Obstacle to Reading:
The Case of the Bible?

Not only is the culture of reading in school often somewhat antithetical to spiritual development, the cultural, religious and literary status of the Bible can militate against it being the "stimulus" for spiritual and moral development. Arguably, the Bible, which is neglected to a great extent

in our schools (Wachlin 1997; Francis 2000; Pike 2002c), is rarely read for
the spiritual experience it can provide and a range of beliefs appear to
account for its neglect (Pike 2003e). Personal response approaches
commonly employed with other texts, especially poetry, that are read
in school are rarely applied to the reading of the Bible. The "special difficulty" of the Bible within education may still be that it is the subject of
"on the one hand, feeling and belief, on the other hand, disbelief and
indifference" (Newbolt 1921: 34).

A way forward would appear to be to promote the activities that have
been so successful with other canonical works that have almost "religious" status. Approaches to Shakespeare teaching and other
pre-twentieth century authors (Pike 2000a; 2003b) could be used with
the Bible as they share a common emphasis on the experience of the
reader. Indeed, one of the "great functions of literature for the young is
to give them models of life which both deepen the experience they have
and suggest explore, ranges of experience they don't have" (Byatt 1998:
45). Reading a literary work, such as the Bible, is entirely different from,
and ultimately more valuable than, any other type of reading because,
unlike other forms, it "diverges from the real experiences of the reader
in that it opens up perspectives in which the empirically known world
of one's own personal experience appears changed" (Iser 1971: 8).

Aligning the Bible with the literary heritage within successive
National Curriculum documents in the UK may, paradoxically, not
have done the Bible any favours. The high status of such heritage works
can lead to a too reverential attitude among readers who become passive
and feel they need to be told the text's meaning rather than constructing
their own interpretation of it (Pike 2000a). Further, locating a text such
as the Bible within "heritage literature" situates it, in the perception of
many teachers of literature, at the opposite end of the reading spectrum
to the sort of literature that can foster "personal growth" (Pike 2002b)
and this perception can result in resistance.

The teaching of the Bible and other classic works should focus on the
potential of such texts for fostering the spiritual, aesthetic, imaginative
and creative lives of students (Pike 2003f). That the Bible is never read
by two-thirds of thirteen to fifteen year olds in secondary schools in the
UK cannot be justified (Francis 2000: 165). Even when the Bible is
studied it is often as an information text rather than as one which can
foster spiritual development. In many classrooms art and literature
often "replace written biblical revelation to interpret life for us"
(Seerveld 1995: 33) and yet the Bible *is* art and literature and can be
responded to as such. That the Bible should be neglected "at the sharp
edge of schooling, where matters of power, self identity, gender and all
questions of the greatest importance in our social and political lives are
to be found" (Jasper 1999: 14) is a situation requiring urgent redress.

A Pedagogy for Biblical Reading that Fosters Spiritual Growth

The kind of teaching that legitimates personal response, and is especially valuable when children are reading the Bible, is informed by reader response theory (Tompkins 1980; Freund 1987), the broad range of literary perspectives which have in common an emphasis upon the experience of the reader. For Rosenblatt, a leading reader response theorist, aesthetic reading occurs when "the reader's primary purpose is fulfilled during the reading event, as he (sic) fixes his attention on the actual experience he is living through" (Rosenblatt 1978: 27). In other words, the reader applies the literary work to his or her own life and responds to the text as a "stimulus"; such reading is vital as it activates "elements of the reader's past experience" (Rosenblatt 1978: 11).

Influenced by reader response theory, a number of biblical scholars have advocated the importance of personal interpretation. Clines' position is that if we are to take the existence of the Bible seriously in the modern world we should concentrate on "what people are making of the Bible, what reception it is receiving, how it is being understood, what it is capable of meaning to real live people" (Clines 1997: 17) and Powell points out that "literature that is worth reading transcends contextual interests specific to its production" because "texts come to mean things their authors did not consciously intend" (Powell 2001: 3). Arguably, we should focus upon what the Bible *means* rather than exclusively upon what it *meant*.

A "deeper encounter with the Bible" (Shortt and Smith 2002: 167) is possible if the reader is freed to respond individually to the biblical text so that it can become personally relevant. Yet, the study of the Bible in many classrooms may rely too exclusively on the telling of Bible stories which "have remained with us in a quite unconnected way – unconnected , that is, both from each other and from the stuff of our own lives" (Cox 2001: 41). Personal response is undoubtedly open to abuse but we should consider what the alternative is: for dependant readers always to be told what the text means by someone else?

It has, however, been argued that there is a "price to be paid" for fostering active reading and personal response and that reader response theory depends upon a conception of texts as "open" rather than "closed" as the reader only becomes more active "at the price of permitting less clarity and wider boundaries of possible meaning" (Thiselton 1992: 153). Thiselton's view that a text can "achieve greater force" and permit "greater engagement" only "at the price of a degree of ambiguity" can be problematized because the engagement of the reader may stem, not from *interpretation* alone but from *application*. Engagement can be fostered when a text is perceived to be personally relevant and is *applied* to the reader's own situation. The aesthetic distance can be between the experience of the reader and his or her expectations of and response to the text.

Approaches informed by reader response theory include the annotation of the biblical passage as a "stimulus" initially so that readers are encouraged to engage personally with the passage by noting what they think and feel in response to the words. Following such annotation in response to text as "stimulus", journal entries can be kept to accompany particular texts so that the development of the child's responses over time and throughout successive engagements can be witnessed. How the text is applied personally can be the basis of these journal entries and such activity ensures the relevance of the text is perceived by the reader.

Reading and Responding to the Bible at Bradford Christian School

According to Schneiders (1991), understanding meaning as *appropriation* involves more than "aesthetic surrender" and requires a personal engagement with the truth-claims of a text:

> the interpretation by which we appropriate the meaning of the text by a fusion of horizons with the world the text projects, is essentially an enterprise within the area of spirituality, that is, of the conscious effort toward life – integration through self-transcendence toward the horizon of ultimate value. (Schneiders 1991: 174)

As the New Testament addresses questions of ultimate significance and its truth claims offer us away of being I decided to investigate the reading of the Bible in a Christian school with an unmistakeable sense of itself as a spiritual community. Bradford Christian School is one of the new Christian schools in the UK (Walford 1994). Its pupils come from forty different churches as well as non-church attending families and the Bible has a central place in the life of the school. For instance, I observed a Year 7 (aged 11) class being registered and participating in their daily devotional which was on the subject of not worrying (Luke 12: 22–6). The teacher asked children what they worried about so that there was an immediate connection between the world of the text and that of the reader and they were responding to the text as "stimulus". One boy described his worries about a science test and another pupil, a girl, said she was worried about their home (it was being renovated, her father was "grumpy" and a kitchen was due to be delivered while she was at school!). As well as entering into the text personally the teacher focussed on the truth claims of the text and explained that a relationship with and faith in God was required if they were to be able to trust him with the issues troubling them. In a similar way, the Headteacher's Barmitzvah project with Year 8 focuses on key biblical characters who had to change and face challenges because children at this age, in particular, are rapidly changing and have many challenges to face.

As the "existential question raised by the New Testament about Jesus is whether or not he is the Messiah, the Son of God, the Saviour of the world" (Schneiders 1991: 173) and the response of a reader to this question is likely to influence their reading, I wanted to see how readers in such a Christian school would respond to biblical texts I had selected. After reading a paper I had written in an English journal advocating the greater use of the Bible as literature in schools (Pike 2002c) the headteacher invited me to take a Year 11 class. My aim was to foster an "aesthetic" and personal reading of biblical texts by encouraging readers to respond to the text as a "stimulus". Such an approach was, in any case, congruent with the ethos of the school where children are encouraged to apply the Bible to their lives.

Sitting around a table with half a dozen Year 11 pupils I explained that I wanted them to annotate the biblical passage, but that the aim was not to focus on genre, rhetoric, style or literary features but simply on what it meant to them. One of the selected extracts was from I Corinthians 13:

> Though I speak with the tongues of men and angels, and have not charity, I am become as sounding brass, or a tinkling cymbal. And though I have the gift of prophecy, and understand all mysteries, and all knowledge; and though I have all faith, so that I could remove mountains, and have not charity, I am nothing. And though I bestow all my goods to feed the poor, and though I give my body to be burned, and have not charity, it profiteth me nothing. Charity suffereth long and is kind, charity envieth not; charity vaunteth not itself, is not puffed up, doth not behave itself unseemly, seeketh not her own, is not easily provoked, thinketh no evil; rejoiceth not in iniquity, but rejoiceth in the truth; beareth all things, believeth all things, hopeth all things, endureth all things, charity never faileth.

Many of the initial annotations to text as "stimulus" that students made were no different from those I would have expected from reasonably mature, well adjusted children of any religious persuasion (or none at all) in any state school classroom in which I had taught. For instance, after focussing on giving one's goods to the poor but not having "charity" one girl wrote "you can't just do things that look good – you gotta do things for love". Another passage chosen was from the fourth chapter of Paul's epistle to the Phillipians:

> Rejoice in the Lord always: and again I say, rejoice. Let your moderation

be known unto all men. The Lord is at hand. Be careful for nothing; but in every thing by prayer and supplication with thanksgiving let your requests be made known unto God. And the peace of God, which passeth all understanding, shall keep your hearts and minds through Christ Jesus. Finally, brethren, whatsoever things are true, whatsoever things are honest, whatsoever things are just, whatsoever things are pure, whatsoever things are of good report; if there be any virtue, and if there be any praise, think on these things. (Philippians 4: 4–7)

These sixteen year old students annotated the text as "stimulus", and jotted down how it applied to them. One girl commented on the second half of the extract above, the exhortation to dwell on "whatsoever things are of good report" by noting "Don't have bad thoughts about anything or anyone – always think on the good things...don't always be negative'". Another reader realized that her friend possessed fine attributes and also less desirable qualities and found in the text encouragement to see the best in her: "I really need to concentrate on the good factors of her, not the bad". Another reader, a student who had confided in me that she lacked confidence when I had visited previously, applied aspects of the latter half of the passage to herself and not to others; the admonition to focus on the "true", "honest", "just'" and "good" was related to the way she saw herself as she wrote "don't focus on the bad – low self worth and esteem – focus on the good things about yourself".

An added dimension was apparent, however, in the responses of most of these readers that one would not expect to find to such a degree in a state school. As well as engaging in "aesthetic reading" and applying the texts to their own lives they also engaged with the truth-claims of the texts and participated in what might be termed specifically "Christian" reading. One girl responded to "the Lord is at hand" by writing "He is near to me" and to "by prayer and supplication" with the comment "keep lines of communication open". She responded to "peace of God" with the affirmation "He knows the situation, his hand is upon it and he gives me a peace I can't comprehend". Similarly, another reader responded to the same phrase "the Lord is at hand" by writing "whenever I need him I can talk to him" and referred to a medical matter concerning a friend which she had faith would be resolved. This was reading in line with a clear faith-commitment. One girl wrote next to the first passage's final declaration that love never fails, "God and love are the only things that I can really rely on...everything, for me, comes back to God and love".

Conclusion

Even among these readers who shared the same faith-commitment, *application* was an individual matter. One reader was stimulated to think about her relationship with a boyfriend, another reflected on conflict with parents, another on a friend's medical condition and another on her relationship with God. The approach of allowing young readers to respond to the biblical text as "stimulus" and to make time for this would appear, however, to be equally applicable in state schools because the reader is given the opportunity to respond to the text and to relate it to his or her life in whatever way and at whatever level he or she chooses. Such an approach is sensitive to a mixed audience in terms of beliefs, spiritual commitment and orientation. Differentiation by outcome is built into teaching which privileges the unique nature of personal, aesthetic and spiritual response and does not seek to legislate or to enforce conformity.

By giving children the opportunity to read the Bible as a "stimulus" and to respond personally ensures that individuality is respected (Pike 2000d). Many readers responded devotionally in the lesson I taught but others simply responded to a moral message. Promoting the reading of the Bible as a "stimulus" is so valuable because it "permits students to have a spiritual encounter but does not force them to do so" (Pike 2003c). Reading a biblical text as a "stimulus" connects the text with readers' experiences so that it becomes relevant to all and spiritually significant for some. The equivalent of reading the biblical text as a "stimulus" would be to take children around an art gallery or sculpture park and to encourage them to stop and stare. Some may have fully fledged aesthetic encounters where a work of art becomes significant and is applied personally, which happens when some readers read the Bible, but others would not. The distance travelled during the spiritual journey can help bring about profound horizonal change. Our task is to provide the opportunity for especially significant long-distance travel.

References

Bible, the Authorized Version 1611. Cambridge: Cambridge University Press.
Byatt, A. S. 1998: Hauntings. In B. Cox (ed.), *Literacy Is Not Enough – Essays on the importance of reading.* Manchester: Manchester University Press, 41–6.
Clines, D. J. A. 1997: *The Bible and the Modern World.* Sheffield: Sheffield Academic Press.
Cox, R. 2001: Using the Bible with Children. *Journal of Education and Christian Belief* 5 (1).
Derewianka, B. 1990: *Exploring How Texts Work NSW.* Australia: PETA.

DfEE 2001: *Key Stage 3 National Strategy: Framework for teaching English: Years 7, 8 and 9.* London: HMSO.

DfEE 1998: *The National Literacy Strategy.* London: HMSO.

Francis, L.J. 2000: Who reads the Bible? A study among 13–15 year olds. *British Journal of Religious Education* 22(3).

Freund E. 1987: *The Return of the Reader: Reader-response criticism.* London & New York: Methuen.

Halliday, M. 1978: *Language as Social Semiotic.* London: Edward Arnold.

Heidegger, M. 1936/1977: The Origin of the Work of Art. In David Krell (ed.), *Martin Heidegger: Basic Writings.* London: Routledge.

Iser, W. 1971: Indeterminacy and the Reader's Response in Prose Fiction. In J. Hillis Miller (ed.), *Aspects of Narrative: Selected papers from the English Institute.* New York: Columbia University Press, 1–45.

Kress, G. 1989: *Linguistic Processes in Sociocultural Practice.* Oxford: Oxford University Press.

Jasper, D. 1999: How Can We Read the Bible? In L. Gearon (ed.), *English Literature, Theology and the Curriculum.* London: Cassell.

Jauss, H. R. 1982: *Toward an Aesthetic of Reception.* Minneapolis: University of Minnesota Press.

Langford, M. 2001: Is education for spirituality compatible with a managerial approach to schooling? *Prospero* 7 (2), 3–7.

Littlefair, A. 1991: *Reading All Types of Writing.* Milton Keynes: Open University Press.

Littlefair, A. 1992: Reading and Writing Across the Curriculum. In C. Harrison and M. Coles (eds.), *The Reading for Real Handbook.* London: Routledge.

Marshall, B. 1998: English Teachers and the Third Way. In B. Cox (ed.), *Literacy Is Not Enough: Essays on the importance of reading.* Manchester: Manchester University Press, 109–15.

Newbolt Committee 1921: *The Teaching of English in England.* London: HMSO.

Palmer, P. J. 1993: *To Know as We are Known: A Spirituality of Education.* New York: HarperCollins.

Pike, M. A. 2000a: Keen Readers: adolescents and pre-twentieth century poetry. *Educational Review* 52 (1), 13–28.

Pike, M. A. 2000b: Pupils Poetics. *Changing English – studies in reading and culture,*7(1), 45– 54.

Pike, M. A. 2000c: Spirituality, Morality and Poetry *International Journal of Children's Spirituality* 5(2), 177–92.

Pike, M. A. 2000d: Boys, Poetry and the Individual Talent. *English in Education* 52(1), 41–52.

Pike, M. A. 2001 Adolescents as Active Readers in NFER (ed.), *TOPIC (Practical Applications of Research in Education),* 26. Slough, NFER.

Pike, M. A. 2002a: Aesthetic Distance and the Spiritual Journey: Educating for Morally and Spiritually Significant Events across the Art and Literature Curriculum *International Journal of Children's Spirituality* 7(1), 9–21.

Pike, M.A . 2002b: Action Research and English Teaching: ideology, pedagogy and personal growth, *Educational Action Research* 10(1), 27–44.

Pike, M. A. 2002c: The Most Wanted Text in the West: Rewards Offered for Reading the Bible as Literature. *The Use of English,* 54. 29–42.

Pike, M. A. 2003a: The Bible and the Reader's Response, *Journal of Education and Christian Belief* 7(1), 37–52

Pike, M. A. 2003b: The canon in the classroom: students' experiences of texts from other times. *Journal of Curriculum Studies* 35(3), 335–70.

Pike, M. A. 2003c From the Picture to the Diagram? Literacy and the Art of English Teaching. *The Use of English* 54(3), 211–16.

Pike, M. A. 2003d: From Social to Personal Transaction: A Model of Aesthetic Reading in the Classroom, *Journal of Aesthetic Education* 37(2), 61–72

Pike, M. A. 2003e: Belief as an Obstacle to Reading: The Case of the Bible? *Journal of Beliefs and Values* 24(2), 155–63.

Pike, M. A. 2003f On Being in English Teaching: a time for Heidegger? *Changing English – studies in reading and culture* 10(1), 91–99

Pike, M. A. 2003g: *Teaching Secondary English.* London: Paul Chapman Publishing/Sage.

Powell, M. A. 2001: *Chasing the Eastern Star – adventures in reader response criticism.* Louisville, Kentucky: Westminster John Knox Press.

Rosenblatt, L. 1978: *The Reader, The Text, The Poem: The Transactional Theory of the Literary Work.* Carbondale: Southern Illinois University Press.

Schneiders, S. . 1991: *The Revelatory Text – Interpreting the New Testament as Sacred Scripture.* New York: HarperCollins.

Seerveld, C. 1995: *A Christian Critique of Art and Literature.* Iowa: Dordt College Press, Sioux Center.

Shortt, J and Smith, D. 2002: *The Bible and the Task of Teaching.* Nottingham: The Stapleford Centre.

Steiner, G. 1987: *Martin Heidegger.* Chicago: University of Chicago Press.

Thiselton, A.C. 1992: *New Horizons in Hermeneutics: The Theory and Practice of Transforming Biblical Reading.* Grand Rapids, Michigan: Zondervan Publishing House.

Tompkins, J. 1980: *Reader-Response Criticism.* Baltimore, Maryland: Johns Hopkins University Press.

van Renen C. G. 2003: *Reader Response Approaches to Literature Teaching in a South African OBE Environment.* EdD thesis submitted to the University of Port Elizabeth.

Walford, G. 1994: Weak Choice, Strong Choice and the New Christian Schools. In J. M. Halstead (ed.), *Parental Choice and Education: Principles, policy and practice.* London: Kogan Page, 139–50.

Chapter 13

The Spiritual Dimension of the Curriculum: What are school inspectors looking for and how can we help them find it?

Jack Priestley

IT IS A COMMON ASSUMPTION that any talk of the spiritual is likely to be vague and woolly. There is substance to such a charge for reasons which I shall come to when we look at the whole vexed question of definitions but let me begin by drawing attention to the wording of the title. The key word is "dimension". A dimension is simply an aspect of measurement. It is not an addition to what is already there. I think it is important to make this point right at the beginning because teachers, understandably, are only too ready to react negatively to yet more imposition upon them in terms of curriculum scope and content.

It is, I think, significant that this word "spiritual" has come to the fore again in recent years despite attempts in some quarters to ridicule it (see Flew and Naylor 1996). It is also significant that it would appear to have replaced a term which became very commonplace for a number of years. I refer to that rather dismissive phrase, "the hidden curriculum" – a vague and rather sneering acknowledgement that there was something buzzing around but we could not be bothered to determine what it was. To talk of the spiritual is much more positive and starts to pull back into the light of day something which has been around within educational language in England and Wales for a long time.

In English and Welsh education it is normal to refer back to the Preamble of the 1944 Education Act as the start of the use of the word in the oft quoted sentence, "It shall be the duty of the Local Education Authority so far as its power extends to provide for the spiritual, moral, mental and physical development of the community." In fact R. A.

Butler, the Minister of Education at the time, was merely continuing an emphasis begun by his predecessor H. A. L. Fisher in 1917 when introducing what was to become the 1918 Education Act. I think it is worth quoting the passage from his speech to Parliament on that occasion.

> We assume that education should be the education of the whole man [sic.], spiritually, intellectually and physically, and it is not beyond the resources of civilisation to devise a scheme of education possessing certain common qualities . . . from which the whole youth of the country, male and female, may derive benefit. We assume that the principles upon which well-to-do parents proceed in the education of their families are valid; also *mutatis mutandis* for the families of the poor; that the State has need to secure for its juvenile population conditions under which mind, body and character may be harmoniously developed. (Maclure 1968: 175)

Two things immediately emerge. First, the emphasis, both in 1917 and 1944, came out of a context of war and real threats to national survival. Secondly, the notion of the spiritual was linked to those of civilization and character. If there was a danger point when this emphasis might have been lost it was in the more light-hearted days of the 1960s and 70s when there were serious efforts within the Department of Education and Science to replace "spiritual" with "social", a move ultimately frustrated by the RE inspectorate. Thanks to that initiative the word remained firmly embedded in the 1988 Education Reform Act and on through to the present day.

Teacher Anxieties

But, of course, any such new initiative or resurgence of emphasis on some neglected aspect of education is bound to be yet another cause of teacher anxiety. The profession has been assaulted as never before in recent years with initiatives of every sort. There are now whole battalions of people sitting in government offices dreaming up new initiatives for schools. Is this just one more? What are the main anxieties?

Elaine McCreery (2000), of Manchester Metropolitan University, has produced a study on just this topic in a piece of doctoral research which she undertook in West London while working at the University of Surrey, Roehampton. As a part of that study she asked teachers about their anxieties and perceptions of this new emphasis on the spiritual. The results, although not altogether surprising, benefit from being well researched and documented.

First among the anxieties is that of a lack of definition. How can there be informed discussion if we cannot say what it is that we are talking about? And how can we evaluate what we are doing if we do not really know what is being looked for?

Secondly, and closely related to that, Dr McCreery has documented the evidence for the almost total lack of any attempt to deal with this subject in teacher training. Her findings bear out personal experience. In my own university, for example, the spiritual dimension of education gets an allocation of exactly half an hour in a lecture delivered to the whole postgraduate course at the end of the year. I know because I have been asked to do it. I also know that it is a full thirty minutes more than some other training institutions offer.

Thirdly, and perhaps more surprisingly, Elaine McCreery also discovered that older teachers were more comfortable with the concept of the spiritual than younger ones. The question then arises as to whether that is because of maturity or because of cultural changes over a generation? Anxiety comes about, she also discovered, not just from feelings of ignorance but also from feelings of it being at heart an intensely personal thing, causing wariness because expression of it might be potentially divisive in the staffroom.

However, not all reactions are negative. Some teachers see in the concept an enhancing of their own status, a recognition that teachers are not only human beings as well but that, being seen as spirited themselves, was perhaps an acknowledgement that they retain their age old power to adapt or even sabotage anything that comes down from a higher authority.

Elaine McCreery's study showed also one final important consideration for my purposes, namely, that whilst class teachers automatically turn their attention to their pupils, heads and deputies incline towards relating the concept to the idea of the whole school. For them it becomes an essential part of the whole philosophy of education. Perhaps somewhere in the muddle of groping for the meaning of this word "spiritual" there is an unconscious indication that there is a muted rebellion against the 1980s' removal of philosophical and historical content from the professional training of teachers and that they are no longer content to be seen merely as curriculum delivery agents.

Two more questions with which I want to deal also arise implicitly out of this sort of enquiry. "Spiritual development" is a nice phrase, for example, but "development to what end?" is a key question. Where are the models and who determines them? And secondly there is the vexed question of assessment. How does one measure this thing called the spiritual? Surely it is not quantifiable in the way all our other forms of assessment are.

The Demands of School Inspectors

What is it then that school inspectors say they are looking for? In England and Wales it is no secret. It is quite explicitly stated in the official Handbooks. Let me quote extensively from page 71 of the *Handbook For Inspecting Primary and Nursery School* (Ofsted 1999) given under the heading, "How the school cultivates pupils' personal – including spiritual, moral, social and cultural – development."

> Although each aspect of spiritual, moral, social and cultural development can be viewed separately, the provision is likely to be interconnected and your evaluation should reflect this.
>
> A good deal of your evidence in this section will come from your classroom observations. You need to be alert to situations which contribute . . . so that you have a range of examples for possible inclusion in the written report.
>
> Assess how well the staff provide opportunities that help pupils explore the values of others. Young children will only be able to develop insights into the values and beliefs of others if their own ideas are valued by their peers, parents and teachers. As they get older, acceptance of these ideas continues in importance and spreads across all aspects of the curriculum, for example in stories, drama, art, music, history and religious education.

It seems, at first sight, quite clear and straightforward but the more we examine it the more we become aware that there is a significant degree of hesitancy about some of the phrases used and some comment is called for.

First, we note that, "the provision is likely to be interconnected", for it is seen as bound up with other aspects such as the moral, social and cultural, which themselves are all regarded as being within the overall concept of personal development. This serves to reinforce the point I made at the beginning that the spiritual is not to be regarded as an entity in itself. It is not another bit of stuff to be taught, another lump of curriculum to be delivered. It can be "viewed separately" but it is within the person – the pupil, the student or the teacher – and it may well be that we notice it most of all when it is absent as when a sports' commentator talks of "a spiritless performance".

Secondly, we are told that the "evidence will come from your classroom observations" and that you will need to be alert to "situations which contribute". I deduce two things from this passage, each of which seems to me to be perfectly valid. In the first instance we are being told that such evidence as we can produce will very likely be subjective in nature. By contrast our modern scientific culture increasingly demands that only objective evidence is valid. Here no such assumption is made and the inspectors are to be commended for acknowledging the fact.

Thirdly, we are asked to be alert to "situations which contribute". In short this is a recognition that we are operating in the realm of indirect rather than direct communication, a point which seems to be expanded upon in the third paragraph which talks of assessing teachers' abilities to provide opportunities for helping pupils to "explore the values of others" through taking seriously "their own ideas" in the first instance. This is an extremely subtle process in which we all engage but which we rarely make explicit. Again, it is to acknowledge something which seems to run counter to the dominant forces of our modern Western culture. We like to think that our communications with each other are essentially direct and factual. But is that really the case? Most of our communication with one another, I would suggest, is indirect and conducted not by fact, but by metaphor, narrative, gesture, body language and a whole range of devices which we both have to learn for ourselves and to recognize in others.

The section goes on to acknowledge that, in curriculum terms, such indirect forms are the stuff of story (note our current obsession with soap operas), drama, art, music and history. And then is added "religious education". I find that very interesting. I have no doubt that religious communication is indeed a classic example of all that I have referred to above but it is also the case that many exponents of RE are constantly falling over backwards to make their subject acceptable in terms of direct communication with emphasis on what they term the "phenomenological" and have consequently loosened the ties with story, drama, art and music. In short, if these forms really do characterize the spiritual dimension then it is arguable that much explicit religious education has become as de-spiritualized as other parts of the curriculum.

I want, then, to try and develop these ideas by asking two key questions. What form does development take in the case of this spiritual dimension and why do we have such difficulty in defining what we mean by the spiritual?

Development

The words "develop" and "developing" are everywhere to be found in contemporary educational literature, so much so that we rarely hesitate to think about what the words convey. In fact, as I have written elsewhere (Priestley 2000a), they are relatively modern words, unused before the beginning of the nineteenth century or the late eighteenth at the earliest. Prior to that the word only appeared in its past participle form, "developed". We still use it that way when we talk of having a film developed. It is the opposite of "enveloped" and simply means, "to show what is there or is hidden".

Writing from an Indian context and in a book which is full of insights into this whole subject of the spiritual dimension of education Jane Sahi expands on this very point,

> Development also suggests growth from below, not fashioned from without. The word "development" in its older usage was understood as the opposite of envelopment. It meant "to unwrap" or to "lay open by removal of that which enfolds". In other words it is to reveal more of that which exists. This suggests a process of reaching down, in order to reach out, not unlike the relation of the depth of the roots to the height of the branches. (Sahi 2000: 36)

It is from the relatively new disciplines of psychology and economics that modern educationists have borrowed their usage of the word and with it the strong, and totally unwarranted, assumptions of constant improvement. That is particularly the case with economists who regard any developing economy as synonymous with one which is improving. Psychologists use the term much more guardedly but because educationists deal predominantly with the young the same positive value judgements become assumed. Intelligence, conceptualization and so on "develop" from childhood to adulthood but equally, for a psychologist, dementia, Alzheimer's and a host of other diseases often "develop" at the other end of the life cycle: educationists, even those nowadays priding themselves on "life long learning", simply ignore those particular connotations where "development" implies mental and conceptual decline.

When we come to the whole notion of spiritual development we would do well to be particularly cautious. For there is a whole school of thought throughout English literature which bears witness not so much to spiritual enrichment as to decline and deterioration with the ageing process, beginning in childhood. And I suspect that with a moment's reflection many teachers would acknowledge it from their own experience. Let me give just three examples.

Those who are familiar with the poetry of Wordsworth will immediately recognize that in two of his best known and major works he records his own inner growth at great length and in unusual depth. I refer, of course, to *The Prelude* and to his *Ode on the Intimations of Immortality*. To quote some random lines from the latter:

> There was a time when meadow, grove and stream,
> The earth and every common sight,
> To me did seem
> Apparelled in celestial light,
> The glory and the freshness of a dream.

It is not now as it hath been of yore;-
Turn wheresoe'er I may,
By night or day,
The things that I once saw I now can see no more.

The Rainbow comes and goes,
And lovely is the Rose,
The Moon doth with delight
Look round her when the heavens are bare,
Waters on a starry night
Are beautiful and fair;
The sunshine is a glorious birth;
And yet I know, where'er I go,
That there hath past away a glory from the earth.

In the fifth stanza he plots the progress (another word we have loaded with ideas of improvement in recent years) of this decline.

Shades of the prison-house begin to close
Upon the growing boy,
But he beholds the light and whence it flows,
He sees it in his joy:
The Youth, who daily farther from the east
Must travel, still is Nature's Priest,
And by his vision splendid
Is on his way attended:
At length the Man perceives it die away,
And fade into the light of common day.

Clearly what he is giving voice to here is the experience of regression from childhood, not of any sort of advancement. Edwin Muir (1938) states the same experience very directly when he says,

A child has a picture of human existence peculiar to himself [sic] which he probably never remembers after he has lost it: the original vision of the world.

It was Edward Robinson who used those words *The Original Vision* (1977) as the title for his book containing the results of a large scale research project which demonstrated the sustaining power of early childhood insights of this sort in many lives. That vision, Muir suggests, contains for the child, "a completer harmony of all things with each other than he will ever know again."

Finally, from my own experience (Priestley 1990) let me try very briefly to describe two inter-related incidents which I think add weight to this.

It began with a university seminar with second year undergraduates as part of a general course on religious education for non-specialists. I was trying to give examples of the nature of religious language and the dangers of literalism when dealing with various forms of mythology where fundamental religious and moral ideas are communicated through story. I took the Adam and Eve creation myth as an example. It was hard work but finally I prevailed upon them that no-one could possibly have assumed that any observer was there to write it down. Satisfaction, however, was short lived when, as we broke up, a student commented, "Well, it hardly matters anyway. If it's taken you an hour to persuade a class of undergraduates what hope do we have in persuading a class of seven year olds? We just can't use this sort of material with young children."

By pure chance, on the very next morning I was working with a class of seven year olds. They were in the middle of a project on India and I had been invited to tell them stories that Indian children would all know. Entering the classroom while the teacher was on playground duty I met with a surprise. The Indian scene which had been on the back wall during my previous visit had been removed. In its place was a large paper tree with a snake coiled through its branches and an unclothed man and woman half hidden behind them. As the children crowded in I just had time to say to the class teacher, "My students tell me this can't be done with young children". She laughed and told me to sit down and listen. The children immediately gave me a blow by blow account of the Genesis story interspersed with much laughter. I went on to tell the story of Rama and Sita, which we then acted out and they went out to play.

We went too, standing with our plastic coffee cups in the middle of the maelstrom of an infants' playground in a Devon village school. Suddenly we heard a shout and turned just in time to see a boy kick a girl in the shins and run off to be pursued by half a dozen girls. What happened next seemed, on reflection, to be of the greatest significance. As they chased around the perimeter of the playground the girls started to chant in unison, "You've got the snake; you've got the snake". One was sent over to tell Miss what had happened. As she turned away her final retort was, "He's bit the apple hasn't he Miss?"

The first point of significance is the obvious one. These children had clearly understood that story at a level which went deep below the literal and they had been able, without intellectual analysis, to transfer the imagery into a situation which was at one and the same time both different and similar. It was different in that it was not set in the ancient world but in the here and now, but it was similar in that it was within a concrete moral situation of "dos" and "don'ts". Told that you can do anything except eat the apple any young child knows full well that that is exactly what is going to happen. In exactly the same way when Sita is told not, under any circumstances, to step outside of the ring then they know that that is exactly what she is going to do. Such stories are not time and context bound; they are as timeless as the human spirit which both constructed them and is then instructed by them.

But the second point, although more speculative, is equally important as an educational insight. This incident happened eleven years ago. These seven year olds are now eighteen. Some of them may well be at university and training to become teachers. And I have little doubt that they will be telling some other lecturer that such stories cannot be told to young children either because the stories are "not true" or because infants cannot be expected to be able to understand what "they are really all about". In short, I am suggesting that within our present pseudo scientific culture we actually de-educate our young people in the whole matter of communicating spiritual, religious and moral ideas. And we do so on the basis of what we term "child development theories" which have been well enough tested in terms of mathematical and empirical knowledge, but about which assumptions that these apply equally to all sorts of other forms of knowledge have never been tested.

Definition

So far I have scrupulously avoided the subject of definition despite my full awareness that for most teachers this is a central issue and the most frequently asked question. We clamour after definition but on this particular subject many teachers feel that they themselves have been left to provide the answers. They have plenty of suggestions to make when asked. To select just four is to illustrate the point and also to demonstrate the widespread confusion which exists and which makes communication difficult. I have heard the spiritual variously defined recently as:

- The thoughtful awareness of an inner feature of human experience.
- The non-material dimension of life.
- A contrast with the temporal, physical and intellectual sides of life.
- Synonymous with religious faith.

The first three all have something of merit within them: with the fourth I have some problem, not, I must add, on the grounds that religious faith can exist without it but that it might be regarded as synonymous with it, thus excluding any possibility of its existence outside of a religious context.

The question I want to raise here, however, is much more basic. It is whether anything at all is really gained by any attempted definition. Of course, I recognize the felt need to draw the parameters in order to get a certain conceptual control simply to proceed. But I have long believed that that is best obtained by a cluster of descriptions rather than by striving for a clear definition. And my grounds for arguing that are quite simple. It is to look up the definition of the word "definition". The *Oxford English Dictionary* defines the verb "define" as, "determine the limits of; state exactly what (a thing) is." It goes on to define "definite" as "having fixed limits".

This, of course, is exactly what the spiritual is not. Jesus of Nazareth, for one, claimed that, "it bloweth where it listeth" (John 3: 8). To determine its limits is simply to remove its major characteristic, or to create a paradox like bottling the wind. To state exactly what the thing is is also to pre-suppose that it is a thing and we would be back again to the vexed notion of another bit of stuff to taught. Isn't the whole point of this phenomenon that it is present or absent in any thing but its presence is beyond the capability of all but a tiny proportion of human minds totally to separate it from whatever it is which carries it: that small band of people we call the mystics. For everyone else it is a dimension rather than a substance and we perceive it indirectly rather than directly?

Elsewhere (Priestley 1996: 1997), I have argued that we can proceed much more confidently with description than with definition. There are certain characteristics of the spiritual which we can, I think, all identify. Let me suggest six although the list can undoubtedly be added to. They are:

1   The spiritual is a broader concept than the religious. It was Alfred North Whitehead, a philosopher now almost forgotten in his native Britain, who described religion as "what the individual does with his own solitariness" (Whitehead 1927: 6). Derided at the time, his comment, nevertheless, points to the fact that all religions stem from the deep spiritual experience of a lone individual who communicated that experience through metaphorical language to others who found that it resonated with their experiences also.

2   The central, core attribute of the spiritual is that it is dynamic. The most common imageries of spirit are of wind, fire or running water. Movement is of the essence. We cannot bottle the wind nor, as Buddhists proclaim, can we step into the same water of a running stream twice.

3   The spiritual is connected with being – with what we are – not with what we know or what we can do. To assess someone's spirituality it is necessary to have recourse to biography.

4   An important aspect of the spiritual is that it has to do with what we might term 'utopias', with what we might become and not just with what we are.

5   The spiritual is both personal and communal but today it is the latter

which is more frequently acknowledged. Few question the use of the word in the context of "team spirit". Sport has taken over from religion as the sphere in which the word can be best used without embarrassment.

6   Spiritual and spirituality are holistic concepts. We live nowadays in societies which constantly demand of us that we separate out the entities of which both individuals and groups are comprised. Analysis demands fracture. A concern for the spiritual requires us to see whole beings and to respond to them with our own sense of wholeness.

I argue then for description rather than for definition because the very notion of definition contradicts some of these points. Definition is part of the very process of separation of the parts and by its very nature is static in order to exert a form of control. It murders to dissect.

Something for which life and movement are of the very essence can only be comprehended in terms of a process, not as a thing – another piece of curriculum stuff. So, David Tacey, in his book, *Re-Enchantment: The New Australian Spirituality* (2000) speaks of the spiritual dimension of education simply as "developing a sense of the sacred", communicating in a mere six words something very specific and central to the core activity of educating with this whole concept in mind.

Assessment

It leads us too, I think, to the question of assessment without which, it seems, nothing can be considered valid within today's curriculum considerations. Is the spiritual assessable and, if so, how does one go about it?

If we return to the considerations of school inspectors then we have to recall that they do not assess it within the context of teaching within the classroom. Rather they comment on the school's *provision* for it, by which I assume they mean its sensitivity and awareness of this dimension within the whole life of the school, including the classroom; perhaps even an acknowledgement that when it shows itself it is valued and responded to with approval.

However, such a statement only moves the question one stage further back. If inspectors have difficulty in assessing it why should teachers find it any easier? I think the answer lies in something which is at once very simple but at the same time quite profound. We now live in a culture which puts a high premium on being objective. It is what we proudly call being scientific. And we have been drilled in the associated methodologies to the point where it affects almost everything we do.

In curriculum terms it has come to mean that while we still recognize that there is something of a spectrum between the objective and the subjective those things at the objective end of the scale are given the highest rating. Those subjects, like mathematics and science on the one hand and the factual elements of, say, English on the other (spelling, grammar etc.) which are the most objective to assess because they are simple to measure, assume a greater importance than other things. A recent Methodist Report on Education makes the point very succinctly,

> There is an increasing and worrying tendency for that which is easily measurable to assume importance rather than finding ways of making that which is truly important in terms of individual personality and community, measurable. (Methodist Conference 1999: para. 4.9)

The spiritual is right at the other end of the spectrum. It is as subjective as pure science is objective and we should not apologize for that. The answer to the question of assessment is simply that it has to be essentially subjective. We balk at the very idea but I would suggest that a moment's thought helps us realize that most of life's big decisions are made that way, or, at least, require a large element of it, like choosing a partner or a career.

Moreover there are long-term precedents to go by. While the concept of spirituality is not confined to religion it is religious communities which have the longest practical tradition of coping with it. How do Jewish communities select a person to become a Rabbi? How do Sikhs decide who is worthy of bearing the title of Guru? How has the Christian Church created saints? As soon as we begin to unravel these questions we find that, while attempts are made to introduce an element of objectivity, decisions are generally based on judgement rather than proof, on a sequence of events or a whole life story rather than isolated facts.

Conclusion

It was Carl Jung who summarized the spiritual as "the principle which stands in opposition to matter, an immaterial form of existence" and suggested that its determining characteristic is that it is dynamic, the "classical antithesis of matter – the antithesis, that is, of stasis and inertia" (Jung 1937; 1982: 4).

In the same article Jung also comments that "only the psyche can penetrate the psyche" which is a way of saying that through our teaching, whatever its subject matter, we cannot help but meet our pupils at the basic level of our common humanity at the same time as we communicate the subject matter of the curriculum. Equally, the notion that only the psyche can penetrate the psyche demands of those of us who teach professionally that we recognize that the child or the student possesses an autonomous spirit from which we can learn. The enemy of the spiritual is cynicism and, as we all know, cynicism creeps in at a very young age in our contemporary materialistic society.

Finally, it is, I suggest, significant that Jung's comments are made in the context of an article on the importance of stories which our modern world tends to reduce to the category of entertainment only. The idea that they may teach us and may even teach us how to teach has become strange to us but it was in my own student days that I was first introduced to Morris West's novel *The Devil's Advocate* (West 1959: 1996) which I slowly came to realize attempts, through a process of indirect communication, to answer these very questions of what constitutes the spiritual and its assessibility.

The main character of the book is Blaise Meredith, a Roman Catholic priest based in the Vatican and bearing the title of Promoter of the Faith, known more popularly as the Devil's Advocate. His task is to examine submissions for candidates put forward for canonization and to offer a critique of the facts on which they are based. He has undertaken the task many times before but this account represents what will be his last case because the story begins with his own discovery that he himself has terminal cancer.

His first impulse is to reject the case but then the following exchange takes place, prompted by his Superior.

> I believe this experience may help you. It will take you out of Rome, to one of the most depressed areas of Italy. You will rebuild the life of a dead man from the evidence of those who lived with him – the poor, the ignorant, the dispossessed. You will live and talk with simple people. Among them perhaps you will find a cure for your own sickness of spirit.
>
> "What is my sickness, Eminence?" The pathetic weariness of the voice, the desolate puzzlement of the question, touched the old churchman to pity. He turned back from the window to see Meredith slumped forward in his chair, his face buried in his hands. He waited a moment, weighed his answer and then gave it gravely. "There is no passion in your life my son."

Or, as Søren Kierkegaard once caustically commented, "Take away passion from the thinker and what do you have? You have the university lecturer!"

References

Flew, A. and Naylor, F. 1996: *Spiritual Development and All That Jazz*. York: Campaign for Real Education, 18, Westlands Grove, Stockton Lane.

Grimmit, M. G. (ed.) 2001: *Pedagogies of Religious Education: Case Studies in the Research and Development of Good Practice in RE*. London: McCrimmons.

Jung, C. 1937: The Phenomenology of the Spirit in Fairy Tales. In B. Campbell (eds.), 1982, *Spirit and Nature: Papers from the Eranos Year Books*. Princeton, NJ: Princeton University Press.

McCreery, E. 2000: *Promoting Children's Spiritual Development in Education: A Review of the Literature and an Exploration of Teachers' Attitudes*. University of Surrey, Roehampton: Unpublished Ph.D. thesis.

Maclure, J.S. 1968: *Educational Documents: England and Wales 1816–1967*. Methuen: London.

Methodist Conference 1999: *The Essence of Education: A Report of the Methodist Conference 1999*. Peterborough: Methodist Publishing House.

Muir, E. 1938. *Autobiography*. London: Faber.

Ofsted, 1999: *Handbook for Inspecting Primary and Nursery Schools with guidance on self evaluation, effective from January 2000*. London: Her Majesty's Stationery Office.

Priestley, J. 1990: "I Was God Yesterday, Sir." in *Resource* 12 (3), 1–3: University of Warwick Institute of Education.

Priestley, J. 1996: *Spirituality in the Curriculum, The 1996 Hockerill Lecture*. Frinton-on-Sea, Essex: The Hockerill Education Foundation.

Priestley, J. 1997: Spirituality, Curriculum and Education. *The International Journal of Children's Spirituality* 2 (1), 23–34. (An abbreviated and edited version of the Hockerill Lecture above.)

Priestley, J. 2000a: The Moral and Spiritual Growth of Children. In J. Mills and R. Mills (eds.), *Childhood Studies: A Reader in Perspectives of Childhood*. London: Routledge.

Priestley, J. 2000b: Curriculum and Kierkegaard: Towards Creating a Paradigm for Discerning the Spiritual Dimension of Education. In R. Best (eds.), *Education for Spiritual, Moral, Social and Cultural Education*. London: Cassell.

Robinson, E. 1977: *The Original Vision*. Oxford: Manchester College.

Sahi, Jane. 2000: *Education and Peace*. Pune 411007, India: Vasant Palshikar.

West, M. 1959, 1996: *The Devil's Advocate*. London: Mandarin.

Chapter 14

Teachers' Values and Spiritualities: From Private to Public

MARK CHATER

Is it relevant and legitimate to explore teachers and their beliefs about their work, in the context of a discussion of children's spirituality? This chapter first offers a brief rationale for paying attention to teachers' spirituality, and argues for a spiritual and moral recognition of the difference teachers can make.

Next the chapter examines teachers' spiritualities at the outset and in the middle of their careers, through reference to two small projects and to the continuing tradition of research into teachers' narrative accounts of their work (Richardson 1990; Thomas 1995). There is a particular focus on those teachers whose priorities have been with an open-ended spiritual dimension to children's education and whose writing shows them to be open to their own spirituality. It raises recurring questions: why do teachers want to teach? In their interactions with children, what do they most profoundly value? What is the core of their educational values? What influence does the education system in which they work have on those core vales? How do teachers' values and spirituality, and especially their desire to teach, change from the beginning to the middle of their career?

The dominant education paradigm, that of improvement and effectiveness, is then analysed briefly for its ambiguous influence on teachers and their spirituality. Finally it is suggested that some teachers succeed in moving from relatively private spiritualities of personal vocation to relatively public spiritualities of profession, and that their narratives are highly valuable for the profession.

Why Address the Spirituality of Teachers as Part of a Discourse on Children's Spirituality?

Recurrent themes in the discourse on children's spirituality have raised these issues among others:

* The importance of the subjective – the need to recognize, celebrate and legitimate the subjective and experiential, in balance with the objective and cognitive;
* The importance of the subject–participant – the need to resist, and question, models of research which claim to be "clean" of affect or relationship;
* The primacy of the relational – as against, say, the abstract, the reified or the propositional, as ways of knowing; and therefore the importance of participating relationally;
* The tensions between tradition and experience;
* The damage wrought by a modernist education system, which is suspicious of us, which is the servant of global capital and which insists on structure, definition and control, all processes which eventually do violence to the spirit;
* The ambiguity of spirituality as something not always "nice", "wholesome", "constructive".

These themes show that children's spirituality casts a long shadow into the territory of pedagogics and educational policy. We need to pay attention to teachers, not only because they work with the children a lot of the time, but also because they can unlock the subjective in children, in their own selves and in their research about their work, but do not always do so; because they relate, and so influence; because, if our framework includes a recognition of issues of marginality, voice/voicelessness and power, teachers have these issues too; and because teachers are ambiguous, caught between the centrally-determined "truths" of knowledge as determined by the system and the diverse, creative needs and interests of the children on the other. Teachers wish to be answerable to both, or to one over the other. For all these reasons, teachers are relevant to children's spirits.

The Spirituality of Teachers' Vocation Discourses

I now turn to some contemporary evidence on how some teachers see themselves and their work. The first set of evidence is a compilation of conversations in interviews to select candidates for places on initial teacher training programmes, both undergraduate and postgraduate, in an English training college between 1995 and 2003. The recurrent responses to set questions designed to get them to explain their desire to teach ("why do you want to teach", or "why do you want to teach a particular subject?") are gathered and interpreted. Here I use, not the *ipsissima verba* of particular candidates, but composite statements which summarize the most recurrent points made, and phrases used, by the majority of successful candidates out of approximately 450 interviews over eight years. I offer this evidence as it shows intending teachers speaking, in a very specific moment, the selection interview, about their desire to teach. They are aware that the selection process is the gateway to the profession they seek to enter. This is therefore a moment in which they speak with candour and use language and ideas as articulately as they can. It is a moment of significance, in which they bring their personal aspirations and express them in ways that, they believe, will be approved of by the selectors. For these reasons, the discourse of the selection interview is particularly fruitful for indicating the spiritualities of teachers.

The first and most obvious message from these responses is the strongly recurrent sense of personal vocation, evidenced in responses such as

I love children.

Ever since I was little I have wanted to teach.

Seeing them [children] struggling to understand, and finally getting it, makes me feel as if I am doing something useful.

When I help them [children], and they turn and thank me, or they show me their work with pride, I feel as if I have done something really hugely important.

I feel that when they look back and remember how I helped, they'll remember me and appreciate me.

This type of discourse seems to remove teaching from the external to the internal realm; feelings about teaching as a vocation are private, exalted feelings, separated from the everyday, perhaps untried by further experience. The idea of a vocation to teach seems to calls the person out from the humdrum or unsatisfactory into a special status. The majority of respondents are aged 18 or 21, either about to leave school or about to graduate from university; their life-stage and expected ways of thinking and feeling about themselves [1] must be taken as provisional and subject to further evolution. Perhaps for this reason, there is a latent narcissism in these responses which, when examined, reveals a self-deception too: the rhetoric is of placing little children at the center, of valuing them, but the reality is that the candidate's feelings about themselves are at the center.

There exists another type of discourse, heard more rarely in interviews, but (I suspect) more promising in its imagery of the desire to teach.

In my workplace I am often getting into situations in which I am explaining to other people how to do [a procedure]. One day after this happened, someone said "you know, you'd make a good teacher", and that started me thinking.

Reading [text; often literature or scientific information] I was so enthused by it that I developed this urge to pass it on. I'd love to share the enjoyment.

[Subject] is often misunderstood by the public. It is important that people get a chance to look into it properly. I want to help future generations to understand it better. Then maybe there will be less [ignorance/prejudice/fear/conflict] around.

This type of response focuses on a process somewhat removed, although not totally separate, from the feelings of the individual. It is a process distinguished by interactivity between child as learner, adult as provider of learning experiences, and text (in the broadest sense). It is a narrative demonstrating that the candidate is already fascinated by, and an active participant in, interactive habits which are the ingredients of learning: explanation, getting to the heart of the matter, asking the right question, knowing how to answer it for a particular audience, listening. This type of answer convinces us more of the strengths of the candidate, and contrasts strongly with the narcissism of the previous comments.

Occasionally the question becomes *Why do you want to teach [subject]?*, and this impels the candidate towards a consideration of teaching something, rather than an abstract which tends to default to feelings about teaching. Responses then raise points about the importance of artistic sensibility and expression, or scientific knowledge, or values, or literacy, etc., for children becoming adults.

Teaching is often spoken of as a vocation. In the first set of responses, vocation is unaccountable and suggests an undefined spiritual superiority. As a word, vocation carries ideological baggage: almost always, its connotations are positive, aspirational and dramatic. This seems to be a characteristic inherited from Jewish and Christian scripture, especially from prophetic call-narratives and Jesus' discourses on discipleship. To have a calling seems to mean being called out of the ordinary or unsatisfactory: for instance, Samuel's calling draws him out from among the faithless in Israel (I Samuel 3); Isaiah's seems to call him from his own feelings of unworthiness, incapability and inarticulacy (Isaiah 6: 1–9); Jesus' calling to his disciples is presented as an urgent and radical departure from apathy (Matthew 22: 1–14). In its strongest form, it gives a sense of life-long destiny and empowerment (Jeremiah 1: 4–10). More generally, it is felt that everyone should have a vocation, although it becomes a reality only for the few (Matthew 22: 14). The biblically influenced idea of vocation performs a hidden task by suggesting something of the person's feelings and assumptions about themselves and what makes them different from their fellows.

Thus, in a naïve spirituality of teaching, the vocation to teach is the love of children, the love of sharing knowledge, the hunger to impart, the romantic view of Jesus as the lover and enlightener of little children, the need to be as Jesus seemed – depended on, appreciated, the center of attention. It is a dream of desire, an untested aspiration, a spiritual fantasy – "spiritualized" in the sense of being held artificially apart from earthly reality. A trace of dualism is therefore to be seen in this form of spirituality. Several candidates were from Christian backgrounds, or had values influenced by Christianity. It is possible that even those from entirely secular backgrounds were influenced by Christian ideas absorbed during their own schooling.

In the second set of responses, a less naïve, less self-centred and more engaged spirituality of teaching seems to be at work. Although there is generally no age correlation, respondents of the second type seem to be more experienced. They see their desire to teach less in terms of pure affect and more in terms of skills, human characteristics, the fascination of texts or the social good. They seem to have tested the realities of the teaching profession and found in them some satisfying, important experiences with learners. Their sense of vocation is less high-flown, more earthed, more likely to be accountable, more aware of professionalism.

A key difference between the two responses lies in their intuited intention. One can sense that the first type of respondent, the holder of the special vocation, almost wishes to stand apart from the idea of a profession, seeing it as compromise, as unattractive: the confusion of working with children who are unpredictable, the irritation of having to fit in with under-funded systems and imperfect colleagues, the humiliation of having one's cherished lesson plan criticized, the exhaustion and bewilderment of curricular change.

Since we are exploring teachers' spirituality in its broadest sense, we could ask how the respondents of the first type might move towards the second; what sort of experiences and inner growth might cause them to exchange a romantic and naïve spirituality of vocation for a more earthed, engaged spirituality of professional experience? And whether such a movement is possible, or desirable. And what professional structures might encourage it; or whether the movement is too costly, perhaps perceived as too likely to end in illusionless cynicism.

There is a tension involved in changing from vocation to profession. For instance, in the long tradition of research in Christian ministry, *vocatio* and *professio* are held as contradictory even when they are interpreted as equally necessary (Campbell 1985). The notion of profession may also be vulnerable. A "hurrah" word (Barrow & Milburn 1990: 249), it may either be used emotively to uphold favoured values, or manipulated to demarcate or marginalize any form of attitude or behaviour found to be unacceptable. To profess means to acknowledge, with associations of laying claim to special knowledge or values. Entering a profession is usually understood to be dependent upon satisfying examiners as to one's competence, through a test or series of tests, and being of appropriate character or ethical standards. Here we re-enter the world of the personal vocation. So there appears to be overlap, as well as tension, between vocation and profession.

Moving From a Spirituality of Vocation to a Spirituality of Profession

I now draw on a second source, the continuing tradition of teachers' narratives which reveal their personal, political responses to their own work (Richardson 1990; Thomas 1995; Hargreaves 2000). I include in this my own work on the Teachers' Lives Project, which consists of professional narratives from a small number of established teachers in primary, secondary and tertiary levels of education in the English system between 1998 and 2001. This project, open to any teachers interested in promoting children's spirituality, invited teachers to keep journals and to collate, and interpret, the recurrent issues. The title of the project was deliberately chosen to emphasize a personal element, and the project literature left open the question of where the personal ends and the professional or political begins. The project was in continuity with life-history research on teachers, but had a specific interest in their spirituality as teachers.

The results, some of them quoted directly here, give vent to considerable levels of frustration among serving teachers committed to supporting spirituality (their own and the children's). The evidence suggests that the spirituality of teachers in mid-career has changed very considerably from the naïve sense of vocation described above. The change has been difficult, sometimes traumatic, and has left these teachers less certain, yet still deeply reflective. One wonders, however, whether there are some other teachers for whom the pain of experience has so manhandled their hopes that little or no spirituality is left.

If the earlier spiritualities of the vocation to teach, described above, are to move to a deeper, less self-centred and more earthed spirituality of teaching, this change must be achieved in a way that allows people's spiritual feelings about their desire to teach to be nurtured, but also challenged. This evolution is a movement from a privatized to a public-space spirituality.

Of the many themes and instances treated by participants, the dominant one is the sense of a daily assault on the spirit, and on spirituality. Some teachers blame overwork: "what did I do at the weekend, apart from planning?" (KAL.P.99; Chater 2001). Others point to the frequency with which teachers seem to be blamed for society's ills (SEB.S.99; Chater 2001). There is strong criticism of the inspection regime in England, closely allied to a culture of perfectionism which both oppresses and rules out risk-taking: "I have to prioritize and not panic. It is absolutely not possible to be a perfect tutor any more!" (LJM.T.99; Chater 2001). Implicit in many is a complaint about bureaucracy, causing one writer to use the phrase "drowning in paper" (LJM.T.99; Chater 2001). Each of these phrases is quoted as representative of wider patterns in the journals, indicating negative features of working life that undermine, or distort, or jostle aside the place of the spirit in education.

One excerpt is worth sharing more fully because of the strong sense it gives of a teacher struggling to remain human, and focused on the personal needs of students, not only unsupported by the values of the system but actually marginalized by them. The teacher tells of conversations with two very troubled 16–19 year old students who had just returned to school from unsuccessful work placements.

> My conversation with (Student 1) lasted about half an hour. It took place huddled round the radiator in a cold corridor – the only place where we could find some privacy. The previous half-hour I had spent round the same radiator with (Student 2), the student who had been asked to leave her work placement. . . . I needed (Student 2) to tell me herself the story of what could potentially be a very discouraging, negative experience for her. So – I spent an hour in the corridor with two students while the rest of the class worked on their own with no support from me. Was I right to do so? I've no doubt I had no alternative. But I wonder what would have happened if this had taken place during an . . . inspection . . . (LJM.T.99; Chater 2001)

A teacher having a spirituality which trusts this pattern will be more able to give themselves permission for risks, mistakes, meltdowns, disasters, and recoveries, new insights, losses leading to findings and joy. In this respect, such a spirituality can be a challenge to the regime of fear of mistakes stimulated from inspection agencies and cultures of perfection. The project's investigation of teachers' feelings about themselves and their work revealed both the fear and the willingness to risk professional "death" in the hope of sharing, with pupils' personal "resurrection".

Reflection on other journal passages from the same research reveals a number of other negative themes about moving away from the initial early sense of vocation. These include exhaustion, a sense of the loss of control over one's working life, a sense of losing meaning, a sense that the positive experiences happen marginally to the given framework set by the authorities, and – in a few cases – extreme frustration or extreme anxiety (Chater 2001).

These themes are reflected more widely. In the UK, the bureaucracy theme develops into a critique of the bureaucratization of education, a problem not only for educators but also for management theorists. Bureaucracy is a key feature of teachers' narratives, and is seen as the enemy of the spirit, the destroyer of the life of the spirit.

> Far from being empowered, teachers have become the bearers of the will of their line managers. (Hartley 1997: 102)

Both in teacher narratives and in management theory we have a critique of bureaucracy as eliminating trust. There is a shift from trust to function. People begin to identify themselves, and their colleagues, as functions rather than as being in relationship. While in some healthy organizations this impersonality may be a form of protection, it can also reduce people to roles. Adult managers who only understand themselves as their roles remind us, in life-stage terms, of the adolescent whose identity is shaped by the roles and habits they assume from peers and others (Fowler 1981: 151ff.). Closely associated with bureaucracy is information overload, or data deluge, the miseries of which are well documented (Secretan 1997: 107). Bureaucracy is defined by Belbin as justified only when an administration is served by idiots – we might amend that to read that a bureaucracy often comes into existence, unjustifiably, when an administration *believes* itself to be served by idiots. The essence of bureaucracy is that

> it denies control to those who are capable of meeting their responsibilities. (Belbin 1996: 96)

In view of this, we would do well to look again at our assumptions on the nature of trust. Onora O'Neill in her BBC Reith Lectures of 2002 has called for a more intelligent form of accountability (O'Neill 2002).

The educator or manager in thrall to the bureaucratic mentality is the one who, in David Tracy's telling phrase, when hearing the word religion (one might add values, or spirituality) reaches for their pocket calculator (Tracy 1987: 110). This pithy remark comes in the middle of a sustained analysis of forms of reductionist hermeneutics, of which the technocratic reduction of all experience to quantifiable units is one.

Robert Bellah (1996a), in part of his discourses on American working and cultural life, speaks of the birth of an anxious class of professionals, trapped in perpetual frenzied effort without apparently making any progress beyond survival. A working atmosphere of perpetual change and permanent crisis will sap creativity. Employees are kept busy mastering new information, and fear freezes out visions. Elsewhere he explores how people as citizens deal with the cognitive dissonance of being empowered, whole, happy citizens yet not having control over the workings of the economy, sudden unexplained political developments, or shifts in working life caused by economic or political patterns. He argues that challenges to managerial ethos come from the excluded, the moral critics and the autonomous professionals (Bellah 1996b: 139). Most importantly, he ponders on the contradiction that managers see their role as being to "persuade, inspire, manipulate, cajole, and intimidate" (Bellah 1996b: 45), yet also see themselves as morally neutral, as technicians or engineers.

The evidence seems to be that a spirituality of professionalism, in moving away from naivety, is marked by confusion, and that this unites teachers with, at least, other public sector and service professionals.

School Improvement and Teachers' Spirituality

In both the UK and the USA, a culture of improvement in schools has dominated pedagogy over the last decade and is now being exported globally. The school improvement movement emerged about forty years ago as an educational expression or outworking of social democratic principles. School improvement had its roots in responses to inequality – a realization of social class as a key determinant of school achievement, combined with a determination that it should not be an excuse for failure. Making reference to Holt, Vygotsky, and other mid-century non-stage developmentalists, as well as earlier sources such as Pestalozzi and Montessori, the school improvement movement asked: how can teachers help children to learn, and how can this be spread beyond the areas of privilege, to happen more effectively, more frequently, over a wider, ever wider social spectrum? It was such a simple question, but finding the answers, and spreading them around, was not simple. The English system's Plowden report of 1967 called for the setting up of educational priority areas. The movement believed that it would be possible to move towards equality of opportunity, and to combat poverty and exclusion, through raising accessibility and standards in schools (MacBeath & Mortimore 2001).

It followed that teachers and teaching could make a difference to learners and learning. The difference would not always and only be visible in results: it is a mistake to see school improvement as outcome-dominated. At its best, it was and is about nurturing effective learners (MacBeath & Mortimore, 2001: 113).

Contemporary expressions of school improvement underline a number of themes to which proponents of children's spirituality might be sympathetic: the emphasis on learning having considering implications for teaching; the need to address, and make happen, the deep learning of teachers, changing their beliefs and values in order to change practice; the importance to schools and teachers of having high quality critical friendships – critical in both senses, i.e. as both challenging and essential; and of building communities, networks and partnerships; the necessity of a school leadership which is listening and responsive, capable of hearing the "secret harmonies" of the school (MacBeath & Mortimore 2001: 201).

Where the movement can be open to criticism is in its failure fully to control the outcomes of the standards drive. School improvers believe, perhaps with justified realism, that efforts to make this move must involve centralization. They hold effectiveness (of teaching, learning and school management) to be a central virtue, prompting the philosopher Alasdair MacIntyre to raise moral concerns:

> the whole concept of effectiveness is . . . inseparable from a mode of human existence in which the contrivance of means is in central part the manipulation of human beings into compliant patterns of behaviour . . . (MacIntyre 1984: 71)

School improvers also believe that quality management processes could be appropriately adapted for schools, yet they acknowledge this has not always happened (Detert *et al.* 2001: 183–212). They also acknowledge that rapid, radical top-down initiatives are at odds with the ethical core of education, though they are quick to assert that this does not always have to be the case (Barber 2001: 213–28). This is as close as the exponents of school improvement will come, in public, to any acknowledgement of the feelings of teachers exposed in the narratives quoted above.

School improvement, as the dominant and still growing educational culture, is ambiguous in relation to teachers' spirituality. On the one hand, it aspires, as the teachers do, to values of openness, self-betterment, equality and inclusion. It underlines the importance of nurture and of the whole person. It speaks of teachers' transformation as ongoing "deep learning". It sees schools as communities. But these apparently benign values are contradicted by a centralist, *dirigiste* approach, and by the privileging of the value of effectiveness, in ways that are morally questionable and which teachers (in the life history evidence) appear to find oppressive. This dominant drive towards improvement has transformed teachers' thinking and feeling about their work. It has been the background against which teachers have moved from vocation to profession. It has changed them, and it is (perhaps like all spiritualities) ambiguous.

Private and Public Spiritualities of Teachers

Any move from private to public spirituality is not made easy by the reality of accountability structures in UK education, nor is it supported by publicly-held views of spirituality as purely inward and personal. Inspection agency and other thinking has succeeded in privatizing the spiritual:

> We believe that spiritual development is about discovering the self. (Trainor 1995: 8–9)

Ironically, the privatization of vocation evacuates public spaces and allows the technicist, instrumentalist curriculum to be dominant.

> The technicist values of the national curriculum seem to have obscured the vision of education as a process whereby individuals become more human . . . , deepen their self awareness, . . . examine their desires, attitudes and beliefs, . . . and so transform themselves and the social context. . . . (Lally 1993: 41)

This obscuring of vision continues. The technicist curriculum is implemented termly by teachers who comfort themselves with a private, personal vocation. Instead of turning their sense of vocation outwards towards critical dialogue with the system, they turn it inwards and allow the system to contradict their impulses.

This silencing of the potential public voice of vocation not only drives learning teachers into a private, passive sense of vocation, but maintains them in a passive state in relation to their learning. The age-long tensions between the processes of being trained and being educated (Barrow & Milburn 1990: 316–17) become relevant here: the learning teacher with a privatized vocation has already been manoeuvred into a position in which s/he is more ready to undergo training in a set of technical-rational skills which have been placed beyond ethical enquiry or questioning. Correspondingly, the trained student will be more resistant to any education which demands capacities of critical reflectiveness.

The private–public dichotomy extends into teachers' own narratives of their work once established in the profession (Boxall 1995: 106ff). Themes frequently aired in journals include developing and maintaining a sense of self, resisting bureaucratization, learning to live with the incongruities, painful realizations.

> This entry in my diary is very difficult to write. That's because it's of something I'd rather forget, let alone record for posterity. (Boxall 1995: 112)

Teacher narrators tend to write chiefly for themselves. Even when invited to write journals as part of a research project, they write mainly to clarify thoughts, or to relive feelings, or to record their learning or to affirm something of themselves and their dreams about teaching. Like Peter Woods, they have in mind "the ideal reader – myself" (Woods 1995: 181).

> Anyone that knows me will know that if I am writing about something horrific it can only be about one subject – art! (Boxall 1995: 112)

The student then goes on to relate her humiliation and anger at being unable to draw in a class (in College). She concludes by drawing a lesson which applies to children as learners:

> If a child produced as little work as I did today, it could have been treated very insensitively. What reason has that child got to go to school? When I am teaching my own class, please let no child in my class feel as wretched as I did today. (Boxall 1995: 113)

Boxall's analysis is that the diarists struggle to make sense of chaotic, oppressive or confusing working conditions without compromising themselves by settling into them (Boxall 1995: 118).

Other painful experiences which confront precious private dreams with brutal public realities might be, for example, a trainee or new teacher's first encounter with a colleague's personal racism or with institutional racism; a first encounter with an abusive pupil or parent; or an experience of contradiction, eg. between the content of a tutor's advice and the necessity of accommodating one's self to school conditions. These experiences, and others we could think of, are variant forms of the ongoing conflict between a teacher's ideas – core faith-objects – and the professional experiences and priorities which impact on – we might even say, which batter – the teacher's working life.

A form of conversion often takes place in teachers' lives when the ideas with which they started get abandoned, or changed out of recognition, along the way. Idealism gives place to cynicism, displacement to accommodation. In the case of one Head Teacher of a school doing work on values, a conversion from idealism to cynicism was followed by a second conversion onwards to prioritizing holistic approaches to supporting and celebrating children's spiritual and moral development (Farrer 2000).

An excellent contemporary example of a teacher who dares to shift their clearly personal convictions accountably into the dangerous rewards of the public curriculum domain is to be found in a teacher of history, involved in teaching the *Shoah*, interviewed in 1998 by S. Schweber and quoted in Alexander and Ben-Peretz:

They (pupils) have to have an opportunity to think about the implications
... of what they're learning and . . . build their own meaning out of it and
to share that with other people. It's actually a great vision for what
happens when you have community in the classroom and a rigorous,
intellectual experience. And one or the other, you can't do without... And
it's tough to do. You walk a real line between the particular and the
universal messages and implications of the history . . . and, um, that's
difficult, you sort of sculpt the curriculum on a daily basis; it's not a
programmed-by-the-numbers, kind of curriculum. (Alexander & Ben-
Peretz 2001: 41)

The researchers comment that the humanist curriculum, truly responsive and constructing a holistic knowledge including forms of
meaning-making, cannot be packaged in advance, and if so packaged,
is not humanistic?.

In order to decide what knowledge is most worth knowing, and to
consider how best to impart or construct it, we must first have a conception of what is worthwhile. This requires that we examine our most
fundamental beliefs about the purposes of life and the nature of a good
society. These considerations cannot be merely personal. They call us to
reach beyond ourselves to the communities in which we live, study and
teach, and beyond our communities to transcendent ideals . . .
Consequently, the design . . . of educational materials can and should be
conceived as a sacred task. (Alexander & Ben-Peretz 2001: 45)

Conclusion

Among all the callings, teaching is well qualified to transform naïve,
private spiritualities of vocation into something public. Merely feeling
a vocation to teach is not enough: this alone will almost certainly capitulate to the dualities and oppressions of the education system. What can
be good is to nurture and contextualize a vocation to teach by subjecting
it to professional demands (as given through accountability structures)
with all the risks entailed. Teaching is, after all, the process by which
pure, whole ideas are ground down for treatment so that they can be
offered to smaller, less experienced people. It is a privilege to do this for
people; it is a privilege to do it to ideas; but it also teaches teachers that
ideas, like vocations, can seem less pure after treatment.

Personal narratives of teachers show that they realize the pain of
transformation, recognising how the dominant educational ideology
both helps and hinders their movement. They continue uniting personal
and political motifs in dangerous ways (Erricker 2002). In having these
insights, teachers share (in different languages) some of the insights into
spirituality given to the world through Jewish, Christian and thera-

peutic traditions. In particular, the idea that mourning not only brings comfort but also transforms situations (Brueggemann 1978) is understandable in secular professional contexts through the power of the teachers' shared spiritualities to preserve and strengthen a marginalized set of values. Teachers, as people who come into daily contact with transformation, implicitly share the wisdom of spiritual traditions that change in people and ideas can be painful and productive, and this leads them to reject any belief in improvement or betterment without pain as a "narcissistic pathway" (Empereur 1998: 211). Teachers' narratives of their spirituality can contribute to a long, deep and very powerful tradition of prophetic consciousness.

Note

1   See, for instance, Fowler 1981: 151ff.

References

Alexander, H. and Ben-Peretz, M. 2001: Toward a Pedagogy of the Sacred: Transcendence, ethics, and the curriculum. In J. Erricker, C. Ota & C. Erricker (eds.), *Spiritual Education: Cultural, Religious and Social Differences*. Brighton & Portland: Sussex Academic Press, 34–47.

Barber, M. 2001: The Very Big Picture. In: *School Effectiveness and School Improvement* 12(2), 213–28.

Barrow, R. and Milburn, G. 1990: *A Critical Dictionary of Educational Concepts* (second edition). New York and London: Harvester-Wheatsheaf.

Belbin, M. 1996: *The Coming Shape of Organisation*. London: Butterworth-Heinemann.

Bellah, R. 1996a: Creating Transforming Communities. In *Global Learning*, 1(3).

Bellah, R. *et al.* 1996b: *Habits of the Heart: Individualism and Commitment in American Life*, Berkeley: University of California Press.

Bonhoeffer, D. 1937, Engish translation 1959: *The Cost of Discipleship*. London: SCM Press.

Boxall, W. 1995: Making the Private Public. In: D. Thomas 1995 (ed.), *Teachers' Stories*. Buckingham: Open University Press, 106–20.

Brueggemann, W. 1978: *The Prophetic Imagination*. Minneapolis, MN: Fortress Press.

Campbell, A. 1975: *Paid to Care? The limits of professionalism in pastoral care*. London: SPCK.

Chater, M. 2001: '*It is now 5.45 and the caretaker has come in to throw me out': What the Teachers' Lives Project can tell teachers and managers about the school ethos and values debate*. Unpublished paper for seminars at the Universities of Warwick and Glasgow.

Detert, J., Louis, K. and Schroeder, R. 2001: A Culture Framework for Education: defining quality values and their impact in US high schools. In *School Effectiveness and School Improvement* 12(2), 183–212.

Empereur, J. 1998: *The Enneagram and Spiritual Direction*. New York: Continuum Press.

Erricker, C. 2002: *When Learning becomes Your Enemy*. Nottingham: Educational Heretics Press.

Farrer, F. 2000: *A Quiet Revolution: Encouraging Positive Values in our Children*. London: Rider.

Fowler, J. 1981: *Stages of Faith*. San Francisco: Harper.

Hargreaves, A. 2000: *Changing Teachers, Changing Times: Teachers' Work and Culture in the Postmodern Age*. London: Continuum.

Hartley, J. 1997: *Reschooling Society*. Brighton: Falmer Press.

Lally, V. 1993: *Values and the Curriculum: Theory and Practice*. Leicester: CAVE/NAVET.

MacBeath, J. and Mortimore, P. 2001: *Improving School Effectiveness*. Buckingham: Open University Press.

MacIntyre, A. 1984: *After Virtue*. London: Duckworth.

O'Neill, O. 2002: *A Question of Trust: BBC Reith Lectures*. London: BBC, in: www.bbc.co.uk/radio4/reith2002

Richardson, R. 1990: *Daring to be a Teacher*. Stoke-on-Trent: Trentham Books.

Secretan, L. 1997: *Reclaiming Higher Ground: Building Organisations that Inspire Excellence*. New York: McGraw-Hill.

Thomas, D. 1995: (ed.), *Teachers' Stories*. Buckingham: Open University Press.

Tracy, D. 1987: *Plurality and Ambiguity*. London: SCM.

Trainor, D. 1995: The Inspection of SMSCD in *Governors' Action*, April 1995, pp. 8–9.

Chapter 15

Faith Education of Children in the Context of Adult Migration and Conversion: The Discontinuities of Tradition

CLIVE ERRICKER

RELIGION RELIES UPON TRADITION for historical continuity. This continuity can be challenged by disruptive cultural change, such as migration and conversion. This can be in the case of migration of individuals and groups moving to a new cultural milieu within which their religion and ethnicity are both in a minority, or the "convert migration" of a religion to a new cultural milieu, to which it has to adapt and within which it seeks adherents, converts or influence. This chapter is based on contrasting examples in two religions: Buddhism and Islam. Its focus is on how the inter-relationship between a new national identity or a new religious identity interacts in relation to the upbringing of the next generation. At first I consider some of the generational issues for adults and then move on to questions of how faith education is approached.

The Challenge to Religious Traditions

The world in the twenty-first century is likely to be a time of challenge to religion and by religion. Tradition is central to the character of institutionalized religious life by virtue of being the instrument by which religion achieves stability and, as a result, the ability to meet new challenges as societies develop new forms. Religious traditions are those institutions that seek to preserve the continuing relevance of religion to modern life. But, the place of religion in modern western society is in decline, at least in so far as the influence traditional religion has on the lifestyles of citizens and the politics and values of western nation states is concerned.

Nevertheless, although religious traditions are most usually identified from without as being rigid and solid: immovable rather than flexible objects, their survival demands flexibility. Metaphorically we might usefully understand them as candle flames, in the way in which they seek to preserve their spirit, as well as fortresses, given their tendency to resist change. As the former, in the need to preserve the contour of their form, they shift continually in response to the elemental conditions that prevail on them and within them. Religious traditions have to take account of the new, even if there is a tendency to resist it. Paradoxically, this can even mean they become a part of the new, having an increasing influence in the modern world by virtue of the appeal generated by reconfiguration, or just "re-branding", as for example with the Alpha movement in the Christian Church. Conversion to high-profile forms of militant fundamentalist Islam provides another contemporary example. Crucial to the maintenance of tradition in religion is the relationship that exists between the religion and its "host" culture, its economic base, and its appeal to successive generations. To illustrate these points I offer the specific case studies that follow. To highlight the issues involved these studies throw into relief the problems and possibilities arising from migration and conversion in relation to the faith education of new generations. The binding connection between conversion and migration is that religious traditions migrate not only across geographical boundaries but also through time.

Migrant Religion and Conversion in Buddhism

The growth of the Buddhist presence in the West in the latter half of the twentieth century has been cumulative and diverse, such that it is possible to find, or indeed commit yourself to, a representative range of any form of Buddhism found across the globe: Tibetan, Zen, Pure Land, Nichiren or Theravadin, for example. Beyond this there are also the seeds of seeking to establish forms of western Buddhism, as traditional forms adapt to new cultural settings or, as in the case of the Western Buddhist Order, create a distinct form that attempts to be free of alien cultural characteristics from its inception. There are also Buddhist groups that cross traditional Buddhist divides and welcome the pluralism of the western situation as a positive enriching development. This situation has developed into a fascinating picture of religious, social and cultural change that is still in its infancy. Within this movement to conversion the questioning of contemporary spiritual values is a key factor.

The Buddhist Forest Retreat Order

The Forest Retreat Order represents one of the most traditional forms of Buddhist transplantation and, for that reason, paradoxically perhaps in its new setting, one of the most radical alternatives to conventional western lifestyles and values. How does a Thai *Sangha*[1] based on the strict observance of the *Vinaya*[2] and accustomed to remote rural territory flourish in the west?

Documentation of the growth of Ajahn Chah's Thai Forest Retreat Order in the West is now readily available.[3] Its beginnings resided in his own disaffection with the state of Buddhism in Thailand after receiving monastic ordination at the age of twenty one in 1939. The study of Buddhist doctrine and *Pali* texts within his training brought him no closer to realising the Buddha's emphasis on the teachings having one aim: the cessation of suffering. The laxness of the practice by *bhikkhus*[4] and lay people alike was equally uninspiring. Such disenchantment, which actually threads throughout the movement as an inspiration and is echoed later, led to Ajahn Chah's meeting with the meditation master Ajahn Mun, and his conviction as to the importance of the monastic rule and the practice of mindfulness as 'seeing that everything arises in one's own heart'.[5] The forcefulness of this insight and its abiding presence in the movement is testified to in the prologemia to his western disciple, Ajahn Sumedho's, teachings in *Mindfulness: The Path to the Deathless*[6] and thus alerts us to the significance of the maintenance of tradition in the teachings and practices in the present Order, which gives it its direction and sustenance in its present situation, despite or perhaps because of increasing social and cultural diversity. This insistence on the significance of tradition as a return to the original threads through its western presence. Ajahn Sumedho's comments on this are indicative at both a practical and spiritual level:

> We are a tradition that believes itself to be from the original...and we are limiting our lives to the boundaries of the Vinaya . . . to get us to reflect on our impulsivity, assumptions, cultural habits . . . alms mendicancy is an act of faith. We seek to live within the limitations it confers and reflect daily . . . and be grateful for what we are given: food, clothing, shelter, medicine being made available to you. Our lives have to depend on the good heartedness of the lay community. If the lay community isn't good hearted, then we wouldn't be able to exist . . . this allows us to maintain meditation: the spiritual exercises that we have.[7]

The Forest Retreat Order represents a tale of tradition renewed or reconstructed, having fallen into decline. Adaptation is minimal upon migration. Its characteristics have been referred to as "Protestant Buddhism" because the impetus for renewal in Thailand was originally generated by a western convert and, similar to the inception of the Christian Protestant Churches in Europe, the aim was to restore the "original" faith that had been corrupted and diminished.

The Order's appeal is to a western disaffection with a secularized society that lacks spiritual incentive and motivation. The spiritual example of monks and nuns living the monastic life with a high degree of discipline based on renunciation is the main attraction. This example we might refer to as "regenerated tradition" deliberately setting out not to integrate itself with the norms of its host culture but provide a benignly expressed challenge.

The Japanese Buddhist Church of America

By contrast with the above, in Tetsuden Kashima's study of Japanese Buddhists in the United States (Kashima 1977), we find a story which can be paralleled by other immigrant groups' histories; for example, those of Vietnamese Buddhists, Bangladeshi Muslims, Khojas Shi'a Ithnasheeri Muslims, referred to later, and various Hindu and Sikh communities. The author is of Japanese extraction and the son of a priest, the Reverend Tetsuro Kashima. In this study we can trace an example of Buddhist ethnic transference to the West.

Kashima remarks on how "The Buddhist Church of America (BCA) represents an alien religion in America – one that has continued for seventy-six years". It is predominantly Jodo Shinshu of the West and East School varieties and most emigrated from the Hiroshima area (Prefecture), representing a quarter of the total migrants, who numbered 84,562. The Buddhist Churches of America represents Amida Buddhism, or Pure Land, with its headquarters in San Francisco. It was inaugurated under this name in 1944 after the traumatic events during the Second World War when almost all the Japanese and Nisei (first generation Americans of Japanese ancestry) were interned. This resulted in a complete dislocation of habits and lifestyles. A continual theme in the history of the institution is its importance as a force for ethnic solidarity, 'The Buddhist Church is a place for the Japanese to meet other Japanese' as one Nisei father stated. In this respect it existed solely for the Japanese and their offspring since 1899. The use of the word church has become increasingly problematic for its members during the latter decades of the twentieth century since it does not reflect the purposes or structures of an inherently Japanese Buddhist religious community. As Kashima points out, Temple or Dojo ("a place where the Way is cultivated") is a more proper description of its place of worship, and sangha is a more exact description of its membership (1977: 187).

The history of Japanese immigrants bears some familiar features. Prejudice and willfully ignorant racism such as that propagated by the Western Central Labour Union in Seattle in 1900 whose propagation for restrictions on immigration led to such descriptions of Japanese Buddhists as having the "treacherous, sneaking, insidious, betraying and perfidious nature and characteristics of the Mongolian race" (1977: 18). Kashima suggests that the use of the word "church" was probably an attempt to mitigate against anti-Japanese agitation and is evidence of the Americanization of second and third generation Japanese.

The Japanese bombing of Pearl Harbour in December 1941, despite its condemnation by the Buddhist Mission of North America (as it then was) led to internment. Most of those interned were Buddhists. Even before the bombing "Many Japanese destroyed items that might be regarded as incriminating: some burned sutra books (scriptures), while others concealed their family Buddhist altars" (ibid.: 48).

With generational change from Issei to Nisei to Sansei (3rd generation, but second generation American born) the membership declined in relation to the size of the Japanese American population since the BCA never systematically proselytized and successive generations did not have the same need for its support as members of an isolated ethnic minority. Also, those who still belonged to and supported the organization did not necessarily practice Buddhism. One Nisei minister commenting on why there was continued Nisei involvement with their church suggested:

> Perhaps it could be guilt or family pressure. What my parents have done for the temple, and therefore . . . I must carry on. And the other one would say I must do it for my children. These may be some of the reasons why they do it. But not so much from the religious standpoint. (Ibid.: 188)

And one Nisei said, "I don't know anything about Buddhism, I'll come not to the service but to other things. To carnivals, but not to study class or the *Hondo* [temple hall]" (ibid.: 188).

Kashima remarks on the differences among the three generations as highlighted by the Reverend Koshin Ogui:

> As history shows, the Issei had to work to support their families, nothing but work. The Nisei were educated by the Issei to build up their lives the same as the *hakujin* [Caucasian] people. So you see the majority of Nisei people out to buy cars and homes. They don't think about spiritual matters. They are more satisfied with fancy cars and homes. The Sansei are raised in such a background and getting tired of it. Of course, they respect their families. But they're looking for more importance in life – to go forward to fight for human rights, against racial discrimination

and to help the community instead of building up their abundance. (Ibid.: 197)

If this proves to be the case and the BCA extends its involvement with other non-Japanese Shin-Buddhists, the spiritual heart of the organization could be re-vitalized.

But Kashima's judgement is equivocal, "Looking ahead we may conceive of many futures for the BCA, which is really just another way of saying that the future is uncertain." Kashima suggests that possible futures depend on how a number of present problems are resolved, he cites five: decreasing and changing membership; the ethnic character of membership; economic problems; the proper techniques for teaching Buddhism; interrelated problems with the ministry. All of the problems are ultimately interconnected, as he observes (1977: 207). He also posits that if the BCA comes to include a wider racial representation, as its leaders envision, then "Buddhism will indeed become fully Americanized" (1977: 220).

What is interesting in this study, is the close but shifting connections between ethnicity (Japanese), nationality (American), and religiosity (Buddhist) representing the equation that the community has to balance across three generations. For each generation the balance between these factors is different, in terms of priority. Migration was one of the dominant features of the twentieth century and is likely to be no less dominant in the twenty-first. It determines the issues of particular importance to this Buddhist group, it creates future uncertainty, discrimination, and problems in distinguishing the relationship between religion and culture, a relationship that changes across generations. Is being Buddhist important, as an aspect of identity, in a secularized American environment? Is it better to shed it in the movement towards becoming fully American, or is it the vital commitment to be retained and nurtured, against all others, to preserve identity and values? What does being Buddhist actually mean for this community and how does it relate to larger issues concerning the spiritual and moral condition of a globalized world in the twenty-first century? What does the propagation of the dharma mean for this kind of community when its initial concern for the first, migrant, generation was economic survival and ethnic identity, then, for the next generation, wealth creation and assimilation? The questions that emerge for an immigrant group of this kind differ to those posed for Buddhists in other situations. When Kashima speaks of anticipating Buddhism becoming fully Americanized what sort of Buddhism will this be?

When migration is principally concerned with the preserving of ethnic tradition the result, it seems, is the failure of religious tradition to inspire the same spiritual values and practices in future generations.

Comparing the two Buddhist movements above suggests that religious tradition becomes rejuvenated when there is a renewal of spiritual vision that attracts new blood through conversion. Thus, tradition itself depends for its survival on the correct balance of dynamic and judicious change and stasis. But it must be wary of corroding factors associated with both the preservation of an "ethnic" culture and assimilation into a new "national" culture.

A Muslim Comparison: The Khoja Shia Ithnasheeris

So, what needs to be preserved and what needs to be changed in relation to custom, belief and ritual? How are shifts in identity accomplished without the loss of religious identity? Let's now consider the issues raised by the Buddhist examples in relation to a Muslim group.

> What are we? All our communities are called Khoja Shia Ithnasheeri. But first is Khoja. We are Khojas because that is our tribe, Shias because that is what our belief is and then Ithnasheeri because we follow the 12 Imams.[8]

This statement would not seem to presage an auspicious beginning. It suggests the Khoja (ethnic) identity precedes the Muslim (religious) one. However, this community is taking account of the inherent problems associated with this. Its emphasis is on being Shia, the spiritual values of Shia Islam and the importance it places on religious freedom. This is a familiar theme in its history of migration from India to East Africa and then the West. However, the challenges presented in the West are, arguably, much greater than those presented previously in East Africa. These challenges relate most specifically to the upbringing of first generation British Khoja Shia children. And the problems experienced in the West now seem to bear similarity with those found in traditional Islamic countries, given the influence of globalization.

> "My father says I am free to express myself to him. But I can't because our culture dictates that young people do not assert themselves before their elders," says Hussain. "Heavy metal is my only outlet. All my pent up energy is released when I listen to it." (del Nevo 1992: 3)

Hussain, from Lahore in Pakistan, is a 19-year-old urban, middle class boy with a desire to be a journalist. He further remarks, "In the West a boy of my age can make his own choices . . . He can talk to girls, drink, listen to any type of music. We don't necessarily want to indulge in these things. But we do want the freedom to choose. And our parents don't understand – they feel threatened" (1992: 3).

The significant issue in the difference between his experience and that of his understanding of children in the West is one of being in a culture that you feel you have some ownership of and one where you can create your own separate sub-culture. But Muslim children in the West voice similar concerns to his. For example, this 11 year old Khoja boy:

> Although I agree with my dad, sometimes I feel that we live on two different planets. He has not been to the same school as I have . . . and he has no idea regarding what my friends get up to or watch on TV or read . . . So much fuss being a Muslim. (Erricker 2001: 216)

It falls to the present adult generation to negotiate this sense of difference, and determine the impact of it on tradition. The next generation will have to do likewise. For Khoja Shias the need to preserve identity in the context of new cultural influences has made the Jamaat,[9] as a centre of worship and a place of belonging, a critical force for survival. But the question as to how it competes with wider cultural influences that attract the youth in their search for identity remains an open one. Here we have a situation comparable to that of the Japanese Buddhists in America, but the secular influence has now spread further afield. There is no longer an insularity from it based on religious and national identity, per se. Religious tradition has to cope with the pressures of cultural globalization across the former territorial borders within which nationality and religious identity were more securely related.

The "Faith" of the Next Generation

Here I am concerned with what form a faith education can profitably take, and to what purpose. I wish to introduce a distinction between the "wisdom" tradition and the "doctrinal" tradition. By wisdom tradition I am referring to those teachings which have a universal appeal. Most well known are those within the Jewish bible: e.g. Ecclesiasties and the Song of Solomon. There is a parallel to this in Indian religion with the Sant tradition: holy men who attracted and attract followers across religious (doctrinal) divides. The doctrinal tradition represents the separation of believers into formal religious groups based on key creedal formulas. Thus, Christians are Trinitarian, for example. The doctrinal tradition emphasizes belonging: insiders and outsiders, orthodoxy and heresy. They tend to be exclusivist. The wisdom tradition emphasizes a way of seeing the world that accommodates difference across religious divides by means of a more poetic and individual apprehension: it seeks to guide rather than instruct. It tends to be inclusivist.

Taken to their extremes you find the two different religious models represented today in the phenomena of New Age and Fundamentalism.

The doctrinal traditions can accommodate wisdom literature and teachings to varying degrees, but the wisdom literature and teachings cannot provide the foundation of the doctrinal traditions. Thus, we have wisdom literature within the Jewish Bible but not within Torah itself. Also, there are tensions when this occurs. For example, the tension between acceptance and persecution of the Sufis in Islam and the contemporary issues surrounding anti-realist theology in Christianity. The pedagogy, by which I mean form of faith education, of Sufism and anti-realist theology will be different in design from purely instructional doctrinal methods, it will be more expressive and based on a more "existential" model.

But the key issue in this context that the above over-view seeks to introduce is to what extent should faith education embrace the stance of doctrinalism or wisdom. Can faith education within religious traditions usefully bring the two together or is this impossible?

And, to what extent can the incorporation of a wisdom model help in the context of passing on tradition within the contexts of migration and conversion?

Alternative Pedagogies in Faith Education

How does the above analysis impact upon the case studies reviewed earlier? When religion migrates and converts, as with the Buddhist Forest Retreat Order, despite its traditional manifestations (robed monks, insistence on the Vinaya, ordained and lay separation of roles), what is the pedagogical model that attracts adherents or interest and influence? I suggest that it employs a predominantly wisdom model. The darsanas of the senior monks: Ajahn Sumedho, Ajahn Succhito and others are dependent on their charismatic authority and on challenging conventional cultural and social values. This is done by appealing to a radically different model derived from the Buddha's teaching as an existential enquiry. Ajahn Chah's disillusionment concerning his own training in Thailand was based on the fact that this was precisely what it did not do. The institutionalization of Buddhism in Thailand as a national religion mitigated against this. Thus, we find the call for renewal in his movement and a return to "Original Buddhism". Its migration to the West, with concomitant converts, emphasizes this sense of renewal and return further, along wisdom lines. For example, Stephen Batchelor, a western convert to Buddhism, has called for Buddhism without beliefs (Batchelor 1998). By this he means that religiosity is not important. What is important is the practice of the dharma. This separation of dharma from religion is a manifestation of the influence of the wisdom model.

At the Dhamma (or Dharma) School in Brighton we can witness something of the application of this understanding to a faith pedagogy for children, between three and eleven. According to its literature, the Dhamma School is based on Buddhist principles. The teachers are all Buddhist in conviction. Yet, there is a certain shyness in using this term. The Co-Head, Kevin Fossey, prefers not to speak of himself as a Buddhist, but of trying to develop a "good heart", in effect a different term for affirming what Batchelor calls the practice of the dharma. This is not to say that the school is not Buddhist in its outward manifestations and intentions: it has pujas and shrines and the teaching revolves around the Buddhist concepts of interdependence, impermanence and compassion. It does not draw on just one branch of Buddhist tradition. The Dalai Lama and Theravadin monks and nuns are in evidence in photos within the classrooms, Buddha rupas are used that have differing cultural origins. Perhaps the diffidence of promoting the term "Buddhist" is in part a desire to play down religious connotation and affirm values and principles for a western population that do not relate themselves to traditional western views of religiosity.

Parents who send their children to the school seem to reflect the advantage of this approach. They are western and not "religious". They are attracted by its alternativeness and its emphasis on "spiritual values". One mother replied, in answer to a question I posed, "Why do you bring your son here?" as follows, "The teachers are teaching spiritual values and being aware of the bigger picture . . . more sensitivity and compassion for others". In answer to the question whether she was a Buddhist: "Yeah, sort of finding out about it, learning to." Her son, Solly, is three and three-quarters and has been there since last September. He showed me in detail what it means to "do Buddha". With palms together he demonstrates "touch your forehead, head, nose and chin and bow." The school has an effect on the mother too: "Definitely brilliant, mixing with other like-minded people...just feels lovely...I really like the people I meet here, just feel so lucky."[10] Steve, who is a classroom assistant, brought his daughter eight years ago and has stayed on, but without affirming a sense of allegiance to "Buddhism". Another classroom assistant is training in transpersonal psychology and sees it as complementary to Buddhist practice. My impression is that the school serves a community of parents with values alternative to that of mainstream, capitalist and secularized western culture.

An impromptu puja by Kevin Fossey for a class who were not performing their task well consisted of a brief introductory meditation on the breath followed by a talk (darsana) on interdependence, impermanence and attachment to views that was related to his own immediate experience and that of the children. It was an encouragement to listen in debate as well as express their own opinions. It was a reflection on how windy days change our mood and disposition. It was a reflection on right effort directly related to the immediate classroom problem. His stress on thoughts and feelings rather than "teaching a dogma" reflected the democratic model the school seeks to espouse and the concentration on issues that make it challenging. In conversation he mentioned that

> The worry for me is that people see it as a Buddhist school and see it as all very nice and open but when they come in to do it they realize it is a hundred times more challenging than they actually thought.[11]

In relation to the expectations of being a faith school his worry is that "People mistake me saying no to something or mistake you questioning them as not being very Buddhist . . . in one sense you are putting yourself up for a fall . . . I can't live up to that."[12]

It seems clear that one of the main issues here is the way in which the school represents the adaptation of Buddhism to a different cultural milieu and what it represents within that new situation. The pedagogy of the school, within the classroom and more generally between staff as to how the school is run and what it seeks to achieve and how it becomes successful, is a significant feature.

In relation to the other two case studies we can begin with the Japanese Buddhist Church of America, since it offers us the larger historical perspective in terms of the point of migration to the West. In this case the primary concern was to preserve an ethnic community which continued to practice its religiosity (this being a specific component of its difference in relation to the host community). Across succeeding generations this aim failed due to the process of assimilation. United States nationality, with the incursion of its values, triumphed over ethnic and religious difference. Kashima's hope is for an American Buddhism, within which Japanese Americans can find a sense of Buddhist identity. This depends on them assimilating to a form of Buddhism that is not ethnically based, nor necessarily based on religiosity, per se. It relies upon the trend in terms of conversion to Buddhism in the United States that follows Batchelor's view expressed above (see also Erricker 2001: 197–206). To put it bluntly, the wisdom tradition is once again in evidence and the notion that faith education of the young can be related to a previously assumed ethnicity, nationalism or cultural and doctrinal religiosity is found wanting.

Turning to the Khoja Shias we have an interesting case in transition. The base is ethnic and religious. The challenge is social and cultural assimilation. What can we assume? First, we can acknowledge that religious identity, as Shias, is paramount. And that the desire for the young to retain their religious values and behaviour, in contradistinction to those of the host culture, is a primary endeavour. Does this constitute a different concern from that of the Buddhist examples considered previously? Pedagogically I think there is no difference, insofar as the aim is to bear witness to a different set of values from mainstream host culture. However, the question remains as to how those values are addressed. Why should they still be relevant for the young when the socio-cultural infrastructure within which those values were previously expressed is absent? Pedagogically the situation is complex because it is not just a matter of "spiritual enquiry" within which the model of the wisdom tradition would suffice as a method. There remains a doctrinal insistence circumscribed by the notion of being Shia.

I suggest that the wisdom approach works most usefully within a climate of liberal enquiry and that it is resisted when the need for maintaining boundaries is most prevalent, as in situations that relate to migration. It works when the seminal sub-culture consists of those who come to hear specific teachings by virtue of being already disaffected from mainstream culture and values, but not on the basis of ethnic or religious difference per se. This relates the efficacy of the wisdom model more specifically to conversion. However, the model of the original can be a useful way of applying the wisdom model to both situations. Within both the Buddhist conversionist situation and the Khoja Shia migrationist situation this can be used to significant effect. Here we can recognize the challenge to effective nurture of the next generation being comparable. The common goal is against assimilation into mainstream values. In neither case does it mean that the continuation of Buddhism or Shia Islam is assured but it does provide a basis on which the convictions of the traditions, emanating from their founders and significant figures, can be re-applied to the modern world. In Buddhism the main figures would include the Buddha himself and, particularly in evidence at the Dhamma school, the Dalai Lama – though St. Francis was also present in the foyer. In Shia Islam the significance of the Prophet and his family is paramount and, in particular, the figures of Imams Ali and Hussain. This is something quite different to the maintenance of ethnicity and social cohesion but that is the possible cost of such a survival and development strategy.

With the above considerations in mind, the approach of the leader of medrassa education at the Wessex Jamaat, Yasin Rahim, can be usefully compared to that of Kevin Fossey at the Dhamma School. There are some common themes: reflection on experience, raising of issues, challenge to the children and an acceptance of and adaptation to a new cultural situation from the perspective of how the teachings of the tradition are conveyed and engaged with. The pedagogical issues are paramount. Both play down instruction in favour of preparing the children for living in *their* world with committed values that they can own by conviction. Both take seriously the impact of western culture. Yasin's emphasis on "saying only that which pleases Allah" and Kevin's "having a good heart" have a practical resonance, despite doctrinal difference. Both are prepared to embrace conflictual issues in order to overcome them. Both are charismatic in relation to their own convictions and in presenting their shortcomings, in relation to the ideal, within their own behaviour: both command respect of their students in this way. Both are prepared to take the experiences and opinions of their students seriously for engagement to occur. Again, they attempt to model the original.

Of course, there are differences, regarding the type of community each school serves and the expectations of that community and differences within each community. But even these differences present similar problems. The problems largely revolve around pedagogical expectation in relation to distinctions between instruction, engagement, autonomy and values. We might say that they are an expression of the difference between education as critical and affective engagement and education as a more conformist sense of nurture.

Conclusion

Put into western terminology truth, law or doctrine have no value unless they have clear existential purpose for the individual in relation to values and community. This, we can say, is the first principle of the wisdom tradition because it provides reflection on the issues rather than a repetition of the "answers". Returning to the earlier metaphor of the candle flame, the point of tradition is to keep the flame alight, to provide the conditions for it to burn, rather than to suffocate its movement. And this is not so much about the continuity of tradition but its reconstruction. The difficulty in creating such a reconstruction lies in determining how religious or spiritual conviction distinguishes itself from traditional religiosity and the mores of cultural custom as they relate to values.

The pragmatic need to adapt to change and the internal dissent that can involve is integral to the survival of tradition. Agents of change are also those committed to tradition in that they wish it to continue, albeit within a revitalized form. Here the paradox of tradition is made clear: to abide and provide continuity it must accept change and enforce discontinuity. The forms must change to ensure a spiritual legacy. The interaction with the world, in a social and cultural sense, must reflect the latter's demands but not accede to its values. This tension is paramount in the execution of tradition's task: to raise the next generation in a way such that they understand the culture within which they are embedded but neither accept its demands nor separate themselves off from it such that they cannot influence its direction. Nurture, in relation to this tension, requires some sophistication to be effective. This is where the sophistication of the wisdom model can be of particular value in both contexts. But this is not to deny that attempts to revivify tradition and invigorate spiritual commitment in the young, in this context, are akin to walking a tightrope entailing significant risk of falling away from tradition and into the twin abyss of assimilation and secularity. Balance is everything, and even then it may not be enough.

Notes

1 The term for Buddhist community, in this case a specifically monastic community.
2 The strict code of monastic discipline and the scriptural collection of rules and commentaries.
3 See the sources cited above. Also the issue of the growth, impact and transformation of Buddhism in the West has spawned much research in academic journals on the study of religion as well as in larger research publications and more popular literature.
4 The term for Buddhist monks.
5 Ibid. S. Batchelor, p. 39.
6 Sumedho Ajahn (1987), *Mindfulness: The Path to the Deathless*. Great Gaddesden: Amaravati Publications.
7 Ajahn Sumedho, senior monk of the Forest Retreat Order in Britain, interview 15 December 1999, Amaravati, Hertfordshire.
8 Jaffer Dharamsi, Co-ordinator of the European Khoja communities, Interview on 28 February 2000, Stanmore, Middlesex, UK.
9 The term for the local religious community.
10 Interview, 23 May 2002.
11 Interview, 23 May 2002.
12 Interview, 23 May 2002.

References

Batchelor, S. (1998) *Buddhism Without Beliefs: A Contemporary Guide to Awakening*. London: Bloomsbury
del Nevo, M. (1992) Letter from Lahore: Ozzy and Hussain, *The New Internationalist* 238, December.
Erricker, C. 2001 *Buddhism*. London: Hodder.
Erricker, C. (2001) The Spiritual Education of Khoja Shia Ithnasheeri Youth: The Challenges of Diaspora in J. Erricker, C. Ota and C. Erricker (eds), *Spiritual Education, Cultural, Religious and Social Differences: New Perspectives for the 21st Century*. Brighton & Portland: Sussex Academic Press.
Kashima, Tetsuden (1977) *Buddhism in America: The social organisation of an ethnic religious institution*. Greenwood Press.
Sumedho, Ajahn (1987) *Mindfulness: The Path to the Deathless*. Great Gaddesden, Herts.: Amaravati Publications.

Chapter 16

Metaphors of Spiritual Education: Fight and Blessing

MARIA AZEVEDO AND HELENA GIL COSTA

THIS CHAPTER PRESENTS the text Genesis 32: 24–33 as a metaphor for spiritual education and then it looks at some practical examples extracted from experiences carried out with educators, parents and adults in a Creativity Training Program. The text, even though belonging to a religious tradition, is not the object of a theological approach. It is presented here as belonging to humanity from a pedagogical point of view: from educators to educators. The way we understand spirituality and spiritual education derives from the following perspectives.

The Main Concepts: Understanding Spirituality and Spiritual Education

Spirituality

The concept of *spirituality* seems to be ambiguous. In fact, different cultures and different religions define it according to their own specificities, and sometimes there even exists some confusion between the concepts of spirituality, wisdom, culture, faith and religion. The understanding of spiritual education will differ according to how we define spirituality, and also according to the type of psychological, sociological, philosophical, or other kind of approach adopted (Carr 2001). From a strictly anthropological approach, leaving out any theological considerations, we have tried to construct a definition of spirituality by collecting the most relevant elements from different existing traditions:

A situated perception, emerging out of the onto-teleological basis of the human being, that becomes conscious and is dynamically translated into one's fulfilment and understanding of both other people and the world, as well as in the acceptance of the Transcendent.[1]

Such a definition of spirituality presupposes an anthropological perspective that comes from Bergson, Buber, Ortega and others. It is a point of view in which "being human" results from a permanent flow between nature and action, between being conscious of oneself and of one's circumstance (*the ontological basis*) and from the project of "being more" (one's task of becoming more human, one's theology).

Education

Looking now at the concept of *education*, we should be aware of its evolution since the 1970s. We define it as a continuous process, from birth to death, whose intrinsic purpose is to bestow on each person the means that enables him/her to become more and more autonomous, that is to say, to satisfy their needs and aspirations up to the maximum of their possibilities, as an individual, but also as a member of society.[2] As Paulo Freire[3] has well stressed both in his theory and practice, no one can assume, in exclusive terms, the function of an educator, thinking that he/she has nothing more to learn, just as no one has the exclusive condition of a student.

The ability to educate ourselves reciprocally depends, according to Freire, on *conscientization*, that is to say, on the ability each of us has to read ourselves and to read the world, on our ability to confront ourselves both as a being and as a project, in relation to other people, to the world and to God – whatever idea one may have of God. This perspective is based on the way we look at the teacher's work. Whatever the age of his/her pupils (from nursery school to adult education), the teacher is not someone whose function is only to *teach*; that is to say, someone who transmits knowledge that other people are supposed to learn. The teacher must be someone who "creates conditions for the development of the capacities of human beings who are on the way to their fulfilment as persons, citizens and professionals" (Dias 1997: 7). That is to say, every teacher is an educator.

Affinities between education and spirituality

If we confront both concepts (*education* and *spirituality*), we should be able to identify their affinities. Thus, we perceive in both of them:

- a dynamic nature;
- an attention to the aims, that is to say to the *sense* of human activity; a lasting relationship between *being* and *knowing*;

- a "concrete universality", that is to say, the confrontation with the whole human experience throughout the concrete experience of each person and of each culture.

Education gives rise to the birth of spirituality and, in its radical meaning, education is a spiritual process. So when we say *spiritual education* the adjective almost seems to be redundant. Likewise, moral, aesthetical and religious education (and, generally seen, civic, environment, consumer education) arise as applications of this nuclear ground or didactical starting points. Education, as a spiritual process, assures awareness and personal appropriation that nullifies indoctrination, an eminent danger if education is seen separately from spirituality. So, even when using the word *Education*, the spiritual dimension is always implied.

Teacher's Spiritual Education

Seen in this way, to train teachers towards the spiritual education of children necessarily has a double perspective:

- to train the teachers as persons, by creating conditions that lead to their own personal development as well to a capacity for what might be termed "spiritual performance";[4]
- to train the teachers as "persons who work with persons", that is to say, by means of presenting knowledge, methods and techniques that may help others (namely children) to act similarly.

Although in some contexts this second aspect may be stressed, the first dimension should never be excluded: only someone who tries to know him/herself and to conduct his/her own personal development can help others doing the same.

Sturner (1994) presents a perspective of "creative life" that matches the one presented here; even though it was presented in another context and with differing objectives. He understands creative life as a dynamic and continuous succession of three conditions:

- **Centration**: it is a work of self-attention that leads to the consciousness of oneself as understanding of *who one is* and *what for* (that is, human beings' *onto-teleological* basis). In our experience we implement centration when we apply Silence Education with "writing the self" and relaxation techniques.
- **Action**: results from what, in the previous stage, constituted an anticipation of a possible self-achievement. It consists, thus, in an active vigilance on oneself and in a coherent attitude in various

fields of life (profession, pedagogical relationships, love, relations in the community, etc.).

- **Celebration**: a time and a way of resting, making peace and thanksgiving for all that has been done in the previous phases of the process.

Part 1: Fight and Blessing, Metaphors of Education

The reading of Genesis 32: 24–33 (the fight between Jacob and the Angel) is here proposed as a metaphor of the educational situation (particularly in relation to spiritual education) polarized into *fight* (symbol of the effort of action) and *blessing* (symbol of celebration).

> Jacob was left alone, and wrestled with a man there until the breaking of the day. When he saw that he didn't prevail against him, he touched the hollow of his thigh, and the hollow of Jacob's thigh was strained, as he wrestled.
> The man said, "Let me go, for the day breaks".
> Jacob said, "I won't let you go, unless you bless me".
> He said to him, "What is your name?"
> He said, "Jacob". He said, "Your name will no longer be called Jacob, but Israel; for you have fought with God and with men, and have prevailed".
> Jacob asked him, "Please tell me your name".
> He said, "Why is it that you ask what my name is?" He blessed him there.
> Jacob called the name of the place Peniel: for, he said, "I have seen God face to face, and my life is preserved". The sun rose on him as he passed over Peniel, and he limped because of his thigh. Therefore the children of Israel don't eat the sinew of the hip, which is on the hollow of the thigh, to this day, because he touched the hollow of Jacob's thigh in the sinew of the hip.

The Fight (Action)

The biblical quotation above begins by presenting a situation and its characters. Education as discovery and conquest of one's identity, thus, as spiritual education, is a solitary fight, a fight where it is impossible to expect any external help, a fight that does not happen by chance. It presupposes a journey, a leaving from oneself, from one's home, from one's land, from one's commodities, just as Jacob left the home of his father-in-law. It presupposes courage. Thus, the situation described is a metaphor of education: education is not an intelligence game, but a fight where one plays out one's own life.

This fight materializes itself in *a person*: "Jacob [. . .] wrestled with a man there until the breaking of the day." This man (or angel in other translations) is not identified in any part of the description. We do not know his name or anything about him . . . he is just, first the one who fights and then the one who blesses. It would not be illegitimate to identify him as an image of the *educator*. Always mysterious, the educator for the child and young people incarnates transcendence. This can be understood as *alterity* (each educator is for the young the Other, completely other, but simultaneously a Self, that is, somebody). But he could also be understood as absolutely transcendent, as Jacob himself says: "I have seen God face to face, and my life is preserved."

The passage makes reference to a fight that happens *during the night*. The discovery of oneself is a tactile fight, a fight of mistakes, of false steps, of stumbles. In fact, the fight for intellectual knowledge ends only when the light of comprehension begins. The fight is harder if it is for self-knowledge, autonomy and spiritual maturity. The night is the symbol for centration as referred to above and it is the condition for action and celebration. Descriptions from men and women that conquered and established themselves confirm this way of feeling.[5]

The following phrase of the biblical quotation synthesizes the permanent tension in education in any time and place: "When he saw that he didn't prevail against him, he touched the hollow of his thigh, and the hollow of Jacob's thigh was strained, as he wrestled." Educators do not give up easily. When they realize that they cannot win, they squeeze, move, and leave definitive signs. Such signs are so deep that they become as important as, or even more important than nature itself: "Therefore the children of Israel don't eat the sinew of the hip, which is on the hollow of the thigh, to this day, because he touched the hollow of Jacob's thigh in the sinew of the hip." From Jacob, with his new name Israel, a people is born maintaining as tradition the symbol that preserves the memory of this fight. Education is always a solitary fight where we can see the educator's action, but education is also born from a culture and returns to its roots. The taking off of the nerve from the hip's thigh – necessary for the meat to become tasty when cooked – assumes a new meaning in this context. It becomes a symbol of brotherhood between human beings and nature and makes all of us remember our origins as a people, that is, as a historic and cultural community.

Dialogue on the Name and Blessing (celebration)

Take a look at the dialogue between both characters: "The man said, 'Let me go, for the day breaks' Jacob said, 'I won't let you go, unless you bless me.'" Usually, it is not the educator who asks permission to leave. On the contrary, the educator frequently makes an effort to keep the one he has educated near him, even suffering when the student leaves, when education ends. There is, however, a moment when the educator (parent or teacher) has to leave . . . or has to allow one to leave. This is the moment when one judges the success of education and even of the educator's success. The unknown man of the text (the educator) started a fight where he tried to develop strength and abilities. Once these were guaranteed, his presence was no longer necessary. Frequently, however, the educator is afraid to face his own failure. He/she knows he/she is not divine or celestial. He/she does not trust him/herself very much and trusts even less the results of his/her work. He/she is afraid that, far away, the young people will not be able to maintain the balance: he/she is afraid to see his/her disciple hesitate or fall. If, however, the educator could feel *the breaking of the day*, if he/she knew that the disciples do not want to be alone before the blessing. If the educator could face the situation in this way, he/she would know when to leave and how to anticipate the young's revolt. His/her departure would not be an involuntary rest or a retirement against his/her will, but a contemplation of the one who became stronger as a result of his/her intervention, as a result of the fight he/she initiated. The educator's departure would be the discovery of equality between the two of them. Initiation would make sense for both, considering that – according to ancient tradition – "when the disciple is ready, so will be the master" (Pessoa 1986).

The following words are on the name: "He said to him, 'What is your name?' He said, 'Jacob.' He said, 'Your name will no longer be called Jacob, but Israel; for you have fought with God and with men, and have prevailed.'" The name is a sign of one's own identity and personal dignity. Knowing the name was, for the Jews and other ancient people, the same as knowing deeply the named one. Even today, in certain cultures, calling someone by his/her name is a sign of equality in terms of social, professional or other status, as well as of the most perfect trust. If providing a name is normal for the one who provided the being or secured the creation (parents or godparents), changing the name implies for the one who does it the mastery of being the authority over the one whose name is changed. For the latter, it implies an acceptance of this authority and reverence in the act of adopting the new name, even if used with the original one.

Attributing a new name is just like giving new life, new nature but absolutely different from the former one. That was the meaning of those name changes associated to chrism or to the entrance into a religious order within the Catholic tradition. That is why the *unknown man* of the text – the absolute other – does not say his own name, cannot be known or named, is above the human word; but, because of this, has the power to give a new name to the one he has fought, tested and, by the fight to give again existence. The new name – Israel – given by the mysterious being and accepted by Jacob is a sign of this new birth. *Being born again* is not only an English phrase, but also the recurrent image presented by many authors in literature, philosophy, and spirituality to describe the reaching of a new spiritual maturity.[6]

The dialogue on the name is a blessing mark because it creates a relationship with the Absolute – in the name of God Jacob's name is changed and blessing is given. Blessing is not just to laud or to praise the virtues or the work of someone, it is not just to call attention to who he or she is. Blessing is more than a concern for someone, more than a caring relationship. Caring – being aware of the needs of others and doing whatever we can to fulfil those needs – is a moral attitude and a specific way of moral thought. The bonds of a caring relationship "are valid against other demands and are sometimes felt to be absolute in the sense that to acknowledge possible reasons for which one might betray them is already a betrayal in itself" (Wringe 2000). But blessing someone is to look upon and to come across his original goodness and to appeal to his consciousness of *being loved* (Nowen 1992). Blessing is an attitude that promotes spirituality, as defined earlier.

Part 2: Celebration as a Blessing

Pedagogical Practice

If, up to this point we reflected on the meaning of fight and blessing in spiritual education, then we should try to understand how this metaphor explains the ground of our pedagogical practice; how this metaphor, *coming from life, returns to life and so creates a new life* (Ricoeur 1976). In other words, we shall seek to understand:

1   How we try to make celebration in the work we do with our students, a necessary follow-up for the moments of centration (night) and action (fight).
2   How we try to combine these three moments to work in a flexible and permanent process that leads to plenitude.

In any educational programme (whether it is a short-term course for professionals from different areas, or a course for parents, or even a university curriculum in teacher education – that is, a long-term course), we try to give space to what we call "time to celebrate" – at the end of a session, at the end of a programme, or at any time that it makes sense because celebrating is also a way of resting, making peace and thanksgiving. And if such a time has any relevance it is because it has a deep relationship with the things that happened during the programme. For that reason such a time is consistent and has an impact on people's lives.

However, in order to make things more clear and relevant, we will try to show how a celebration arises in a Creativity Training Program, as well as some effects that it has on those that were part of it. This does not mean that a celebration cannot happen in other kinds of programmes, but as we believe that a Creativity Program is, in itself, a paradigm of the educational process, so it will be presented here.

Pedagogical Practice example: A Creativity Training Program

Using a Systemic Approach to Creativity (Isaksen *et al.* 1994: 7), we usually organize a training programme around its four dimensions: Person, Press (climate or context), Process, and Product.

Working the "Person" dimension, we try:

- To understand that being creative is, "in essence", to realize who we are, what is hidden inside us, and let this grow to a higher level, what it means to be a (more) creative person is to accept that something happens through us.
- To uncover the obstacles that prevent the growth of such a potential that, being innate, is so frequently inhibited by the process of acculturation.

Working the "Press" dimension, we try:

- To understand the elements of the organizational climate that stimulate, or obstruct, the manifestation and development of creative behaviours. That is, in which ways a person can feel more or less capable, more or less creative, more or less confident in him/herself and in his/her capacities according to the situation in which he/she finds him/herself;
- To realize that each one of us is, simultaneously, cause and consequence of our own group climate process generation.

These two dimensions are part of what we call *centration*. Time and silence are needed because observation and reflection are necessary; because we need to empty our mind; because we need to learn to unlearn.

In approaching the "Process" dimension, we try:

- To understand our own creative process.
- To develop specific skills to solve problems in which there is not a known path to follow.

This is a time to learn and practice some generating and focusing creativity tools and techniques. It is a hard, difficult, but also a playful time because, in order to improve our personal and group skills for creative problem-solving, we must combine our divergent, multidirectional and flexible thinking, along with our traditional, convergent, and logical thinking. We are, therefore, giving space for *action* (the *fight* of the metaphor previously analyzed).

And, lastly, the "Product" dimension. According to O' Quin and Besemer (cf. Isaksen *et al*. 1994: 9), creative products are evaluated from three different aspects: Novelty, Resolution, Elaboration and Synthesis.

- Novelty analyzes the level of originality inside the product.
- Resolution looks at the way the product solves the problem or situation for which it was created.
- Elaboration and Synthesis are directed to understanding the product's characteristics that are beyond the basic requirements of the problem solving – namely the importance of things such as appearance, elegance, attractiveness, etc.

A creative product is, in itself, a symbol of the greatest educational goal: namely, the personal self-realization, the total "development of a human being – as a person, as a citizen and as a professional" (Dias 1997: 7). In other words, a symbol of a human being full of novelty, efficiency, elegance, and attractiveness.

Therefore, the fourth dimension, the "Product", is the one that brings us to celebration and blessing. We are the reason for celebrating – and, as "the work is [always] very good" (Gen. 1: 31), it needs to be blessed and sanctified. To do so, we need to allow ourselves to become more at ease, we need to relax and be happy with the way we are – here and now.

Creating different spaces and different situations that challenge each one of us to use the whole of our senses and capacities, we want the celebration to help us:

- To inspire and commit ourselves to action;
- To do more, to do better, to do differently;
- To deepen our interpersonal relationships;
- To transform our reality.

What do we do, then? Very simple things, like the following:

- *We go out from the limited space of a classroom as often as we can.* We believe that getting out of a classroom can be a way of allowing ourselves to behave differently from the socially accepted stereotypes; different from those fake identities that, so often, do not allow us to be ourselves, or, at least be "more ourselves".

- *We play games*, because, during the programme, we use a dynamic methodology to think about the theory with the practice – one in relation to the other, and one because of the other. Games are a way to use a playful methodology, putting each person in a more comfortable situation, avoiding value judgements and anxiety feelings.
- *We use our body. We dance together.* We do not have a body, we are a body, an existential reality that demands that we get closer to it through a deep listening to its sensations – in order to get closer to our true self (Marroquin 1995: 59). Sensibility, beyond the use of the richness of the senses, has something to do with being open, with experiencing, with the capacity to be surprised, of seeing beyond the obvious, of rejuvenating our old ways of seeing people and things (Aldana 1996: 41). Because interpersonal communication is like dancing, our dance is created with the other. Dancing needs, on the one hand, the involvement of the one who dances and, on the other hand, it is a scheme that we create together (Adler *et al.* 1999: 15).
- Sometimes, and going a little further, we dance "in mirror", looking into each other's eyes. Because, in looking into the eyes of the other, I can see my soul. Because considering otherness, I recognize my identity. Because in giving, receiving and trusting the other, I recognise my strengths. Because by proclaiming myself as a sender, I need acceptance on the part of the receiver.
- *We draw, we paint, we write, we create symbols that define us.* We look for the awareness of the path already made – such as one who ends a phase in order to allow a new cycle of life to begin; such as one who, at the end of a fight, takes care of the wounded, buries the dead ("dead" in the sense of what we no longer need, what we need to abandon), celebrates victory (because there are no losers here) and, then, feeds oneself to be ready for the next fight.
- *We talk. We make silence. We laugh together.* Sometimes it happens that we cry together. What matters is to let appear what is inside – it is a way to communicate with the most hidden roots of ourselves.

At the end, when evaluating the way we work, people are asked to put into small phrases their experiences and the most significant learning during the training programme. These are some of those phrases:

- *The training programme helped us to create a team spirit, to break barriers. It showed that sometimes it is worthwhile to be different.*
- *I am learning not to be so afraid of taking risks.*

- *I am getting a new view on old situations.*
- *It made me have more confidence in facing the future. I begin to realize that I am not alone in a crowd.*
- *I remember that a problem is big if we see it that way.*
- *I have learnt that inside of us there is a potential. I do not have to feel sorry for myself but I need to go on fighting. Without risk taking nothing can be gained.*
- *I am learning to know myself. Until now I had not done many things that, after all, I know I can do.*
- *I have learnt more skills for working in a group and I learned more about myself.*
- *I had the chance to recognize that, sometimes, the small (and normal) can be very meaningful.*
- *I have realized that one cannot be restricted to "yes" and "no", to "black and white". "Maybe" and other colours are also an option.*

These are not things that they did not know before . . . *in their minds.* But, perhaps, for the very first time, they began to realize them in their being.

Conclusion

As we have seen in theory and in practice, blessing – in the context of spiritual education – is the attitude and the behaviour by which educators confirm the ontological goodness of someone's acts. This is to say, fixing a moment of transition of someone's growth as a person, blessing drives him/her towards new actions aiming the development of his potentialities. However, and we have to stress this, according to our reading of Genesis 32: 24–33, only the educator who is a *master* can promote reconciliation and plenitude. The name of the Unnamed is the peace that he communicates. The name of the educator is the plenitude that he promotes. And one should still ask how can the educator testify to a peace, a plenitude, that he/she does not have or how can the educator testify to it if he/she did not allow himself to be owned by it? Remember that the wish for a blessing was the condition that Jacob made in order to give in to the unknown fighter. But at this point the text does not say that he/she had left. No educator truly departs from the ones he/she educates after have giving them peace. If, as already said, he/she lives, incarnates, is the peace he/she transmits to his/her disciples, he/she will remain with them in the same harmony he/she preaches. An endemic narcissism makes the educator feel him/herself to be a prophet, an angel . . . or even a little god. The Pygmalion temptation does not ever leave the educator . . . unless he/she considers him/herself as Jacob. If the building up of oneself is never complete, if *nobody educates nobody but we educate each other mutually*, as Paulo Freire used to say, then those who want, or feel a call, to become educators are also Jacob in a fight with their angel. One gives up fighting against one's previous generation, but never gives up fighting against one's own insufficiency, one's own ignorance. One gives up fighting against images of the past (ours and others') but one must not give up fighting for one's own being and human achievement. To fulfil our function as educators, we must feel our own way to become aware of the hurts experienced in the fight, of our limitations, and to receive the blessing that has to possess us.

Notes

1   This definition is related with what other authors call *faith*, not as worship or tradition but as an act of the total personality: "trust and loyalty to what a person or community accepts as an ultimate center of value" (Niebuhr) or "what concerns people ultimately (. . .) that to which they direct their lives and that from which they expect fulfilment" (Paul Tillich) (Fernhout 1989: 188).

2   As the Hamburg Declaration on Adult Learning stressed, "The objectives of youth and adult education, viewed as a lifelong process, are to develop the autonomy and the sense of responsibility of people and communities, to reinforce the capacity to deal with the transformations taking place in the economy, in culture and in society as a whole, and to promote coexistence, tolerance and the informed and creative participation of citizens in their communities, in short to enable people and communities to take control of their destiny and society in order to face the challenges ahead. It is essential that approaches to adult learning be based on people's own heritage, culture, values and prior experiences and that the diverse ways in which these approaches are implemented enable and encourage every citizen to be actively involved and to have a voice." Online: <http://www.unesco.org/education/uie/ confintea/declaeng.htm>; 2003–02–04).

3   Paulo Freire presented this idea in almost all his books. The last one, that can be seen as his pedagogical and spiritual testament is Freire, Paulo 1997: *Pedagogia da Autonomia: Saberes necessários à prática educativa*. S. Paulo: Paz e Terra.

4   We use this expression to name the spiritual growth in terms of affective attitudes, awareness to the sublime in moral, aesthetic or religious aspects of human experience, as well as an intellectual capacity "as a matter of the acquisition of certain kinds of problem solving skills" or "as initiation in the wisdom of received traditions of thought and evaluation" (Carr 1996: 166).

5   Jesus Christ and Buddda are presented by their traditions as having two phases in their lives, separated by a period of centration (Jesus fasted forty days and forty nights in the desert and was tempted by the devil before beginning preaching; Buddha sat down in meditation under the Bodygaya

and 49 days later was illuminated). Some mystics from the Roman Catholic tradition, such as Teresa de Avila or Juan de la Cruz, wrote about similar experiences.

6   Fernando Pessoa (1888–1935), the Portuguese poet, can be seen as an example of this way of thinking. He left a personal note, written down after the spiritual crisis after which he created his major works: "Today, assuming definitely the decision to be myself, to live accordingly to my work, I re-entered forever, back from my sensory journey around other people, getting the full command of my Genius and with the divine aware-ness of my Mission. Today I only want myself exactly as my innate character wants me to be; and my Genius, with whom I was born, imposes me to be. A thunderbolt today blinded me in brightness. I was born". (Fernando Pessoa 1966: *Páginas Íntimas e de Auto-Interpretação*, Textos esta-belecidos e prefaciados por Georg Rudolf Lind e Jacinto do Prado Coelho, pp. 63–4).

References

Adler, R. B. and Towne, N. 1999: *Looking Out Looking In*. Orlando: Harcourt Brace.

Aldana, G. 1996: *La Travesia Creativa – Assumiendo las Riendas del Cambio*. Santafé de Bogotá: Creatividad e Innovación Ediciones.

Carr, D. 1996: "Rival conceptions of Spiritual Education", *Journal of Philosophy of Education* 30 (2), 159–78.

Dias, J. R. 1997: A educação de infância como primeira fase da educação perma-nente. *Perspectivar Educação: Revista para Educadores* 3/4, 5–14.

Dias, J. R. 2000: *A Realização do Ser Humano*. Porto: Didáctica Editora.

Fernhout, H. 1989: "Moral Education as Grounded in Faith", *Journal of Moral Education* 18 (3), 186–98.

Freire, P. 1997: *Pedagogia da Autonomia: Saberes necessários à prática educativa*. S. Paulo: Paz e Terra.

Gusdorf, G. 1991: *Les Écritures du moi: Lignes de Vie I*. Paris: Editions Odile Jacob.

Isaksen, S., Dorval, B. and Treffinger, D. 1994: *Creative Approaches to Problem Solving*. Buffalo: Kendall/Hunt Publishing Company.

Marroquín, M. and Villa, A. 1995: *La Comunicación Interpersonal – Medicion y Estrategias para su Desarrollo*. Bilbao: Ediciones Mensajero.

Niebuhr, H. R. 1985: *Radical Monotheism and Western Culture*. New York: Harper and Row.

Nowen, H. 1992: *Life of the Beloved – Spiritual Living in a Secular World*. The Crossroad Publishing Company.

Pessoa, F. 1966: *Páginas Íntimas e de Auto-Interpretação*, Textos estabelecidos e prefaciados por Georg Rudolf Lind e Jacinto do Prado Coelho. Lisboa: Ática.

Pessoa, F. 1986: *Obras de Fernando Pessoa*. Porto: Lello & Irmão – Editores.

Ricoeur, P. 1975: *La Métaphore Vive. L'ordre philosophique*. Paris: Seuil.

Sturner, W. 1994: *Mystic in a marketplace: a spiritual journey*. Buffalo: Creative Education Foundation Press.

Tillich, P. 1957: *Dynamics of Faith*. New York: Seabury Press.

Contributors

Maria da Conceição Azevedo is Associate Professor at Universidade de Trás-os-Montes e Alto Douro, Portugal, where she teaches philosophy of education in teacher education courses. Her research interests also include moral education and spiritual development of children and adults. She has written a book about the Portuguese poet Fernando Pessoa as an educator and she is now working on dying and death education.

Joyce Bellous teaches at McMaster Divinity College, McMaster University, in the areas of education, ethics and culture. Her current research is in children and spirituality, particularly in the nature of spirituality itself. She also writes on faith education and has published over thirty essays in books and journals.

Jerome Berryman is an Episcopal priest who founded and directs the Centre for the Theology of Childhood in Houston, Texas, USA. He served for ten years as Canon Educator at Christ Church Cathedral in Houston and spent a further decade in the Texas Medical Centre in Houston teaching medical ethics and developing paediatric pastoral care, as well as many years in various school and parish settings. His training includes Princeton Theological Seminary (M.Div., D. Min.) and Tulsa University Law School (J.D.) and his publications include some 30 articles, 10 chapters in books, and four books, among which is *Godly Play* (1991). The first five volumes of *The Complete Guide To Godly Play* are now available.

Mark Chater is Principal Lecturer and programme leader for the secondary PGCE and Graduate Teacher Programme at Bishop Grosseteste College, a Church of England College of Higher Education in Lincoln, U.K. His teaching and research covers theology, spirituality, values in education, educational management and ethical / human issues in management.

Clive Erricker is Hampshire County Inspector for Religious Education, co-director of the Children and Worldviews Project and co-editor of the *International Journal of Children's Spirituality*. His recent publications include joint authorship of *The Education of the Whole Child*, Cassell, 1997 and co-authorship of *Reconstructing Religious, Spiritual and Moral Education*, Routledge, 2000. He is also co-editor of and contributor to *Contemporary Spiritualities*, Continuum, 2001 and *Meditation in Education: Calmer Classrooms, Clearer Minds*, Continuum, 2001. He lives in Lee on Solent, Hampshire, UK with Jane and his three children: Katy, Sam and Polly.

Jane Erricker is a principle lecturer in the School of Education at University College Winchester. She lectures on science and education studies programmes and her research on children's spirituality and identity has been carried out with the Children and Worldviews Project team. Her most recent work has been on Muslim girls' identity construc-tions.

J. Mark Halstead is Professor of Moral Education and Associate Dean (Research and Enterprise) in the Faculty of Education, University of Plymouth. His research interests include faith schools, Islamic educa-tion, values education, multicultural education and citizenship. His latest book (co-authored with Michael J. Reiss) is *Values in Sex Education* (RoutledgeFalmer, 2003).

Maria Helena Gil da Costa has a Master in Creativity, a Degree in Sociology, and a Pre-School Teacher Course. She teaches at Universidade Católica (Portugal) and at Escola Superior de Educação Santa Maria, where she served as Head for sixteen years. Her teaching and research covers education, creativity, spirituality, sociology and communication.

Mark A. Pike is Senior Lecturer in Education at the University of Leeds, England where his research and scholarship centres on spiritual, aesthetic and literary education. Mark has recently contributed papers to *Journal of Curriculum Studies, Educational Review, Journal of Aesthetic Education, Changing English, English in Education, Journal of Education and Christian Belief* and *Journal of Beliefs and Values*. Mark is Guest Editor of a special issue of the *International Journal of Children's Spirituality* on 'Literature, Literacy and Spirituality' (Summer 2004) and is the author of *Teaching Secondary English* (2004). After teaching English for ten years, finally as Head of English, Communications and Drama in a large Hampshire comprehensive school, and writing his Ph.D thesis on teenagers' reading at Southampton University, Mark is now Course

Leader for PGCE English in the School of Education at the University of Leeds where he also teaches on masters and doctoral programmes.

John Pridmore is an Anglican priest and is Rector of Hackney in the East End of London. He was previously on the staff of St. Martin-in-the-Fields where he was responsible for the church's international work. He has taught Religious Studies, English, and philosophy in schools in England and Tanzania. He taught Christian Ethics at Ridley Hall, Cambridge, an Anglican theological college. His research interests focus on the theology of childhood and children's spirituality.

Until 1997 **Jack Priestley** was Principal of Westhill College of Higher Education, now fully integrated into the University of Birmingham. He has returned as a Research Fellow to his former institution, the School of Education at the University of Exeter. Freed from administration, he has begun to produce a string of papers centred around the notion of the spiritual dimension of education, offering a critique of the business dominated values which he sees as endangering the concepts of education, culture and religion throughout the Western world. He is concerned to see the current 'teaching and learning' mantra extended to include concepts like 'inspiring and thinking'. He has a particular interest in the prophetic voices of the nineteenth and twentieth centuries such as those of Kierkegaard, Coleridge, William James, Whitehead and Wittgenstein. He is increasingly interested in exploring what it means to educate pupils and students to think religiously as distinct from thinking scientifically about religious phenomena.

Daniel Scott is an Assistant Professor and Graduate Advisor in the School of Child and Youth Care, University of Victoria, Victoria BC. He is currently facilitating a participatory research project with a group of women who are examining their adolescent writings for expressions of spirituality. The working title is "Writing Ourselves Into Being" and a chapter based on this material to be published in *Youth* with Girls is currently in press. He continues to collect narratives of early life spiritual experience and is currently co-authoring a chapter (with Dr Doug Magnuson) entitled "Integrating Spiritual Development into Child and Youth Care Programs and Institutions" for the *Handbook of Spiritual Development in Childhood and Adolescence* to be published by Sage.

Marian de Souza is a Lecturer and Student Adviser in the School of Religious Education, Australian Catholic University, Aquinas Campus, Ballarat where she teaches in undergraduate and post graduate teacher education programs. Marian is interested in researching the elements that nurture young people's spirituality in contemporary contexts and the implications for education; recognizing and addressing the spiritual dimension in the learning process; using the arts to promote cognition, creativity and imagination in learning and teaching across the curriculum; and investigating how new ethnic communities hand on their religious and cultural heritage to their young members.

David Tacey is Associate Professor and Reader in Arts and Critical Enquiry at La Trobe University, Melbourne. He is an author, lecturer, public speaker, and occasional journalist, who addresses such topics as popular spirituality, youth experience, ecology, Aboriginal reconciliation, and contemporary religion. His books include "Jung and the New Age" (London: Routledge, 2001), "ReEnchantment: The New Australian Spirituality" (Sydney: HarperCollins 2000), "Remaking Men: Jung, Spirituality, and Social Change" (London: Routledge 1997), "Edge of the Sacred: Transformation in Australia" (HarperCollins 1995), and "Patrick White, Fiction and the Unconscious" (Oxford University Press 1988). His new book, "The Spirituality Revolution", is a psychological and sociological study of popular spirituality, with emphasis on the spiritual lives of university students today. It will be published by Routledge in London and New York, April 2004.

Ann Trousdale is an associate professor at Louisiana State University, where she teaches courses in children's literature and storytelling. She is also a candidate for ordination in the United Methodist Church. Her research interests include using children's literature to foster children's spiritual development, religious, socio-political and feminist analysis of children's literature; studies of readers' response to literature; oral interpretation of literature; and storytelling. Among her publications are an edited book on storytelling, *Give a Listen: Stories of Storytelling in School*; articles in such journals as *Research in the Teaching of English, International Journal of Qualitative Studies in Education, Language Arts, The New Advocate, Feminist Teacher, Storytelling Magazine* and *Children's Literature in Education*; and chapters in books on children's literature and children's spirituality.

Christina Welch is currently completing her AHRB funded PhD at King Alfred's College in Winchester, Hampshire (UK) looking at the role that popular visual representation plays in the construction of spiritual identities with a focus upon North American Indian peoples and Western alternative spiritual practitioners. To date she has published "Appropriating the Didjeridu and the Sweat Lodge: New Age Baddies and Indigenous Victims?", *Journal of Contemporary Religion*, 17(1): 21-38 (2002).

Wong Ping Ho is a Senior Lecturer at the Department of Educational Psychology, Counselling and Learning Needs, the Hong Kong Institute of Education, Hong Kong, China. He had been a secondary school teacher for ten years before moving into teacher education. He studied for his M.Ed. in religious and moral education at the University of Hong Kong. He is now also a PhD student at the University of Hull working on the issue of spirituality in education.

Index

—